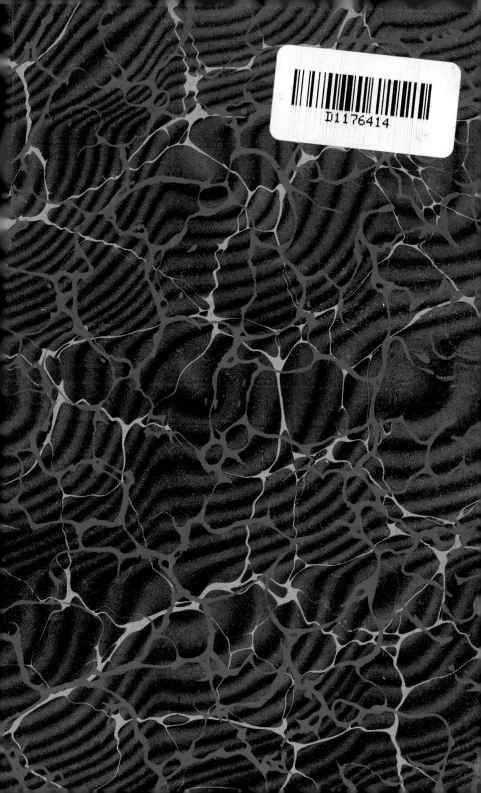

Ex-Libris

Hillcrest Edition

THE WRITINGS OF
MARK TWAIN
VOLUME II

This is the authorized
Uniform Edition of all
my books.

Mark Twain

A corner in the Capuchin convent

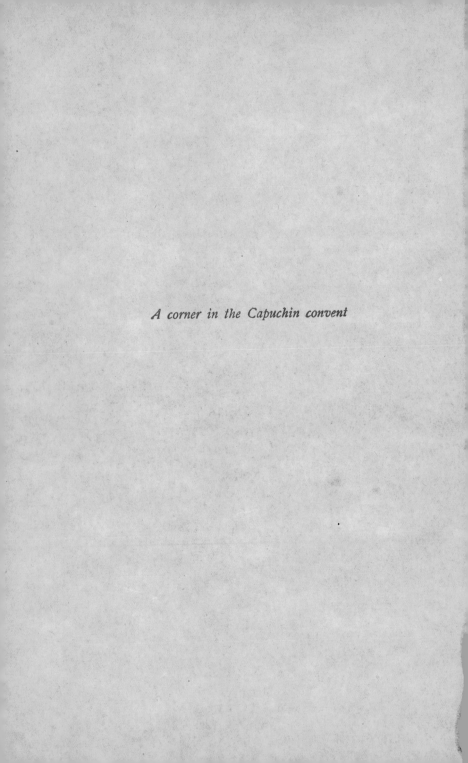

A corner in the Capuchin convent

THE

INNOCENTS ABROAD

OR

The New Pilgrims' Progress

BEING SOME ACCOUNT OF THE STEAMSHIP QUAKER CITY'S PLEASURE
EXCURSION TO EUROPE AND THE HOLY LAND

BY

MARK TWAIN
(Samuel L. Clemens)

IN TWO VOLUMES
VOL. II

NEW YORK AND LONDON
HARPER & BROTHERS PUBLISHERS

ILLUSTRATIONS

PHOTOGRAVURE

(iii)

CONTENTS

(v)

THE INNOCENTS ABROAD

CHAPTER I.

FROM the sanguinary sports of the Holy Inquisition; the slaughter of the Coliseum; and the dismal tombs of the Catacombs, I naturally pass to the picturesque horrors of the Capuchin Convent. We stopped a moment in a small chapel in the church to admire a picture of St. Michael vanquishing Satan — a picture which is so beautiful that I cannot but think it belongs to the reviled "*Renaissance*," notwithstanding I believe they told us one of the ancient old masters painted it — and then we descended into the vast vault underneath.

Here was a spectacle for sensitive nerves! Evidently the old masters had been at work in this place. There were six divisions in the apartment, and each division was ornamented with a style of decoration peculiar to itself — and these decorations were in every instance formed of human bones! There were shapely arches, built wholly of thigh bones; there were startling pyramids, built wholly of grinning skulls; there were quaint architectural structures of various kinds, built of shin bones and the bones of the arm; on the wall were elaborate frescoes, whose

(9)

curving vines were made of knotted human vertebræ; whose delicate tendrils were made of sinews and tendons; whose flowers were formed of knee-caps and toe-nails. Every lasting portion of the human frame was represented in these intricate designs (they were by Michael Angelo, I think), and there was a careful finish about the work, and an attention to details that betrayed the artist's love of his labors as well as his schooled ability. I asked the good-natured monk who accompanied us, who did this? And he said, " *We* did it " — meaning himself and his brethren up stairs. I could see that the old friar took a high pride in his curious show. We made him talkative by exhibiting an interest we never betrayed to guides.

" Who were these people? "

" We — up stairs — Monks of the Capuchin order — my brethren."

" How many departed monks were required to upholster these six parlors? "

" These are the bones of four thousand."

" It took a long time to get enough? "

" Many, many centuries."

" Their different parts are well separated — skulls in one room, legs in another, ribs in another — there would be stirring times here for a while if the last trump should blow. Some of the brethren might get hold of the wrong leg, in the confusion, and the wrong skull, and find themselves limping, and looking through eyes that were wider apart or closer

together than they were used to. You cannot tell
any of these parties apart, I suppose?"

"Oh, yes, I know many of them."

He put his finger on a skull. "This was Brother
Anselmo — dead three hundred years — a good
man."

He touched another. "This was Brother Alexander — dead two hundred and eighty years. This
was Brother Carlo — dead about as long."

Then he took a skull and held it in his hand, and
looked reflectively upon it, after the manner of the
grave-digger when he discourses of Yorick.

"This," he said, "was Brother Thomas. He
was a young prince, the scion of a proud house that
traced its lineage back to the grand old days of Rome
well nigh two thousand years ago. He loved beneath
his estate. His family persecuted him; persecuted
the girl, as well. They drove her from Rome; he
followed; he sought her far and wide; he found no
trace of her. He came back and offered his broken
heart at our altar and his weary life to the service of
God. But look you. Shortly his father died, and
likewise his mother. The girl returned, rejoicing.
She sought everywhere for him whose eyes had used
to look tenderly into hers out of this poor skull,
but she could not find him. At last, in this coarse
garb we wear, she recognized him in the street. He
knew her. It was too late. He fell where he stood.
They took him up and brought him here. He never
spoke afterward. Within the week he died. You

can see the color of his hair — faded, somewhat —
by this thin shred that clings still to the temple.
This [taking up a thigh bone] was his. The
veins of this leaf in the decorations over your head,
were his finger-joints, a hundred and fifty years ago.''

This business-like way of illustrating a touching
story of the heart by laying the several fragments of
the lover before us and naming them, was as grotesque a performance, and as ghastly, as any I ever
witnessed. I hardly knew whether to smile or shudder. There are nerves and muscles in our frames
whose functions and whose methods of working it
seems a sort of sacrilege to describe by cold physio-
logical names and surgical technicalities, and the
monk's talk suggested to me something of this kind.
Fancy a surgeon, with his nippers lifting tendons,
muscles, and such things into view, out of the complex machinery of a corpse, and observing, ''Now
this little nerve quivers — the vibration is imparted
to this muscle — from here it is passed to this fibrous
substance; here its ingredients are separated by the
chemical action of the blood — one part goes to the
heart and thrills it with what is popularly termed
emotion, another part follows this nerve to the brain
and communicates intelligence of a startling character — the third part glides along this passage and
touches the spring connected with the fluid recep-
tacles that lie in the rear of the eye. Thus, by this
simple and beautiful process, the party is informed
that his mother is dead, and he weeps.'' Horrible!

I asked the monk if all the brethren up stairs expected to be put in this place when they died. He answered quietly:

"We must all lie here at last."

See what one can accustom himself to. The reflection that he must some day be taken apart like an engine or a clock, or like a house whose owner is gone, and worked up into arches and pyramids and hideous frescoes, did not distress this monk in the least. I thought he even looked as if he were thinking, with complacent vanity, that his own skull would look well on top of the heap and his own ribs add a charm to the frescoes which possibly they lacked at present.

Here and there, in ornamental alcoves, stretched upon beds of bones, lay dead and dried-up monks, with lank frames dressed in the black robes one sees ordinarily upon priests. We examined one closely. The skinny hands were clasped upon the breast; two lusterless tufts of hair stuck to the skull; the skin was brown and shrunken; it stretched tightly over the cheek bones and made them stand out sharply; the crisp dead eyes were deep in the sockets; the nostrils were painfully prominent, the end of the nose being gone; the lips had shriveled away from the yellow teeth; and brought down to us through the circling years, and petrified there, was a weird laugh a full century old!

It was the jolliest laugh, but yet the most dreadful, that one can imagine. Surely, I thought, it must

have been a most extraordinary joke this veteran
produced with his latest breath, that he has not got
done laughing at it yet.   At this moment I saw that
the old instinct was strong upon the boys, and I said
we had better hurry to St. Peter's.   They were trying to keep from asking, " Is — is he dead? "

It makes me dizzy to think of the Vatican — of
its wilderness of statues, paintings, and curiosities of
every description and every age.   The " old
masters " (especially in sculpture) fairly swarm,
there.   I cannot write about the Vatican.   I think
I shall never remember anything I saw there distinctly but the mummies, and the Transfiguration,
by Raphael, and some other things it is not necessary
to mention now.   I shall remember the Transfiguration partly because it was placed in a room almost
by itself; partly because it is acknowledged by all
to be the first oil-painting in the world; and partly
because it was wonderfully beautiful.   The colors
are fresh and rich, the " expression," I am told, is
fine, the " feeling " is lively, the " tone " is good,
the " depth " is profound, and the width is about
four and a half feet, I should judge.   It is a picture
that really holds one's attention; its beauty is fascinating.   It is fine enough to be a *Renaissance*.   A
remark I made a while ago suggests a thought — and
a hope.   Is it not possible that the reason I find such
charms in this picture is because it is out of the crazy
chaos of the galleries?   If some of the others were
set apart, might not they be beautiful?   If this were

set in the midst of the tempest of pictures one finds
in the vast galleries of the Roman palaces, would I
think it so handsome? If, up to this time, I had
seen only one " old master " in each palace, instead
of acres and acres of walls and ceilings fairly papered
with them, might I not have a more civilized opinion
of the old masters than I have now? I think so.
When I was a schoolboy and was to have a new
knife, I could not make up my mind as to which was
the prettiest in the showcase, and I did not think
any of them were particularly pretty; and so I chose
with a heavy heart. But when I looked at my purchase, at home, where no glittering blades came into
competition with it, I was astonished to see how
handsome it was. To this day my new hats look
better out of the shop than they did in it with other
new hats. It begins to dawn upon me, now, that
possibly, what I have been taking for uniform ugli-
ness in the galleries may be uniform beauty after all.
I honestly hope it is, to others, but certainly it is not
to me. Perhaps the reason I used to enjoy going to
the Academy of Fine Arts in New York was because
there were but a few hundred paintings in it, and it
did not surfeit me to go through the list. I suppose
the Academy was bacon and beans in the Forty-Mile
Desert, and a European gallery is a state dinner of
thirteen courses. One leaves no sign after him of
the one dish, but the thirteen frighten away his
appetite and give him no satisfaction.

There is one thing I am certain of, though. With
2**

all the Michael Angelos, the Raphaels, the Guidos, and the other old masters, the sublime history of Rome remains unpainted! They painted Virgins enough, and Popes enough, and saintly scare-crows enough, to people Paradise, almost, and these things are all they did paint. "Nero fiddling o'er burning Rome," the assassination of Cæsar, the stirring spectacle of a hundred thousand people bending forward with rapt interest, in the Coliseum, to see two skillful gladiators hacking away each others' lives, a tiger springing upon a kneeling martyr — these and a thousand other matters which we read of with a living interest, must be sought for only in books — not among the rubbish left by the old masters — who are no more, I have the satisfaction of informing the public.

They did paint, and they did carve in marble, one historical scene, and one only (of any great historical consequence). And what was it and why did they choose it, particularly? It was the Rape of the Sabines, and they chose it for the legs and busts.

I like to look at statues, however, and I like to look at pictures, also — even of monks looking up in sacred ecstasy, and monks looking down in meditation, and monks skirmishing for something to eat — and therefore I drop ill-nature to thank the papal government for so jealously guarding and so industriously gathering up these things; and for permitting me, a stranger and not an entirely friendly one, to roam at will and unmolested among them, charg-

ing me nothing, and only requiring that I shall behave myself simply as well as I ought to behave in
any other man's house. I thank the Holy Father
right heartily, and I wish him long life and plenty of
happiness.

The Popes have long been the patrons and pre-
servers of art, just as our new, practical Republic is
the encourager and upholder of mechanics. In their
Vatican is stored up all that is curious and beautiful
in art; in our Patent Office is hoarded all that is
curious or useful in mechanics. When a man invents
a new style of horse-collar or discovers a new and
superior method of telegraphing, our government
issues a patent to him that is worth a fortune; when
a man digs up an ancient statue in the Campagna,
the Pope gives him a fortune in gold coin. We can
make something of a guess at a man's character by
the style of nose he carries on his face. The Vatican and the Patent Office are governmental noses,
and they bear a deal of character about them.

The guide showed us a colossal statue of Jupiter,
in the Vatican, which he said looked so damaged
and rusty — so like the God of the Vagabonds —
because it had but recently been dug up in the Campagna. He asked how much we supposed this
Jupiter was worth. I replied, with intelligent
promptness, that he was probably worth about four
dollars — may be four and a half. "A hundred thousand dollars!" Ferguson said. Ferguson said,
further, that the Pope permits no ancient work of

2**

this kind to leave his dominions. He appoints a commission to examine discoveries like this and report upon the value; then the Pope pays the discoverer one-half of that assessed value and takes the statue. He said this Jupiter was dug from a field which had just been bought for thirty-six thousand dollars, so the first crop was a good one for the new farmer. I do not know whether Ferguson always tells the truth or not, but I suppose he does. I know that an exorbitant export duty is exacted upon all pictures painted by the old masters, in order to discourage the sale of those in the private collections. I am satisfied, also, that genuine old masters hardly exist at all, in America, because the cheapest and most insignificant of them are valued at the price of a fine farm. I proposed to buy a small trifle of a Raphael, myself, but the price of it was eighty thousand dollars, the export duty would have made it considerably over a hundred, and so I studied on it awhile and concluded not to take it.

I wish here to mention an inscription I have seen, before I forget it:

" Glory to God in the highest, peace on earth TO MEN OF GOOD WILL!" It is not good scripture, but it is sound Catholic and human nature.

This is in letters of gold around the apsis of a mosaic group at the side of the *scala santa*, church of St. John Lateran, the Mother and Mistress of all the Catholic churches of the world. The group represents the Saviour, St. Peter, Pope Leo, St. Sil-

but chiefly on account of the fatigue of the journey. Two or three of us had been resting ourselves among the tranquil and beautiful scenery of the island of Ischia, eighteen miles out in the harbor, for two days; we called it " resting," but I do not remember now what the resting consisted of, for when we got back to Naples we had not slept for forty-eight hours. We were just about to go to bed early in the evening, and catch up on some of the sleep we had lost, when we heard of this Vesuvius expedition. There were to be eight of us in the party, and we were to leave Naples at midnight. We laid in some provisions for the trip, engaged carriages to take us to Annunciation, and then moved about the city, to keep awake, till twelve. We got away punctually, and in the course of an hour and a half arrived at the town of Annunciation. Annunciation is the very last place under the sun. In other towns in Italy, the people lie around quietly and wait for you to ask them a question or do some overt act that can be charged for — but in Annunciation they have lost even that fragment of delicacy; they seize a lady's shawl from a chair and hand it to her and charge a penny; they open a carriage door, and charge for it — shut it when you get out, and charge for it; they help you to take off a duster — two cents; brush your clothes and make them worse than they were before — two cents; smile upon you — two cents; bow, with a lickspittle smirk, hat in hand — two cents; they volunteer all information, such as that the mules will

arrive presently — two cents — warm day, sir — two
cents — take you four hours to make the ascent —
two cents. And so they go. They crowd you —
infest you — swarm about you, and sweat and smell
offensively, and look sneaking and mean, and ob-
sequious. There is no office too degrading for them
to perform, for money. I have had no opportunity
to find out anything about the upper classes by my
own observation, but from what I hear said about
them I judge that what they lack in one or two of the
bad traits the *canaille* have, they make up in one or
two others that are worse. How the people beg! —
many of them very well dressed, too.

I said I knew nothing against the upper classes by
personal observation. I must recall it! I had forgotten. What I saw their bravest and their fairest
do last night, the lowest multitude that could be
scraped up out of the purlieus of Christendom would
blush to do, I think. They assembled by hundreds,
and even thousands, in the great Theater of San
Carlo, to do — what? Why, simply, to make fun of
an old woman — to deride, to hiss, to jeer at an
actress they once worshiped, but whose beauty is
faded now and whose voice has lost its former richness. Everybody spoke of the rare sport there was
to be. They said the theater would be crammed,
because Frezzolini was going to sing. It was said
she could not sing well, now, but then the people
liked to see her, anyhow. And so we went. And
every time the woman sang they hissed and laughed

— the whole magnificent house — and as soon as she left the stage they called her on again with applause. Once or twice she was encored five and six times in succession, and received with hisses when she appeared, and discharged with hisses and laughter when she had finished — then instantly encored and insulted again! And how the high-born knaves enjoyed it! White-kidded gentlemen and ladies laughed till the tears came, and clapped their hands in very ecstasy when that unhappy old woman would come meekly out for the sixth time, with uncomplaining patience, to meet a storm of hisses! It was the cruelest exhibition — the most wanton, the most unfeeling. The singer would have conquered an audience of American rowdies by her brave, unflinching tranquillity (for she answered encore after encore, and smiled and bowed pleasantly, and sang the best she possibly could, and went bowing off, through all the jeers and hisses, without ever losing countenance or temper) : and surely in any other land than Italy her sex and her helplessness must have been an ample protection to her — she could have needed no other. Think what a multitude of small souls were crowded into that theater last night. If the manager could have filled his theater with Neapolitan souls alone, without the bodies, he could not have cleared less than ninety millions of dollars. What traits of character must a man have to enable him to help three thousand miscreants to hiss, and jeer, and laugh at one friendless old woman, and shamefully humiliate her? He must have *all* the vile, mean traits there are. My observation persuades me (I do not like to venture beyond my own personal observation) that the upper classes of Naples possess those traits of character. Otherwise they may be very good people; I cannot say.

ASCENT OF VESUVIUS — CONTINUED.

In this city of Naples, they believe in and support one of the wretchedest of all the religious impostures one can find in Italy — the miraculous liquefaction of the blood of St. Januarius. Twice a year the priests assemble all the people at the Cathedral, and get out this vial of clotted blood and let them see it slowly dissolve and become liquid — and every day for eight days this dismal farce is repeated, while the priests go among the crowd and collect money for the exhibition. The first day, the blood liquefies in forty-seven minutes — the church is crammed, then, and time must be allowed the collectors to get around: after that it liquefies a little quicker and a little quicker, every day, as the houses grow smaller, till on the eighth day, with only a few dozen present to see the miracle, it liquefies in four minutes.

And here, also, they used to have a grand procession, of priests, citizens, soldiers, sailors, and the high dignitaries of the City Government, once a year, to shave the head of a made up Madonna — a stuffed and painted image, like a milliner's dummy — whose hair miraculously grew and restored itself every twelve months. They still kept up this shaving procession as late as four or five years ago. It was a source of great profit to the church that possessed the remarkably effigy, and the ceremony of the public barbering of her was always carried out with the greatest possible éclat and display — the more the better, because the more excitement there was about it the larger the crowds it drew and the heavier the revenues it produced — but at last a day came when the Pope and his servants were unpopular in Naples, and the City Government stopped the Madonna's annual show.

There we have two specimens of these Neapolitans — two of the silliest possible frauds, which half the population religiously and faithfully believed, and the other half either believed also or else said nothing about, and thus lent themselves to the support of the imposture. I am very well satisfied to think the whole population believed in those poor, cheap, miracles — a people who want two cents every time they bow to you, and who abuse a woman, are capable of it, I think.

ASCENT OF VESUVIUS — CONTINUED.

These Neapolitans always ask four times as much money as they intend to take, but if you give them what they first demand, they feel ashamed of themselves for aiming so low, and immediately ask more. When money is to be paid and received, there is always some vehement jawing and gesticulating

about it. One cannot buy and pay for two cents'
worth of clams without trouble and a quarrel. One
"course," in a two-horse carriage, costs a franc —
that is law — but the hackman always demands more,
on some pretense or other, and if he gets it he
makes a new demand. It is said that a stranger
took a one-horse carriage for a course — tariff, half
a franc. He gave the man five francs, by way of
experiment. He demanded more, and received
another franc. Again he demanded more, and got
a franc — demanded more, and it was refused. He
grew vehement — was again refused, and became
noisy. The stranger said, "Well, give me the
seven francs again, and I will see what I can do " —
and when he got them, he handed the hackman half
a franc, and he immediately asked for two cents to
buy a drink with. It may be thought that I am
prejudiced. Perhaps I am. I would be ashamed
of myself if I were not.

ASCENT OF VESUVIUS — CONTINUED.

Well, as I was saying, we got our mules and
horses, after an hour and a half of bargaining with
the population of Annunciation, and started sleepily
up the mountain, with a vagrant at each mule's tail
who pretended to be driving the brute along, but was
really holding on and getting himself dragged up instead. I made slow headway at first, but I began to
get dissatisfied at the idea of paying my minion five
francs to hold my mule back by the tail and keep

him from going up the hill, and so I discharged him. I got along faster then.

We had one magnificent picture of Naples from a high point on the mountain side. We saw nothing but the gas lamps, of course — two-thirds of a circle, skirting the great Bay — a necklace of diamonds glinting up through the darkness from the remote distance — less brilliant than the stars overhead, but more softly, richly beautiful — and over all the great city the lights crossed and recrossed each other in many and many a sparkling line and curve. And back of the town, far around and abroad over the miles of level campagna, were scattered rows, and circles, and clusters of lights, all glowing like so many gems, and marking where a score of villages were sleeping. About this time, the fellow who was hanging on to the tail of the horse in front of me and practicing all sorts of unnecessary cruelty upon the animal, got kicked some fourteen rods, and this incident, together with the fairy spectacle of the lights far in the distance, made me serenely happy, and I was glad I started to Vesuvius.

ASCENT OF MOUNT VESUVIUS — CONTINUED.

This subject will be excellent matter for a chapter, and to-morrow or next day I will write it.

CHAPTER III.

"SEE Naples and die." Well, I do not know that one would necessarily die after merely seeing it, but to attempt to live there might turn out a little differently. To see Naples as we saw it in the early dawn from far up on the side of Vesuvius, is to see a picture of wonderful beauty. At that distance its dingy buildings looked white — and so, rank on rank of balconies, windows, and roofs, they piled themselves up from the blue ocean till the colossal castle of St. Elmo topped the grand white pyramid and gave the picture symmetry, emphasis, and completeness. And when its lilies turned to roses — when it blushed under the sun's first kiss — it was beautiful beyond all description. One might well say, then, "See Naples and die." The frame of the picture was charming, itself. In front, the smooth sea — a vast mosaic of many colors; the lofty islands swimming in a dreamy haze in the distance; at our end of the city the stately double peak of Vesuvius, and its strong black ribs and seams of lava stretching down to the limitless level campagna

(30)

— a green carpet that enchants the eye and leads it on and on, past clusters of trees, and isolated houses, and snowy villages, until it shreds out in a fringe of mist and general vagueness far away. It is from the Hermitage, there on the side of Vesuvius, that one should "see Naples and die."

But do not go within the walls and look at it in detail. That takes away some of the romance of the thing. The people are filthy in their habits, and this makes filthy streets and breeds disagreeable sights and smells. There never was a community so prejudiced against the cholera as these Neapolitans are. But they have good reason to be. The cholera generally vanquishes a Neapolitan when it seizes him, because, you understand, before the doctor can dig through the dirt and get at the disease the man dies. The upper classes take a sea-bath every day, and are pretty decent.

The streets are generally about wide enough for one wagon, and how they do swarm with people! It is Broadway repeated in every street, in every court, in every alley! Such masses, such throngs, such multitudes of hurrying, bustling, struggling humanity! We never saw the like of it, hardly even in New York, I think. There are seldom any sidewalks, and when there are, they are not often wide enough to pass a man on without caroming on him. So everybody walks in the street — and where the street is wide enough, carriages are forever dashing

3**

along. Why a thousand people are not run over and crippled every day is a mystery that no man can solve.

But if there is an eighth wonder in the world, it must be the dwelling-houses of Naples. I honestly believe a good majority of them are a hundred feet high! And the solid brick walls are seven feet through. You go up nine flights of stairs before you get to the "first" floor. No, not nine, but there or thereabouts. There is a little bird-cage of an iron railing in front of every window clear away up, up, up, among the eternal clouds, where the roof is, and there is always somebody looking out of every window — people of ordinary size looking out from the first floor, people a shade smaller from the second, people that look a little smaller yet from the third — and from thence upward they grow smaller and smaller by a regularly graduated diminution, till the folks in the topmost windows seem more like birds in an uncommonly tall martin-box than anything else. The perspective of one of these narrow cracks of streets, with its rows of tall houses stretching away till they come together in the distance like railway tracks; its clothes-lines crossing over at all altitudes and waving their bannered raggedness over the swarms of people below; and the white-dressed women perched in balcony railings all the way from the pavement up to the heavens — a perspective like that is really worth going into Neapolitan details to see.

ASCENT OF VESUVIUS — CONTINUED.

Naples, with its immediate suburbs, contains six hundred and twenty-five thousand inhabitants, but I am satisfied it covers no more ground than an American city of one hundred and fifty thousand. It reaches up into the air infinitely higher than three American cities, though, and there is where the secret of it lies. I will observe here, in passing, that the contrasts between opulence and poverty, and magnificence and misery, are more frequent and more striking in Naples than in Paris even. One must go to the Bois de Boulogne to see fashionable dressing, splendid equipages, and stunning liveries, and to the Faubourg St. Antoine to see vice, misery, hunger, rags, dirt — but in the thoroughfares of Naples these things are all mixed together. Naked boys of nine years and the fancy-dressed children of luxury; shreds and tatters, and brilliant uniforms; jackass carts and state carriages; beggars, princes, and bishops, jostle each other in every street. At six o'clock every evening, all Naples turns out to drive on the *Riviera di Chiaja* (whatever that may mean); and for two hours one may stand there and see the motliest and the worst-mixed procession go by that ever eyes beheld. Princes (there are more princes than policemen in Naples — the city is infested with them) — princes who live up seven flights of stairs and don't own any principalities, will keep a carriage and go hungry; and clerks,

3**

mechanics, milliners, and strumpets will go without their dinners and squander the money on a hack-ride in the Chiaja; the rag-tag and rubbish of the city stack themselves up, to the number of twenty or thirty, on a rickety little go-cart hauled by a donkey not much bigger than a cat, and *they* drive in the Chiaja; dukes and bankers, in sumptuous carriages and with gorgeous drivers and footmen, turn out, also, and so the furious procession goes. For two hours rank and wealth, and obscurity and poverty, clatter along side by side in the wild procession, and then go home serene, happy, covered with glory!

I was looking at a magnificent marble staircase in the King's palace, the other day, which, it was said, cost five million francs, and I suppose it did cost half a million, may be. I felt as if it must be a fine thing to live in a country where there was such comfort and such luxury as this. And then I stepped out musing, and almost walked over a vagabond who was eating his dinner on the curbstone — a piece of bread and a bunch of grapes. When I found that this mustang was clerking in a fruit establishment (he had the establishment along with him in a basket), at two cents a day, and that he had no palace at home where he lived, I lost some of my enthusiasm concerning the happiness of living in Italy.

This naturally suggests to me a thought about wages here. Lieutenants in the army get about a dollar a day, and common soldiers a couple of cents. I only know one clerk — he gets four dollars a month. Printers get six dollars and a half a month, but I have heard of a foreman who gets thirteen. To be growing suddenly and violently rich, as this man is, naturally makes him a bloated aristocrat. The airs he puts on are insufferable.

And, speaking of wages, reminds me of prices of merchandise. In Paris you pay twelve dollars a dozen for Jouvin's best kid gloves; gloves of about as good quality sell here at three or four dollars a dozen. You pay five and six dollars apiece for fine linen shirts in Paris; here and in Leghorn you pay two and a half. In Marseilles you pay forty dollars for a first-class dress coat made by a good tailor, but in Leghorn you can get a full dress suit for the same money. Here you get handsome business suits at from ten to twenty dollars, and in Leghorn you can get an overcoat for fifteen dollars that would cost you seventy in New York. Fine kid boots are worth eight dollars in Marseilles and four dollars here. Lyons velvets rank higher in America than those of Genoa. Yet the bulk of Lyons velvets you buy in the States are made in Genoa and imported into Lyons, where they receive the Lyons stamp and are then exported to America. You can buy enough velvet in Genoa for twenty-five dollars to make a five hundred dollar cloak in New York — so the ladies tell me. Of course, these things bring me back, by a natural and easy transition, to the

C**

ASCENT OF VESUVIUS — CONTINUED.

And thus the wonderful Blue Grotto is suggested to me. It is situated on the island of Capri, twenty-two miles from Naples. We chartered a little steamer and went out there. Of course, the police boarded us and put us through a health examination, and inquired into our politics, before they would let us land. The airs these little insect governments put on are in the last degree ridiculous. They even put a policeman on board of our boat to keep an eye on us as long as we were in the Capri dominions. They thought we wanted to steal the grotto, I suppose. It was worth stealing. The entrance to the cave is four feet high and four feet wide, and is in the face of a lofty perpendicular cliff — the sea wall. You enter in small boats — and a tight squeeze it is, too. You cannot go in at all when the tide is up. Once within, you find yourself in an arched cavern about one hundred and sixty feet long, one hundred and twenty wide, and about seventy high. How deep it is no man knows. It goes down to the bottom of the ocean. The waters of this placid subterranean lake are the brightest, loveliest blue that can be imagined. They are as transparent as plate glass, and their coloring would shame the richest sky that ever bent over Italy. No tint could be more ravishing, no luster more superb. Throw a stone into the water, and the myriad of tiny bubbles that are created flash out a brilliant glare like blue theatrical fires. Dip an oar, and its blade turns to splendid frosted silver, tinted with blue.   Let a man jump in, and instantly he is cased in an armor more gorgeous than ever kingly Crusader wore.

Then we went to Ischia, but I had already been to that island and tired myself to death "resting" a couple of days and studying human villainy, with the landlord of the Grande Sentinelle for a model. So we went to Procida, and from thence to Pozzuoli, where St. Paul landed after he sailed from Samos. I landed at precisely the same spot where St. Paul landed, and so did Dan and the others.   It was a remarkable coincidence.   St. Paul preached to these people seven days before he started to Rome.

Nero's Baths, the ruins of Baiæ, the Temple of Serapis; Cumæ, where the Cumæan Sibyl interpreted the oracles, the Lake Agnano, with its ancient submerged city still visible far down in its depths — these and a hundred other points of interest we examined with critical imbecility, but the Grotto of the Dog claimed our chief attention, because we had heard and read so much about it.   Everybody has written about the Grotto del Cane and its poisonous vapors, from Pliny down to Smith, and every tourist has held a dog over its floor by the legs to test the capabilities of the place.   The dog dies in a minute and a half — a chicken instantly.   As a general thing, strangers who crawl in there to sleep do not get up until they are called.   And then they don't, either.   The stranger that ventures to sleep there takes a permanent contract.   I longed to see this grotto. I resolved to take a dog and hold him myself; suffocate him a little, and time him; suffocate him some more, and then finish him. We reached the grotto about three in the afternoon, and proceeded at once to make the experiments. But now, an important difficulty presented itself. We had no dog.

ASCENT OF VESUVIUS — CONTINUED.

At the Hermitage we were about fifteen or eighteen hundred feet above the sea, and thus far a portion of the ascent had been pretty abrupt. For the next two miles the road was a mixture — sometimes the ascent was abrupt and sometimes it was not; but one characteristic it possessed all the time, without failure — without modification — it was all uncompromisingly and unspeakably infamous. It was a rough, narrow trail, and led over an old lava-flow — a black ocean which was tumbled into a thousand fantastic shapes — a wild chaos of ruin, desolation, and barrenness — a wilderness of billowy upheavals, of furious whirlpools, of miniature mountains rent asunder — of gnarled and knotted, wrinkled and twisted masses of blackness that mimicked branching roots, great vines, trunks of trees, all interlaced and mingled together; and all these weird shapes, all this turbulent panorama, all this stormy, far-stretching waste of blackness, with its thrilling suggestiveness of life, of action, of boiling, surging, furious motion, was petrified! — all stricken dead and cold in the instant of its maddest rioting! —

fettered, paralyzed, and left to glower at heaven in impotent rage forevermore!

Finally we stood in a level, narrow valley (a valley that had been created by the terrific march of some old-time eruption) and on either hand towered the two steep peaks of Vesuvius. The one we had to climb — the one that contains the active volcano — seemed about eight hundred or one thousand feet high, and looked almost too straight-up-and-down for any man to climb, and certainly no mule could climb it with a man on his back. Four of these native pirates will carry you to the top in a sedan chair, if you wish it, but suppose they were to slip and let you fall,— is it likely that you would ever stop rolling? Not this side of eternity, perhaps. We left the mules, sharpened our finger nails, and began the ascent I have been writing about so long, at twenty minutes to six in the morning. The path led straight up a rugged sweep of loose chunks of pumice-stone, and for about every two steps forward we took, we slid back one. It was so excessively steep that we had to stop, every fifty or sixty steps, and rest a moment. To see our comrades, we had to look very nearly straight up at those above us, and very nearly straight down at those below. We stood on the summit at last — it had taken an hour and fifteen minutes to make the trip.

What we saw there was simply a circular crater — a circular ditch, if you please — about two hundred feet deep, and four or five hundred feet wide, whose inner wall was about half a mile in circumference. In the center of the great circus-ring thus formed was a torn and ragged upheaval a hundred feet high, all snowed over with a sulphur crust of many and many a brilliant and beautiful color, and the ditch inclosed this like the moat of a castle, or surrounded it as a little river does a little island, if the simile is better. The sulphur coating of that island was gaudy in the extreme — all mingled together in the richest confusion were red, blue, brown, black, yellow, white — I do not know that there was a color, or shade of a color, or combination of colors, unrepresented — and when the sun burst through the morning mists and fired this tinted magnificence, it topped imperial Vesuvius like a jeweled crown!

The crater itself — the ditch — was not so variegated in coloring, but yet, in its softness, richness, and unpretentious elegance, it was more charming, more fascinating to the eye. There was nothing "loud" about its well-bred and well-dressed look. Beautiful? One could stand and look down upon it for a week without getting tired of it. It had the semblance of a pleasant meadow, whose slender grasses and whose velvety mosses were frosted with a shining dust, and tinted with palest green that deepened gradually to the darkest hue of the orange leaf, and deepened yet again into gravest brown, then faded into orange, then into brightest gold, and culminated in the delicate pink of a new-blown rose. Where portions of the meadow had sunk, and where other portions had been broken up like an ice-floe, the cavernous openings of the one, and the ragged upturned edges exposed by the other, were hung with a lacework of soft-tinted crystals of sulphur that changed their deformities into quaint shapes and figures that were full of grace and beauty.

The walls of the ditch were brilliant with yellow banks of sulphur and with lava and pumice-stone of many colors. No fire was visible anywhere, but gusts of sulphurous steam issued silently and invisibly from a thousand little cracks and fissures in the crater, and were wafted to our noses with every breeze. But so long as we kept our nostrils buried in our handkerchiefs, there was small danger of suffocation.

Some of the boys thrust long slips of paper down into holes and set them on fire, and so achieved the glory of lighting their cigars by the flames of Vesuvius, and others cooked eggs over fissures in the rocks and were happy.

The view from the summit would have been superb but for the fact that the sun could only pierce the mists at long intervals. Thus the glimpses we had of the grand panorama below were only fitful and unsatisfactory.

THE DESCENT.

The descent of the mountain was a labor of only four minutes. Instead of stalking down the rugged path we ascended, we chose one which was bedded knee-deep in loose ashes, and plowed our way with prodigious strides that would almost have shamed the performance of him of the seven-league boots.

The Vesuvius of to-day is a very poor affair compared to the mighty volcano of Kilauea, in the Sandwich Islands, but I am glad I visited it. It was well worth it.

It is said that during one of the grand eruptions of Vesuvius it discharged massy rocks weighing many tons a thousand feet into the air, its vast jets of smoke and steam ascended thirty miles toward the firmament, and clouds of its ashes were wafted abroad and fell upon the decks of ships seven hundred and fifty miles at sea! I will take the ashes at a moderate discount, if any one will take the thirty miles of smoke, but I do not feel able to take a commanding interest in the whole story by myself.

CHAPTER IV.

THE BURIED CITY OF POMPEII.

THEY pronounce it Pom-*pay*-e. I always had
an idea that you went down into Pompeii with
torches, by the way of damp, dark stairways, just
as you do in silver mines, and traversed gloomy
tunnels with lava overhead and something on either
hand like dilapidated prisons gouged out of the solid
earth, that faintly resembled houses. But you do
nothing of the kind. Fully one-half of the buried
city, perhaps, is completely exhumed and thrown
open freely to the light of day; and there stand the
long rows of solidly-built brick houses (roofless)
just as they stood eighteen hundred years ago, hot
with the flaming sun; and there lie their floors,
clean-swept, and not a bright fragment tarnished or
wanting of the labored mosaics that pictured them
with the beasts and birds and flowers which we
copy in perishable carpets to-day; and there are the
Venuses and Bacchuses and Adonises, making love
and getting drunk in many-hued frescoes on the
walls of saloon and bedchamber; and there are the
narrow streets and narrower sidewalks, paved with

flags of good hard lava, the one deeply rutted with
the chariot-wheels, and the other with the passing
feet of the Pompeiians of by-gone centuries; and
there are the bake-shops, the temples, the halls of
justice, the baths, the theaters — all clean-scraped
and neat, and suggesting nothing of the nature of a
silver mine away down in the bowels of the earth.
The broken pillars lying about, the doorless door-
ways, and the crumbled tops of the wilderness of
walls, were wonderfully suggestive of the "burnt
district" in one of our cities, and if there had been
any charred timbers, shattered windows, heaps of
débris, and general blackness and smokiness about
the place, the resemblance would have been perfect.
But no — the sun shines as brightly down on old
Pompeii to-day as it did when Christ was born in
Bethlehem, and its streets are cleaner a hundred
times than ever Pompeiian saw them in her prime.
I know whereof I speak — for in the great, chief
thoroughfares (Merchant Street and the Street of
Fortune) have I not seen with my own eyes how for
two hundred years at least the pavements were not
repaired ! — how ruts five and even ten inches deep
were worn into the thick flagstones by the chariot-
wheels of generations of swindled taxpayers? And
do I not know by these signs that street commissioners of Pompeii never attended to their business,
and that if they never mended the pavements they
never cleaned them? And, besides, is it not the
inborn nature of street commissioners to avoid their

duty whenever they get a chance? I wish I knew the name of the last one that held office in Pompeii so that I could give him a blast. I speak with feeling on this subject, because I caught my foot in one of those ruts, and the sadness that came over me when I saw the first poor skeleton, with ashes and lava sticking to it, was tempered by the reflection that may be that party was the street commissioner.

No — Pompeii is no longer a buried city. It is a city of hundreds and hundreds of roofless houses, and a tangled maze of streets where one could easily get lost, without a guide, and have to sleep in some ghostly palace that had known no living tenant since that awful November night of eighteen centuries ago.

We passed through the gate which faces the Mediterranean (called the " Marine Gate "), and by the rusty, broken image of Minerva, still keeping tireless watch and ward over the possessions it was powerless to save, and went up a long street and stood in the broad court of the Forum of Justice. The floor was level and clean, and up and down either side was a noble colonnade of broken pillars, with their beautiful Ionic and Corinthian columns scattered about them. At the upper end were the vacant seats of the judges, and behind them we descended into a dungeon where the ashes and cinders had found two prisoners chained on that memorable November night, and tortured them to death. How they must have tugged at the pitiless fetters as the fierce fires surged around them!

Then we lounged through many and many a sumptuous private mansion which we could not have entered without a formal invitation in incomprehensible Latin, in the olden time, when the owners lived there — and we probably wouldn't have got it. These people built their houses a good deal alike. The floors were laid in fanciful figures wrought in mosaics of many-colored marbles. At the threshold your eyes fall upon a Latin sentence of welcome, sometimes, or a picture of a dog, with the legend, " Beware of the Dog," and sometimes a picture of a bear or a faun with no inscription at all. Then you enter a sort of vestibule, where they used to keep the hat-rack, I suppose; next a room with a large marble basin in the midst and the pipes of a fountain; on either side are bedrooms; beyond the fountain is a reception-room, then a little garden, dining-room, and so forth and so on. The floors were all mosaic, the walls were stuccoed, or frescoed, or ornamented with bas-reliefs, and here and there were statues, large and small, and little fish-pools, and cascades of sparkling water that sprang from secret places in the colonnade of handsome pillars that surrounded the court, and kept the flower beds fresh and the air cool. Those Pompeiians were very luxurious in their tastes and habits. The most exquisite bronzes we have seen in Europe came from the exhumed cities of Herculaneum and Pompeii, and also the finest cameos and the most delicate engravings on precious stones; their pictures,

eighteen or nineteen centuries old, are often much
more pleasing than the celebrated rubbish of the old
masters of three centuries ago. They were well up
in art. From the creation of these works of the
first, clear up to the eleventh century, art seems
hardly to have existed at all — at least no remnants
of it are left — and it was curious to see how far (in
some things, at any rate) these old-time pagans ex-
celled the remote generations of masters that came
after them. The pride of the world in sculptures
seem to be the Laocoön and the Dying Gladiator,
in Rome. They are as old as Pompeii, were dug
from the earth like Pompeii; but their exact age or
who made them can only be conjectured. But
worn and cracked, without a history, and with the
blemishing stains of numberless centuries upon
them, they still mutely mock at all efforts to rival
their perfections.

It was a quaint and curious pastime, wandering
through this old silent city of the dead — lounging
through utterly deserted streets where thousands and
thousands of human beings once bought and sold,
and walked and rode, and made the place resound
with the noise and confusion of traffic and pleasure.
They were not lazy. They hurried in those days.
We had evidence of that. There was a temple on
one corner, and it was a shorter cut to go between
the columns of that temple from one street to the
other than to go around — and behold, that pathway
had been worn deep into the heavy flagstone floor

4**

of the building by generations of time-saving feet! They would not go around when it was quicker to go through. We do that way in our cities.

Everywhere, you see things that make you wonder how old these old houses were before the night of destruction came — things, too, which bring back those long-dead inhabitants and place them living before your eyes. For instance: The steps (two feet thick — lava blocks) that lead up out of the school, and the same kind of steps that lead up into the dress circle of the principal theater, are almost worn through! For ages the boys hurried out of that school, and for ages their parents hurried into that theater, and the nervous feet that have been dust and ashes for eighteen centuries have left their record for us to read to-day. I imagined I could see crowds of gentlemen and ladies thronging into the theater, with tickets for secured seats in their hands, and on the wall, I read the imaginary placard, in infamous grammar, "POSITIVELY NO FREE LIST, EXCEPT MEMBERS OF THE PRESS!" Hanging about the doorway (I fancied) were slouchy Pompeiian street boys uttering slang and profanity, and keeping a wary eye out for checks. I entered the theater, and sat down in one of the long rows of stone benches in the dress circle, and looked at the place for the orchestra, and the ruined stage, and around at the wide sweep of empty boxes, and thought to myself, "This house won't pay." I tried to imagine the music in full blast,

the leader of the orchestra beating time, and the
"versatile" So-and-So (who had "just returned
from a most successful tour in the provinces to play
his last and farewell engagement of positively six
nights only, in Pompeii, previous to his departure
for Herculaneum") charging around the stage and
piling the agony mountains high — but I could not
do it with such a "house" as that; those empty
benches tied my fancy down to dull reality. I said,
these people that ought to be here have been dead,
and still, and moldering to dust for ages and ages,
and will never care for the trifles and follies of life
any more forever — "Owing to circumstances, etc.,
etc., there will not be any performance to-night."
Close down the curtain. Put out the lights.

And so I turned away and went through shop
after shop and store after store, far down the long
street of the merchants, and called for the wares of
Rome and the East, but the tradesmen were gone,
the marts were silent, and nothing was left but the
broken jars all set in cement of cinders and ashes;
the wine and the oil that once had filled them were
gone with their owners.

In a bake-shop was a mill for grinding the grain,
and the furnaces for baking the bread; and they
say that here, in the same furnaces, the exhumers
of Pompeii found nice, well-baked loaves which the
baker had not found time to remove from the ovens
the last time he left his shop, because circumstances
compelled him to leave in such a hurry.

4*

In one house (the only building in Pompeii which no woman is now allowed to enter) were the small rooms and short beds of solid masonry, just as they were in the old times, and on the walls were pictures which looked almost as fresh as if they were painted yesterday, but which no pen could have the hardihood to describe; and here and there were Latin inscriptions — obscene scintillations of wit, scratched by hands that possibly were uplifted to Heaven for succor in the midst of a driving storm of fire before the night was done.

In one of the principal streets was a ponderous stone tank, and a waterspout that supplied it, and where the tired, heated toilers from the Campagna used to rest their right hands when they bent over to put their lips to the spout, the thick stone was worn down to a broad groove an inch or two deep. Think of the countless thousands of hands that had pressed that spot in the ages that are gone, to so reduce a stone that is as hard as iron!

They had a great public bulletin-board in Pompeii — a place where announcements for gladiatorial combats, elections, and such things, were posted — not on perishable paper, but carved in enduring stone. One lady, who, I take it, was rich and well brought up, advertised a dwelling or so to rent, with baths and all the modern improvements, and several hundred shops, stipulating that the dwellings should not be put to immoral purposes. You can find out who lived in many a house in Pompeii by the carved stone door-plates affixed to them: and in the same way you can tell who they were that occupy the tombs. Everywhere around are things that reveal to you something of the customs and history of this forgotten people. But what would a volcano leave of an American city, if it once rained its cinders on it? Hardly a sign or a symbol to tell its story.

In one of these long Pompeiian halls the skeleton of a man was found, with ten pieces of gold in one hand and a large key in the other. He had seized his money and started toward the door, but the fiery tempest caught him at the very threshold, and he sank down and died. One more minute of precious time would have saved him. I saw the skeletons of a man, a woman, and two young girls. The woman had her hands spread wide apart, as if in mortal terror, and I imagined I could still trace upon her shapeless face something of the expression of wild despair that distorted it when the heavens rained fire in these streets, so many ages ago. The girls and the man lay with their faces upon their arms, as if they had tried to shield them from the enveloping cinders. In one apartment eighteen skeletons were found, all in sitting postures, and blackened places on the walls still mark their shapes and show their attitudes, like shadows. One of them, a woman, still wore upon her skeleton throat a necklace, with her name engraved upon it — JULIE DI DIOMEDE.

But perhaps the most poetical thing Pompeii has yielded to modern research, was that grand figure of

D**

a Roman soldier, clad in complete armor; who, true to his duty, true to his proud name of a soldier of Rome, and full of the stern courage which had given to that name its glory, stood to his post by the city gate, erect and unflinching, till the hell that raged around him *burned out* the dauntless spirit it could not conquer.

We never read of Pompeii but we think of that soldier; we cannot write of Pompeii without the natural impulse to grant to him the mention he so well deserves. Let us remember that he was a soldier — not a policeman — and so, praise him. Being a soldier, he stayed, — because the warrior instinct forbade him to fly. Had he been a policeman he would have stayed, also — because he would have been asleep.

There are not half a dozen flights of stairs in Pompeii, and no other evidences that the houses were more than one story high. The people did not live in the clouds, as do the Venetians, the Genoese and Neapolitans of to-day.

We came out from under the solemn mysteries of this city of the Venerable Past — this city which perished, with all its old ways and its quaint old fashions about it, remote centuries ago, when the Disciples were preaching the new religion, which is as old as the hills to us now — and went dreaming among the trees that grow over acres and acres of its still buried streets and squares, till a shrill whistle and the cry of "*All aboard — last train for Naples!*" woke me

up and reminded me that I belonged in the nine-
teenth century, and was not a dusty mummy, caked
with ashes and cinders, eighteen hundred years old.
The transition was startling.   The idea of a railroad
train actually running to old dead Pompeii, and
whistling irreverently, and calling for passengers in
the most bustling and business-like way, was as
strange a thing as one could imagine, and as unpoetical and disagreeable as it was strange.

Compare the cheerful life and the sunshine of this
day with the horrors the younger Pliny saw here,
the 9th of November, A.D. 79, when he was so
bravely striving to remove his mother out of reach
of harm, while she begged him, with all a mother's
unselfishness, to leave her to perish and save himself.

"By this time the murky darkness had so increased that one might
have believed himself abroad in a black and moonless night, or in a
chamber where all the lights had been extinguished. On every hand
was heard the complaints of women, the wailing of children, and the
cries of men. One called his father, another his son, and another his
wife, and only by their voices could they know each other. Many in
their despair begged that death would come and end their distress.

"Some implored the gods to succor them, and some believed that
this night was the last, the eternal night which should engulf the
universe!

"Even so it seemed to me — and I consoled myself for the coming
death with the reflection: BEHOLD! THE WORLD IS PASSING AWAY!"

.   .   .   .

After browsing among the stately ruins of Rome,
of Baiæ, of Pompeii, and after glancing down the
long marble ranks of battered and nameless imperial
heads that stretch down the corridors of the Vatican,
one thing strikes me with a force it never had be-

fore: the unsubstantial, unlasting character of fame. Men lived long lives, in the olden time, and struggled feverishly through them, toiling like slaves, in oratory, in generalship, or in literature, and then laid them down and died, happy in the possession of an enduring history and a deathless name. Well, twenty little centuries flutter away, and what is left of these things? A crazy inscription on a block of stone, which snuffy antiquaries bother over and tangle up and make nothing out of but a bare name (which they spell wrong)—no history, no tradition, no poetry— nothing that can give it even a passing interest. What may be left of General Grant's great name forty centuries hence? This — in the Encyclopedia for A.D. 5868, possibly.

"URIAH S. (or Z.) GRAUNT— popular poet of ancient times in the Aztec provinces of the United States of British America. Some authors say flourished about A.D. 742; but the learned Ah-ah Foo-foo states that he was a cotemporary of Scharkspyre, the English poet, and flourished about A.D. 1328, some three centuries *after* the Trojan war instead of before it. He wrote ' Rock me to Sleep, Mother.' "

These thoughts sadden me. I will to bed.

CHAPTER V.

HOME, again! For the first time, in many weeks, the ship's entire family met and shook hands on the quarter-deck. They had gathered from many points of the compass and from many lands, but not one was missing; there was no tale of sickness or death among the flock to dampen the pleasure of the reunion. Once more there was a full audience on deck to listen to the sailors' chorus as they got the anchor up, and to wave an adieu to the land as we sped away from Naples.

The seats were full at dinner again, the domino parties were complete, and the life and bustle on the upper deck in the fine moonlight at night was like old times — old times that had been gone weeks only, but yet they were weeks so crowded with incident, adventure, and excitement, that they seemed almost like years. There was no lack of cheerfulness on board the *Quaker City*. For once, her title was a misnomer.

At seven in the evening, with the western horizon all golden from the sunken sun, and specked with distant ships, the full moon sailing high over head,

(55)

the dark blue of the sea under foot, and a strange
sort of twilight affected by all these different lights
and colors around us and about us, we sighted superb
Stromboli.   With what majesty the monarch held
his lonely state above the level sea!   Distance
clothed him in a purple gloom, and added a veil of
shimmering mist that so softened his rugged features
that we seemed to see him through a web of silver
gauze.   His torch was out; his fires were smolder-
ing; a tall column of smoke that rose up and lost itself in the growing moonlight was all the sign he
gave that he was a living Autocrat of the Sea and not
the specter of a dead one.

At two in the morning we swept through the
Straits of Messina, and so bright was the moonlight
that Italy on the one hand and Sicily on the other
seemed almost as distinctly visible as though we
looked at them from the middle of a street we were
traversing.   The city of Messina, milk-white, and
starred and spangled all over with gaslights, was a
fairy spectacle.   A great party of us were on deck
smoking and making a noise, and waiting to see
famous Scylla and Charybdis.   And presently the
Oracle stepped out with his eternal spy-glass and
squared himself on the deck like another Colossus
of Rhodes.   It was a surprise to see him abroad at
such an hour.   Nobody supposed he cared anything
about an old fable like that of Scylla and Charybdis.
One of the boys said:

"Hello, doctor, what are you doing up here at

this time of night? — What do you want to see this place for?"

"What do *I* want to see this place for? Young man, little do you know me, or you wouldn't ask such a question. I wish to see *all* the places that's mentioned in the Bible."

"Stuff! This place isn't mentioned in the Bible."

"It ain't mentioned in the Bible! — *this* place ain't — well now, what place *is* this, since you know so much about it?"

"Why it's Scylla and Charybdis."

"Scylla and Cha—confound it, I thought it was Sodom and Gomorrah!"

And he closed up his glass and went below. The above is the ship story. Its plausibility is marred a little by the fact that the Oracle was not a biblical student, and did not spend much of his time instructing himself about Scriptural localities.— They say the Oracle complains, in this hot weather, lately, that the only beverage in the ship that is passable, is the butter. He did not mean butter, of course, but inasmuch as that article remains in a melted state now since we are out of ice, it is fair to give him the credit of getting one long word in the right place, anyhow, for once in his life. He said, in Rome, that the Pope was a noble-looking old man, but he never *did* think much of his Iliad.

We spent one pleasant day skirting along the Isles of Greece. They are very mountainous. Their prevailing tints are gray and brown, approaching to

red.   Little white villages, surrounded by trees,
nestle in the valleys or roost upon the lofty perpendicular sea-walls.

We had one fine sunset — a rich carmine flush
that suffused the western sky and cast a ruddy glow
far over the sea.   Fine sunsets seem to be rare in
this part of the world — or at least, striking ones.
They are soft, sensuous, lovely — they are exquisite,
refined, effeminate, but we have seen no sunsets here
yet like the gorgeous conflagrations that flame in the
track of the sinking sun in our high northern
latitudes.

But what were sunsets to us, with the wild excitement upon us of approaching the most renowned of
cities!   What cared we for outward visions, when
Agamemnon, Achilles, and a thousand other heroes
of the great Past were marching in ghostly procession
through our fancies?   What were sunsets to us, who
were about to live and breathe and walk in actual
Athens; yea, and go far down into the dead centuries
and bid in person for the slaves, Diogenes and Plato,
in the public market-place, or gossip with the neighbors about the siege of Troy or the splendid deeds
of Marathon?   We scorned to consider sunsets.

We arrived, and entered the ancient harbor of the
Piræus at last.   We dropped anchor within half a
mile of the village.   Away off, across the undulat-
ing Plain of Attica, could be seen a little square-topped hill with a something on it, which our glasses
soon discovered to be the ruined edifices of the

citadel of the Athenians, and most prominent among them loomed the venerable Parthenon. So exquisitely clear and pure is this wonderful atmosphere that every column of the noble structure was discernible through the telescope, and even the smaller ruins about it assumed some semblance of shape. This at a distance of five or six miles. In the valley, near the Acropolis (the square-topped hill before spoken of), Athens itself could be vaguely made out with an ordinary lorgnette. Everybody was anxious to get ashore and visit these classic localities as quickly as possible. No land we had yet seen had aroused such universal interest among the passengers.

But bad news came. The commandant of the Piræus came in his boat, and said we must either depart or else get outside the harbor and remain imprisoned in our ship, under rigid quarantine, for eleven days! So we took up the anchor and moved outside, to lie a dozen hours or so, taking in supplies, and then sail for Constantinople. It was the bitterest disappointment we had yet experienced. To lie a whole day in sight of the Acropolis, and yet be obliged to go away without visiting Athens! Disappointment was hardly a strong enough word to describe the circumstances.

All hands were on deck, all the afternoon, with books and maps and glasses, trying to determine which " narrow rocky ridge " was the Areopagus, which sloping hill the Pnyx, which elevation the

Museum Hill, and so on. And we got things confused. Discussion became heated, and party spirit
ran high. Church members were gazing with emotion upon a hill which they said was the one St.
Paul preached from, and another faction claimed
that that hill was Hymettus, and another that it was
Pentelicon! After all the trouble, we could be
certain of only one thing — the square-topped hill
was the Acropolis, and the grand ruin that crowned
it was the Parthenon, whose picture we knew in
infancy in the schoolbooks.

We inquired of everybody who came near the
ship, whether there were guards in the Piræus,
whether they were strict, what the chances were
of capture should any of us slip ashore, and in case
any of us made the venture and were caught, what
would be probably done to us? The answers were
discouraging: There was a strong guard or police
force; the Piræus was a small town, and any stranger
seen in it would surely attract attention — capture
would be certain. The commandant said the punishment would be " heavy"; when asked " How
heavy?" he said it would be " very severe "— that
was all we could get out of him.

At eleven o'clock at night, when most of the
ship's company were abed, four of us stole softly
ashore in a small boat, a clouded moon favoring the
enterprise, and started two and two, and far apart,
over a low hill, intending to go clear around the
Piræus, out of the range of its police. Picking our

way so stealthily over that rocky, nettle-grown eminence, made me feel a good deal as if I were on my way somewhere to steal something. My immediate comrade and I talked in an undertone about quarantine laws and their penalties, but we found nothing cheering in the subject. I was posted. Only a few days before, I was talking with our captain, and he mentioned the case of a man who swam ashore from a quarantined ship somewhere, and got imprisoned six months for it; and when he was in Genoa a few years ago, a captain of a quarantined ship went in his boat to a departing ship, which was already outside of the harbor, and put a letter on board to be taken to his family, and the authorities imprisoned him three months for it, and then conducted him and his ship fairly to sea, and warned him never to show himself in that port again while he lived. This kind of conversation did no good, further than to give a sort of dismal interest to our quarantine-breaking expedition, and so we dropped it. We made the entire circuit of the town without seeing anybody but one man, who stared at us curiously, but said nothing, and a dozen persons asleep on the ground before their doors, whom we walked among and never woke—but we woke up dogs enough, in all conscience—we always had one or two barking at our heels, and several times we had as many as ten and twelve at once. They made such a preposterous din that persons aboard our ship said they could tell how we were progressing for a long time, and where we were, by the barking of the dogs. The clouded moon still favored us. When we had made the whole circuit, and were passing among the houses on the further side of the town, the moon came out splendidly, but we no longer feared the light. As we approached a well, near a house, to get a drink, the owner merely glanced at us and went within. He left the quiet, slumbering town at our mercy. I record it here proudly, that we didn't do anything to it.

Seeing no road, we took a tall hill to the left of the distant Acropolis for a mark, and steered straight for it over all obstructions, and over a little rougher piece of country than exists anywhere else outside of the State of Nevada, perhaps. Part of the way it was covered with small, loose stones—we trod on six at a time, and they all rolled. Another part of it was dry, loose, newly-plowed ground. Still another part of it was a long stretch of low grapevines, which were tanglesome and troublesome, and which we took to be brambles. The Attic Plain, barring the grapevines, was a barren, desolate, unpoetical waste — I wonder what it was in Greece's Age of Glory, five hundred years before Christ?

In the neighborhood of one o'clock in the morning, when we were heated with fast walking and parched with thirst, Denny exclaimed, "Why, these weeds are grapevines!" and in five minutes we had a score of bunches of large, white, delicious grapes, and were reaching down for more when a dark shape

rose mysteriously up out of the shadows beside us
and said " Ho!" And so we left.

In ten minutes more we struck into a beautiful
road, and unlike some others we had stumbled upon
at intervals, it led in the right direction. We followed it. It was broad and smooth and white —
handsome and in perfect repair, and shaded on both
sides for a mile or so with single ranks of trees, and
also with luxuriant vineyards. Twice we entered
and stole grapes, and the second time somebody
shouted at us from some invisible place. Whereupon we left again. We speculated in grapes no
more on that side of Athens.

Shortly we came upon an ancient stone aqueduct,
built upon arches, and from that time forth we had
ruins all about us — we were approaching our journey's end. We could not see the Acropolis now or
the high hill, either, and I wanted to follow the road
till we were abreast of them, but the others overruled
me, and we toiled laboriously up the stony hill immediately in our front — and from its summit saw
another — climbed it and saw another! It was an
hour of exhausting work. Soon we came upon a
row of open graves, cut in the solid rock — (for a
while one of them served Socrates for a prison) —
we passed around the shoulder of the hill, and the
citadel, in all its ruined magnificence, burst upon
us! We hurried across the ravine and up a winding
road, and stood on the old Acropolis, with the prodigious walls of the citadel towering above our

5**

heads. We did not stop to inspect their massive blocks of marble, or measure their height, or guess at their extraordinary thickness, but passed at once through a great arched passage like a railway tunnel, and went straight to the gate that leads to the ancient temples. It was locked! So, after all, it seemed that we were not to see the great Parthenon face to face. We sat down and held a council of war. Result: The gate was only a flimsy structure of wood — we would break it down. It seemed like desecration, but then we had traveled far, and our necessities were urgent. We could not hunt up guides and keepers — we must be on the ship before daylight. So we argued. This was all very fine, but when we came to break the gate, we could not do it. We moved around an angle of the wall and found a low bastion — eight feet high without — ten or twelve within. Denny prepared to scale it, and we got ready to follow. By dint of hard scrambling he finally straddled the top, but some loose stones crumbled away and fell with a crash into the court within. There was instantly a banging of doors and a shout. Denny dropped from the wall in a twinkling, and we retreated in disorder to the gate. Xerxes took that mighty citadel four hundred and eighty years before Christ, when his five millions of soldiers and camp-followers followed him to Greece, and if we four Americans could have remained unmolested five minutes longer, we would have taken it too.

The garrison had turned out — four Greeks. We clamored at the gate, and they admitted us. [Bribery and corruption.]

We crossed a large court, entered a great door, and stood upon a pavement of purest white marble, deeply worn by footprints. Before us, in the flooding moonlight, rose the noblest ruins we had ever looked upon — the Propylæa; a small temple of Minerva; the Temple of Hercules, and the grand Parthenon. [We got these names from the Greek guide, who didn't seem to know more than seven men ought to know.] These edifices were all built of the whitest Pentelic marble, but have a pinkish stain upon them now. Where any part is broken, however, the fracture looks like fine loaf sugar. Six caryatides, or marble women, clad in flowing robes, support the portico of the Temple of Hercules, but the porticoes and colonnades of the other structures are formed of massive Doric and Ionic pillars, whose flutings and capitals are still measurably perfect, notwithstanding the centuries that have gone over them and the sieges they have suffered. The Parthenon, originally, was two hundred and twenty-six feet long, one hundred wide, and seventy high, and had two rows of great columns, eight in each, at either end, and single rows of seventeen each down the sides, and was one of the most graceful and beautiful edifices ever erected.

Most of the Parthenon's imposing columns are still standing, but the roof is gone. It was a perfect

5₊₊

building two hundred and fifty years ago, when a shell dropped into the Venetian magazine stored here, and the explosion which followed wrecked and unroofed it. I remember but little about the Parthenon, and I have put in one or two facts and figures for the use of other people with short memories. Got them from the guide-book.

As we wandered thoughtfully down the marble-paved length of this stately temple, the scene about us was strangely impressive. Here and there, in lavish profusion, were gleaming white statues of men and women, propped against blocks of marble, some of them armless, some without legs, others headless — but all looking mournful in the moonlight, and startlingly human! They rose up and confronted the midnight intruder on every side — they stared at him with stony eyes from unlooked-for nooks and recesses; they peered at him over fragmentary heaps far down the desolate corridors; they barred his way in the midst of the broad forum, and solemnly pointed with handless arms the way from the sacred fane; and through the roofless temple the moon looked down, and banded the floor and darkened the scattered fragments and broken statues with the slanting shadows of the columns.

What a world of ruined sculpture was about us! Set up in rows — stacked up in piles — scattered broadcast over the wide area of the Acropolis — were hundreds of crippled statues of all sizes and of the most exquisite workmanship; and vast fragments of marble that once belonged to the entablatures, covered with bas-reliefs representing battles and sieges, ships of war with three and four tiers of oars, pageants and processions — everything one could think of. History says that the temples of the Acropolis were filled with the noblest works of Praxiteles and Phidias, and of many a great master in sculpture besides — and surely these elegant fragments attest it.

We walked out into the grass-grown, fragment-strewn court beyond the Parthenon. It startled us, every now and then, to see a stony white face stare suddenly up at us out of the grass with its dead eyes. The place seemed alive with ghosts. I half expected to see the Athenian heroes of twenty centuries ago glide out of the shadows and steal into the old temple they knew so well and regarded with such boundless pride.

The full moon was riding high in the cloudless heavens now. We sauntered carelessly and unthinkingly to the edge of the lofty battlements of the citadel, and looked down — a vision! And such a vision! Athens by moonlight! The prophet that thought the splendors of the New Jerusalem were revealed to him, surely saw this instead! It lay in the level plain right under our feet — all spread abroad like a picture — and we looked down upon it as we might have looked from a balloon. We saw no semblance of a street, but every house, every window, every clinging vine, every projection, was

E**

as distinct and sharply marked as if the time were noonday; and yet there was no glare, no glitter, nothing harsh or repulsive — the noiseless city was flooded with the mellowest light that ever streamed from the moon, and seemed like some living creature wrapped in peaceful slumber. On its further side was a little temple, whose delicate pillars and ornate front glowed with a rich luster that chained the eye like a spell; and nearer by, the palace of the king reared its creamy walls out of the midst of a great garden of shrubbery that was flecked all over with a random shower of amber lights — a spray of golden sparks that lost their brightness in the glory of the moon, and glinted softly upon the sea of dark foliage like the pallid stars of the milky-way. Overhead the stately columns, majestic still in their ruin — under foot the dreaming city — in the distance the silver sea — not on the broad earth is there another picture half so beautiful!

As we turned and moved again through the temple, I wished that the illustrious men who had sat in it in the remote ages could visit it again and reveal themselves to our curious eyes — Plato, Aristotle, Demosthenes, Socrates, Phocion, Pythagoras, Euclid, Pindar, Xenophon, Herodotus, Praxiteles and Phidias, Zeuxis the painter. What a constellation of celebrated names! But more than all, I wished that old Diogenes, groping so patiently with his lantern, searching so zealously for one solitary honest man in all the world, might meander along and stumble on our party. I ought not to say it, may be, but still I suppose he would have put out his light.

We left the Parthenon to keep its watch over old Athens, as it had kept it for twenty-three hundred years, and went and stood outside the walls of the citadel. In the distance was the ancient, but still almost perfect, Temple of Theseus, and close by, looking to the West, was the Bema, from whence Demosthenes thundered his philippics and fired the wavering patriotism of his countrymen. To the right was Mars Hill, where the Areopagus sat in ancient times, and where St. Paul defined his position, and below was the market-place where he " disputed daily " with the gossip-loving Athenians. We climbed the stone steps St. Paul ascended, and stood in the square-cut place he stood in, and tried to recollect the Bible account of the matter — but for certain reasons, I could not recall the words. I have found them since:

"Now while Paul waited for them at Athens, his spirit was stirred in him, when he saw the city wholly given up to idolatry.

"Therefore disputed he in the synagogue with the Jews, and with the devout persons, and in the market daily with them that met with him.

. . . .

"And they took him and brought him unto Areopagus, saying, May we know what this new doctrine whereof thou speakest is?

. . . .

"Then Paul stood in the midst of Mars hill, and said, Ye men of Athens, I perceive that in all things ye are too superstitious;

"For as I passed by and beheld your devotions, I found an altar with this inscription: TO THE UNKNOWN GOD. Whom, therefore, ye ignorantly worship, him declare I unto you." — *Acts*, ch. xvii.

It occurred to us, after a while, that if we wanted to get home before daylight betrayed us, we had better be moving. So we hurried away. When far on our road, we had a parting view of the Parthenon, with the moonlight streaming through its open colonnades and touching its capitals with silver. As it looked then, solemn, grand, and beautiful, it will always remain in our memories.

As we marched along, we began to get over our fears, and ceased to care much about quarantine scouts or anybody else. We grew bold and reckless; and once, in a sudden burst of courage, I even threw a stone at a dog. It was a pleasant reflection, though, that I did not hit him, because his master might just possibly have been a policeman. Inspired by this happy failure, my valor became utterly uncontrollable, and at intervals I absolutely whistled, though on a moderate key. But boldness breeds boldness, and shortly I plunged into a vineyard, in the full light of the moon, and captured a gallon of superb grapes, not even minding the presence of a peasant who rode by on a mule. Denny and Birch followed my example. Now I had grapes enough for a dozen, but then Jackson was all swollen up with courage, too, and he was obliged to enter a vineyard presently. The first bunch he seized brought trouble. A frowsy, bearded brigand sprang into the road with a shout, and flourished a musket in the light of the moon! We sidled toward the Piræus — not running, you understand, but only advancing with celerity. The brigand shouted again, but still we advanced. It was getting late, and we had no time to fool away on every ass that wanted to drivel Greek platitudes to us. We would just as soon have talked with him as not if we had not been in a hurry. Presently Denny said, "Those fellows are following us!"

We turned, and, sure enough, there they were — three fantastic pirates armed with guns. We slackened our pace to let them come up, and in the meantime I got out my cargo of grapes and dropped them firmly but reluctantly into the shadows by the wayside. But I was not afraid. I only felt that it was not right to steal grapes. And all the more so when the owner was around — and not only around, but with his friends around also. The villains came up and searched a bundle Dr. Birch had in his hand, and scowled upon him when they found it had nothing in it but some holy rocks from Mars Hill, and these were not contraband. They evidently suspected him of playing some wretched fraud upon them, and seemed half inclined to scalp the party. But finally they dismissed us with a warning, couched in excellent Greek, I suppose, and dropped tranquilly in our wake. When they had gone three hundred yards they stopped, and we went on rejoiced. But behold, another armed rascal came out of the shadows and took their place, and followed us two hundred yards. Then he delivered us over to another miscreant, who emerged from some mys-

terious place, and he in turn to another! For a
mile and a half our rear was guarded all the while
by armed men.   I never traveled in so much state
before in all my life.

It was a good while after that before we ventured
to steal any more grapes, and when we did we stirred
up another troublesome brigand, and then we ceased
all further speculation in that line.   I suppose that
fellow that rode by on the mule posted all the
sentinels, from Athens to the Piræus, about us.

Every field on that long route was watched by an
armed sentinel, some of whom had fallen asleep, no
doubt, but were on hand, nevertheless.   This shows
what sort of a country modern Attica is — a community of questionable characters.   These men were
not there to guard their possessions against strangers,
but against each other; for strangers seldom visit
Athens and the Piræus, and when they do, they go
in daylight, and can buy all the grapes they want
for a trifle.   The modern inhabitants are confiscators
and falsifiers of high repute, if gossip speaks truly
concerning them, and I freely believe it does.

Just as the earliest tinges of the dawn flushed the
eastern sky and turned the pillared Parthenon to a
broken harp hung in the pearly horizon, we closed
our thirteenth mile of weary, round-about marching,
and emerged upon the seashore abreast the ships,
with our usual escort of fifteen hundred Piræan dogs
howling at our heels.   We hailed a boat that was
two or three hundred yards from shore, and discov-

ered in a moment that it was a police-boat on the lookout for any quarantine breakers that might chance to be abroad. So we dodged — we were used to that by this time — and when the scouts reached the spot we had so lately occupied, we were absent. They cruised along the shore, but in the wrong direction, and shortly our own boat issued from the gloom and took us aboard. They had heard our signal on the ship. We rowed noiselessly away, and before the police-boat came in sight again, we were safe at home once more.

Four more of our passengers were anxious to visit Athens, and started half an hour after we returned; but they had not been ashore five minutes till the police discovered and chased them so hotly that they barely escaped to their boat again, and that was all. They pursued the enterprise no further.

We set sail for Constantinople to-day, but some of us little care for that. We have seen all there was to see in the old city that had its birth sixteen hundred years before Christ was born, and was an old town before the foundations of Troy were laid — and saw it in its most attractive aspect. Wherefore, why should *we* worry?

Two other passengers ran the blockade successfully last night. So we learned this morning. They slipped away so quietly that they were not missed from the ship for several hours. They had the hardihood to march into the Piræus in the early dusk and hire a carriage. They ran some danger of adding two or three months' imprisonment to the other novelties of their Holy Land Pleasure Excursion. I admire "cheek."* But they went and came safely, and never walked a step.

---

* Quotation from the Pilgrims.

CHAPTER VI.

FROM Athens all through the islands of the Grecian Archipelago, we saw little but forbidding sea-walls and barren hills, sometimes surmounted by three or four graceful columns of some ancient temple, lonely and deserted — a fitting symbol of the desolation that has come upon all Greece in these latter ages. We saw no plowed fields, very few villages, no trees or grass or vegetation of any kind, scarcely, and hardly ever an isolated house. Greece is a bleak, unsmiling desert, without agriculture, manufactures, or commerce, apparently. What supports its poverty-stricken people or its government, is a mystery.

I suppose that ancient Greece and modern Greece compared, furnish the most extravagant contrast to be found in history. George I, an infant of eighteen, and a scraggy nest of foreign office-holders, sit in the places of Themistocles, Pericles, and the illustrious scholars and generals of the Golden Age of Greece. The fleets that were the wonder of the world when the Parthenon was new, are a beggarly handful of fishing-smacks now, and the manly people that performed such miracles of valor at Marathon are only a tribe of unconsidered slaves to-day. The classic Ilissus has gone dry, and so have all the sources of Grecian wealth and greatness. The nation numbers only eight hundred thousand souls, and there is poverty and misery and mendacity enough among them to furnish forty millions and be liberal about it. Under King Otho the revenues of the state were five millions of dollars — raised from a tax of *one-tenth* of all the agricultural products of the land (which tenth the farmer had to bring to the royal granaries on pack-mules any distance not exceeding six leagues) and from extravagant taxes on trade and commerce. Out of that five millions the small tyrant tried to keep an army of ten thousand men, pay all the hundreds of useless Grand Equerries in Waiting, First Grooms of the Bed-chamber, Lord High Chancellors of the Exploded Exchequer, and all the other absurdities which these puppy-kingdoms indulge in, in imitation of the great monarchies; and in addition he set about building a white marble palace to cost about five millions itself. The result was, simply: Ten into five goes no times and none over. All these things could not be done with five millions, and Otho fell into trouble.

The Greek throne, with its unpromising adjuncts of a ragged population of ingenious rascals who were out of employment eight months in the year because there was little for them to borrow and less to confiscate, and a waste of barren hills and weed-grown deserts, went begging for a good while. It was offered to one of Victoria's sons, and afterward to various other younger sons of royalty who had no thrones and were out of business, but they all had the charity to decline the dreary honor, and veneration enough for Greece's ancient greatness to refuse to mock her sorrowful rags and dirt with a tinsel throne in this day of her humiliation — till they came to this young Danish George, and he took it. He has finished the splendid palace I saw in the radiant moonlight the other night, and is doing many other things for the salvation of Greece, they say.

We sailed through the barren Archipelago, and into the narrow channel they sometimes call the Dardanelles and sometimes the Hellespont. This part of the country is rich in historic reminiscences, and poor as Sahara in everything else. For instance, as we approached the Dardanelles, we coasted along the Plains of Troy and past the mouth of the Scamander; we saw where Troy had stood (in the distance), and where it does not stand now — a city that perished when the world was young. The poor Trojans are all dead now. They were born too late to see Noah's ark, and died too soon to see our menagerie. We saw where Agamemnon's fleets rendezvoused, and away inland a mountain which the map said was Mount Ida. Within the Hellespont we saw where the original first shoddy contract mentioned in history was carried out, and the " parties of the second part " gently rebuked by Xerxes. I speak of the famous bridge of boats which Xerxes ordered to be built over the narrowest part of the Hellespont (where it is only two or three miles wide). A moderate gale destroyed the flimsy structure, and the King, thinking that to publicly rebuke the contractors might have a good effect on the next set, called them out before the army and had them beheaded. In the next ten minutes he let a new contract for the bridge. It has been observed by ancient writers that the second bridge was a very good bridge. Xerxes crossed his host of five millions of men on it, and if it had not been purposely destroyed, it would probably have been there yet. If our government would rebuke some of our shoddy contractors occasionally, it might work much good. In the Hellespont we saw where Leander and Lord Byron swam across, the one to see her upon whom his soul's affections were fixed with a devotion that only death could impair, and the other merely for a flyer, as Jack says. We had two noted tombs near us, too. On one shore slept Ajax, and on the other Hecuba.

We had water batteries and forts on both sides of the Hellespont, flying the crimson flag of Turkey, with its white crescent, and occasionally a village, and sometimes a train of camels; we had all these to look at till we entered the broad sea of Marmora, and then the land soon fading from view, we resumed euchre and whist once more.

We dropped anchor in the mouth of the Golden

Horn at daylight in the morning. Only three or
four of us were up to see the great Ottoman capital.
The passengers do not turn out at unseasonable
hours, as they used to, to get the earliest possible
glimpse of strange foreign cities. They are well
over that. If we were lying in sight of the Pyramids of Egypt, they would not come on deck until
after breakfast, nowadays.

The Golden Horn is a narrow arm of the sea,
which branches from the Bosporus (a sort of broad
river which connects the Marmora and Black Seas),
and, curving around, divides the city in the middle.
Galata and Pera are on one side of the Bosporus,
and the Golden Horn; Stamboul (ancient Byzan-
tium) is upon the other. On the other bank of the
Bosporus is Scutari and other suburbs of Constantinople. This great city contains a million inhabitants,
but so narrow are its streets, and so crowded together are its houses, that it does not cover much
more than half as much ground as New York city.
Seen from the anchorage or from a mile or so up
the Bosporus, it is by far the handsomest city we
have seen. Its dense array of houses swells upward
from the water's edge, and spreads over the domes
of many hills; and the gardens that peep out here
and there, the great globes of the mosques, and the
countless minarets that meet the eye everywhere,
invest the metropolis with the quaint Oriental aspect
one dreams of when he reads books of Eastern
travel. Constantinople makes a noble picture.

6**

But its attractiveness begins and ends with its picturesqueness. From the time one starts ashore till he gets back again, he execrates it. The boat he goes in is admirably miscalculated for the service it is built for. It is handsomely and neatly fitted up, but no man could handle it well in the turbulent currents that sweep down the Bosporus from the Black Sea, and few men could row it satisfactorily even in still water. It is a long, light canoe (caique), large at one end and tapering to a knife blade at the other. They make that long sharp end the bow, and you can imagine how these boiling currents spin it about. It has two oars, and sometimes four, and no rudder. You start to go to a given point and you run in fifty different directions before you get there. First one oar is backing water, and then the other; it is seldom that both are going ahead at once. This kind of boating is calculated to drive an impatient man mad in a week. The boatmen are the awkwardest, the stupidest, and the most unscientific on earth, without question.

Ashore, it was — well, it was an eternal circus. People were thicker than bees, in those narrow streets, and the men were dressed in all the outrageous, outlandish, idolatrous, extravagant, thunder-and-lightning costumes that ever a tailor with the delirium tremens and seven devils could conceive of. There was no freak in dress too crazy to be indulged in; no absurdity too absurd to be tolerated; no frenzy in ragged diabolism too fantastic to be attempted. No two men were dressed alike. It was a wild masquerade of all imaginable costumes — every struggling throng in every street was a dissolving view of stunning contrasts. Some patriarchs wore awful turbans, but the grand mass of the infidel horde wore the fiery red skull-cap they call a fez. All the remainder of the raiment they indulged in was utterly indescribable.

The shops here are mere coops, mere boxes, bathrooms, closets — anything you please to call them — on the first floor. The Turks sit cross-legged in them, and work and trade and smoke long pipes, and smell like — like Turks. That covers the ground. Crowding the narrow streets in front of them are beggars, who beg forever, yet never collect anything; and wonderful cripples, distorted out of all semblance of humanity, almost; vagabonds driving laden asses; porters carrying drygoods boxes as large as cottages on their backs; peddlers of grapes, hot corn, pumpkin seeds, and a hundred other things, yelling like fiends; and sleeping happily, comfortably, serenely, among the hurrying feet, are the famed dogs of Constantinople; drifting noiselessly about are squads of Turkish women, draped from chin to feet in flowing robes, and with snowy veils bound about their heads, that disclose only the eyes and a vague, shadowy notion of their features. Seen moving about, far away in the dim, arched aisles of the Great Bazaar, they look as the shrouded dead must have looked when they walked forth from their

6**

graves amid the storms and thunders and earthquakes that burst upon Calvary that awful night of the Crucifixion. A street in Constantinople is a picture which one ought to see once — not oftener.

And then there was the goose-rancher — a fellow who drove a hundred geese before him about the city, and tried to sell them. He had a pole ten feet long, with a crook in the end of it, and occasionally a goose would branch out from the flock and make a lively break around the corner, with wings half lifted and neck stretched to its utmost. Did the goose-merchant get excited? No. He took his pole and reached after that goose with unspeakable *sang froid* — took a hitch round his neck, and "yanked" him back to his place in the flock without an effort. He steered his geese with that stick as easily as another man would steer a yawl. A few hours afterward we saw him sitting on a stone at a corner, in the midst of the turmoil, sound asleep in the sun, with his geese squatting around him, or dodging out of the way of asses and men. We came by again, within the hour, and he was taking account of stock, to see whether any of his flock had strayed or been stolen. The way he did it was unique. He put the end of his stick within six or eight inches of a stone wall, and made the geese march in single file between it and the wall. He counted them as they went by. There was no dodging that arrangement.

If you want dwarfs — I mean just a few dwarfs

for a curiosity — go to Genoa. If you wish to buy
them by the gross, for retail, go to Milan. There
are plenty of dwarfs all over Italy, but it did seem
to me that in Milan the crop was luxuriant. If you
would see a fair average style of assorted cripples,
go to Naples, or travel through the Roman states.
But if you would see the very heart and home of
cripples and human monsters, both, go straight to
Constantinople. A beggar in Naples who can show
a foot which has all run into one horrible toe, with
one shapeless nail on it, has a fortune — but such
an exhibition as that would not provoke any notice
in Constantinople. The man would starve. Who
would pay any attention to attractions like his among
the rare monsters that throng the bridges of the
Golden Horn and display their deformities in the
gutters of Stamboul? Oh, wretched impostor!
How could he stand against the three-legged woman,
and the man with his eye in his cheek? How would
he blush in presence of the man with fingers on his
elbow? Where would he hide himself when the
dwarf with seven fingers on each hand, no upper
lip, and his under-jaw gone, came down in his
majesty? Bismillah! The cripples of Europe are
a delusion and a fraud. The truly gifted flourish
only in the by-ways of Pera and Stamboul.

That three-legged woman lay on the bridge, with
her stock in trade so disposed as to command the
most striking effect — one natural leg, and two long,
slender, twisted ones with feet on them like some-

F**

body else's forearm. Then there was a man further along who had no eyes, and whose face was the color of a fly-blown beefsteak, and wrinkled and twisted like a lava-flow — and verily so tumbled and distorted were his features that no man could tell the wart that served him for a nose from his cheek-bones. In Stamboul was a man with a prodigious head, an uncommonly long body, legs eight inches long, and feet like snow-shoes. He traveled on those feet and his hands, and was as sway-backed as if the Colossus of Rhodes had been riding him. Ah, a beggar has to have exceedingly good points to make a living in Constantinople. A blue-faced man, who had nothing to offer except that he had been blown up in a mine, would be regarded as a rank impostor, and a mere damaged soldier on crutches would never make a cent. It would pay him to get a piece of his head taken off, and culti-vate a wen like a carpet sack.

The Mosque of St. Sophia is the chief lion of Constantinople. You must get a firman and hurry there the first thing. We did that. We did not get a firman, but we took along four or five francs apiece, which is much the same thing.

I do not think much of the Mosque of St. Sophia. I suppose I lack appreciation. We will let it go at that. It is the rustiest old barn in heathendom. I believe all the interest that attaches to it comes from the fact that it was built for a Christian church and then turned into a mosque, without much alteration, by the Mohammedan conquerors of the land. They made me take off my boots and walk into the place in my stocking feet. I caught cold, and got myself so stuck up with a complication of gums, slime, and general corruption, that I wore out more than two thousand pair of boot-jacks getting my boots off that night, and even then some Christian hide peeled off with them. I abate not a single boot-jack.

St. Sophia is a colossal church, thirteen or fourteen hundred years old, and unsightly enough to be very, very much older. Its immense dome is said to be more wonderful than St. Peter's, but its dirt is much more wonderful than its dome, though they never mention it. The church has a hundred and seventy pillars in it, each a single piece, and all of costly marbles of various kinds, but they came from ancient temples at Baalbec, Heliopolis, Athens, and Ephesus, and are battered, ugly, and repulsive. They were a thousand years old when this church was new, and then the contrast must have been ghastly — if Justinian's architects did not trim them any. The inside of the dome is figured all over with a monstrous inscription in Turkish characters, wrought in gold mosaic, that looks as glaring as a circus bill; the pavements and the marble balustrades are all battered and dirty; the perspective is marred everywhere by a web of ropes that depend from the dizzy height of the dome, and suspend countless dingy, coarse oil lamps, and ostrich-eggs, six or seven feet above the floor. Squatting and sitting in groups, here and there and far and near, were ragged Turks reading books, hearing sermons, or receiving lessons like children, and in fifty places were more of the same sort bowing and straightening up, bowing again and getting down to kiss the earth, muttering prayers the while, and keeping up their gymnastics till they ought to have been tired, if they were not.

Everywhere was dirt and dust and dinginess and gloom; everywhere were signs of a hoary antiquity, but with nothing touching or beautiful about it; everywhere were those groups of fantastic pagans; overhead the gaudy mosaics and the web of lamp-ropes — nowhere was there anything to win one's love or challenge his admiration.

The people who go into ecstasies over St. Sophia must surely get them out of the guide-book (where every church is spoken of as being " considered by good judges to be the most marvelous structure, in many respects, that the world has ever seen "). Or else they are those old connoisseurs from the wilds of New Jersey who laboriously learn the difference between a fresco and a fire-plug, and from that day forward feel privileged to void their critical bathos on painting, sculpture, and architecture forevermore.

We visited the Dancing Dervishes. There were twenty-one of them. They wore a long, light-colored loose robe that hung to their heels. Each in his turn went up to the priest (they were all

within a large circular railing) and bowed profoundly
and then went spinning away deliriously and took
his appointed place in the circle, and continued to
spin. When all had spun themselves to their places,
they were about five or six feet apart — and so situated, the entire circle of spinning pagans spun itself
three separate times around the room. It took
twenty-five minutes to do it. They spun on the
left foot, and kept themselves going by passing the
right rapidly before it and digging it against the
waxed floor. Some of them made incredible
" time." Most of them spun around forty times in
a minute, and one artist averaged about sixty-one
times a minute, and kept it up during the whole
twenty-five. His robe filled with air and stood out
all around him like a balloon.

They made no noise of any kind, and most of
them tilted their heads back and closed their eyes,
entranced with a sort of devotional ecstasy. There
was a rude kind of music, part of the time, but the
musicians were not visible. None but spinners were
allowed within the circle. A man had to either spin
or stay outside. It was about as barbarous an exhibition as we have witnessed yet. Then sick persons came and lay down, and beside them women
laid their sick children (one a babe at the breast),
and the patriarch of the Dervishes walked upon
their bodies. He was supposed to cure their diseases by trampling upon their breasts or backs or
standing on the back of their necks. This is well

enough for a people who think all their affairs
are made or marred by viewless spirits of the
air — by giants, gnomes, and genii — and who
still believe, to this day, all the wild tales in the
Arabian Nights. Even so an intelligent missionary
tells me.

We visited the Thousand and One Columns. I
do not know what it was originally intended for, but
they said it was built for a reservoir. It is situated
in the center of Constantinople. You go down a
flight of stone steps in the middle of a barren place,
and there you are. You are forty feet underground,
and in the midst of a perfect wilderness of tall,
slender, granite columns, of Byzantine architecture.
Stand where you would, or change your position as
often as you pleased, you were always a center from
which radiated a dozen long archways and colonnades that lost themselves in distance and the somber twilight of the place. This old dried-up reservoir is occupied by a few ghostly silk-spinners now,
and one of them showed me a cross cut high up in
one of the pillars. I suppose he meant me to
understand that the institution was there before the
Turkish occupation, and I thought he made a remark to that effect; but he must have had an im-
pediment in his speech, for I did not understand
him.

We took off our shoes and went into the marble
mausoleum of the Sultan Mahmoud, the neatest
piece of architecture, inside, that I have seen lately.

Mahmoud's tomb was covered with a black velvet pall, which was elaborately embroidered with silver; it stood within a fancy silver railing; at the sides and corners were silver candlesticks that would weigh more than a hundred pounds, and they supported candles as large as a man's leg; on the top of the sarcophagus was a fez, with a handsome diamond ornament upon it, which an attendant said cost a hundred thousand pounds, and lied like a Turk when he said it. Mahmoud's whole family were comfortably planted around him.

We went to the Great Bazaar in Stamboul, of course, and I shall not describe it further than to say it is a monstrous hive of little shops — thousands, I should say — all under one roof, and cut up into innumerable little blocks by narrow streets which are arched overhead. One street is devoted to a particular kind of merchandise, another to another, and so on. When you wish to buy a pair of shoes you have the swing of the whole street — you do not have to walk yourself down hunting stores in different localities. It is the same with silks, antiquities, shawls, etc. The place is crowded with people all the time, and as the gay-colored Eastern fabrics are lavishly displayed before every shop, the Great Bazaar of Stamboul is one of the sights that are worth seeing. It is full of life, and stir, and business, dirt, beggars, asses, yelling peddlers, porters, dervishes, high-born Turkish female shoppers, Greeks, and weird-looking and weirdly-dressed Mohammedans from the mountains and the far provinces — and the only solitary thing one does not smell when he is in the Great Bazaar, is something which smells good.

CHAPTER VII.

MOSQUES are plenty, churches are plenty, grave-yards are plenty, but morals and whisky are scarce. The Koran does not permit Mohammedans to drink. Their natural instincts do not permit them to be moral. They say the Sultan has eight hundred wives. This almost amounts to bigamy. It makes our cheeks burn with shame to see such a thing permitted here in Turkey. We do not mind it so much in Salt Lake, however.

Circassian and Georgian girls are still sold in Constantinople by their parents, but not publicly. The great slave marts we have all read so much about — where tender young girls were stripped for inspection, and criticised and discussed just as if they were horses at an agricultural fair — no longer exist. The exhibition and the sales are private now. Stocks are up, just at present, partly because of a brisk demand created by the recent return of the Sultan's suite from the courts of Europe; partly on account of an unusual abundance of breadstuffs, which leaves holders untortured by hunger and enables them to hold back for high prices; and partly because buyers are too weak to bear the market, while sellers are amply prepared to bull it. Under these circumstances, if the American metropolitan newspapers were published here in Constantinople, their next commercial report would read about as follows, I suppose:

SLAVE GIRL MARKET REPORT.

"Best brands Circassians, crop of 1850, £200; 1852, £250; 1854, £300. Best brands Georgian, none in market; second quality, 1851, £180. Nineteen fair to middling Wallachian girls offered at £130 @ 150, but no takers; sixteen prime A1 sold in small lots to close out — terms private.

"Sales of one lot Circassians, prime to good, 1852 to 1854, at £240 @ 242½, buyer 30; one forty-niner — damaged — at £23, seller ten, no deposit. Several Georgians, fancy brands, 1852, changed hands to fill orders. The Georgians now on hand are mostly last year's crop, which was unusually poor. The new crop is a little backward, but will be coming in shortly. As regards its quantity and quality, the accounts are most encouraging. In this connection we can safely say, also, that the new crop of Circassians is looking extremely well. His Majesty the Sultan has already sent in large orders for his new harem, which will be finished within a fortnight, and this has naturally strengthened the market and given Circassian stock a strong upward tendency. Taking advantage of the inflated market, many of our shrewdest operators are selling short. There are hints of a 'corner' on Wallachians.

"There is nothing new in Nubians. Slow sale.

"Eunuchs — none offering; however, large cargoes are expected from Egypt to-day."

I think the above would be about the style of the commercial report. Prices are pretty high now, and holders firm; but, two or three years ago, parents in a starving condition brought their young daughters down here and sold them for even twenty and thirty dollars, when they could do no better, simply to save themselves and the girls from dying of want. It is sad to think of so distressing a thing as this, and I for one am sincerely glad the prices are up again.

Commercial morals, especially, are bad. There is no gainsaying that. Greek, Turkish, and Armenian morals consist only in attending church regularly on the appointed Sabbaths, and in breaking the ten commandments all the balance of the week. It comes natural to them to lie and cheat in the first place, and then they go on and improve on nature until they arrive at perfection. In recommending his son to a merchant as a valuable salesman, a father does not say he is a nice, moral, upright boy, and goes to Sunday-school and is honest, but he says, "This boy is worth his weight in broad pieces of a hundred — for behold, he will cheat whomsoever hath dealings with him, and from the Euxine to the waters of Marmora there abideth not so gifted a liar!" How is that for a recommendation? The missionaries tell me that they hear encomiums like that passed upon people every day. They say of a person they admire, "Ah, he is a charming swindler, and a most exquisite liar!"

Everybody lies and cheats — everybody who is in business, at any rate. Even foreigners soon have to come down to the custom of the country, and they do not buy and sell long in Constantinople till they lie and cheat like a Greek. I say like a Greek, because the Greeks are called the worst transgressors in this line. Several Americans, long resident in Constantinople, contend that most Turks are pretty trustworthy, but few claim that the Greeks have any virtues that a man can discover — at least without a fire assay.

I am half willing to believe that the celebrated dogs of Constantinople have been misrepresented — slandered. I have always been led to suppose that they were so thick in the streets that they blocked the way; that they moved about in organized companies, platoons, and regiments, and took what they wanted by determined and ferocious assault; and that at night they drowned all other sounds with their terrible howlings. The dogs I see here cannot be those I have read of.

I find them everywhere, but not in strong force. The most I have found together has been about ten or twenty. And night or day a fair proportion of them were sound asleep. Those that were not asleep always looked as if they wanted to be. I never saw such utterly wretched, starving, sad-visaged, broken-hearted looking curs in my life. It seemed a grim satire to accuse such brutes as these of taking things by force of arms. They hardly seemed to have strength enough or ambition enough to walk across the street — I do not know that I have seen one walk that far yet. They are mangy and bruised and mutilated, and often you see one with the hair singed off him in such wide and well-defined tracts that he looks like a map of the new Territories. They are the sor-

riest beasts that breathe — the most abject — the
most pitiful. In their faces is a settled expression
of melancholy, an air of hopeless despondency.
The hairless patches on a scalded dog are preferred
by the fleas of Constantinople to a wider range on a
healthier dog; and the exposed places suit the fleas
exactly. I saw a dog of this kind start to nibble at
a flea — a fly attracted his attention, and he made a
snatch at him; the flea called for him once more,
and that forever unsettled him; he looked sadly at
his flea-pasture, then sadly looked at his bald spot.
Then he heaved a sigh and dropped his head re-
signedly upon his paws. He was not equal to the
situation.

The dogs sleep in the streets, all over the city.
From one end of the street to the other, I suppose
they will average about eight or ten to a block.
Sometimes, of course, there are fifteen or twenty to
a block. They do not belong to anybody, and they
seem to have no close personal friendships among
each other. But they district the city themselves,
and the dogs of each district, whether it be half a
block in extent, or ten blocks, have to remain within
its bounds. Woe to a dog if he crosses the line!
His neighbors would snatch the balance of his hair
off in a second. So it is said. But they don't
look it.

They sleep in the streets these days. They are my
compass — my guide. When I see the dogs sleep
placidly on, while men, sheep, geese, and all moving
7 **

things turn out and go around them, I know I am not in the great street where the hotel is, and must go further. In the Grand Rue the dogs have a sort of air of being on the lookout — an air born of being obliged to get out of the way of many carriages every day — and that expression one recognizes in a moment. It does not exist upon the face of any dog without the confines of that street. All others sleep placidly and keep no watch. They would not move, though the Sultan himself passed by.

In one narrow street (but none of them are wide) I saw three dogs lying coiled up, about a foot or two apart. End to end they lay, and so they just bridged the street neatly, from gutter to gutter. A drove of a hundred sheep came along. They stepped right over the dogs, the rear crowding the front, impatient to get on. The dogs looked lazily up, flinched a little when the impatient feet of the sheep touched their raw backs — sighed, and lay peacefully down again. No talk could be plainer than that. So some of the sheep jumped over them and others scrambled between, occasionally chipping a leg with their sharp hoofs, and when the whole flock had made the trip, the dogs sneezed a little, in the cloud of dust, but never budged their bodies an inch. I thought I was lazy, but I am a steam engine compared to a Constantinople dog. But was not that a singular scene for a city of a million inhabitants?

These dogs are the scavengers of the city. That is their official position, and a hard one it is. However, it is their protection. But for their usefulness in partially cleansing these terrible streets, they would not be tolerated long. They eat anything and everything that comes in their way, from melon rinds and spoiled grapes up through all the grades and species of dirt and refuse to their own dead friends and relatives — and yet they are always lean, always hungry, always despondent. The people are loth to kill them — do not kill them, in fact. The Turks have an innate antipathy to taking the life of any dumb animal, it is said. But they do worse. They hang and kick and stone and scald these wretched creatures to the very verge of death, and then leave them to live and suffer.

Once a Sultan proposed to kill off all the dogs here, and did begin the work — but the populace raised such a howl of horror about it that the massacre was stayed. After a while, he proposed to remove them all to an island in the Sea of Marmora. No objection was offered, and a ship-load or so was taken away. But when it came to be known that somehow or other the dogs never got to the island, but always fell overboard in the night and perished, another howl was raised and the transportation scheme was dropped.

So the dogs remain in peaceable possession of the streets. I do not say that they do not howl at night, nor that they do not attack people who have not a red fez on their heads. I only say that it would be mean for *me* to accuse them of these unseemly

7**

things who have not seen them do them with my own eyes or heard them with my own ears.

I was a little surprised to see Turks and Greeks playing newsboy right here in the mysterious land where the giants and genii of the Arabian Nights once dwelt — where winged horses and hydra-headed dragons guarded enchanted castles — where Princes and Princesses flew through the air on carpets that obeyed a mystic talisman — where cities whose houses were made of precious stones sprang up in a night under the hand of the magician, and where busy marts were suddenly stricken with a spell! and each citizen lay or sat, or stood with weapon raised or foot advanced, just as he was, speechless and motionless, till time had told a hundred years!

It was curious to see newsboys selling papers in so dreamy a land as that. And, to say truly, it is comparatively a new thing here. The selling of newspapers had its birth in Constantinople about a year ago, and was a child of the Prussian and Austrian war.

There is one paper published here in the English language — *The Levant Herald* — and there are generally a number of Greek and a few French papers rising and falling, struggling up and falling again. Newspapers are not popular with the Sultan's Government. They do not understand journalism. The proverb says, "The unknown is always great." To the court, the newspaper is a mysterious and rascally institution. They know what a pestilence is, because

they have one occasionally that thins the people out
at the rate of two thousand a day, and they regard a
newspaper as a mild form of pestilence.   When it
goes astray, they suppress it — pounce upon it without warning, and throttle it.   When it don't go
astray for a long time, they get suspicious and
throttle it anyhow, because they think it is hatching
deviltry.   Imagine the Grand Vizier in solemn council with the magnates of the realm, spelling his way
through the hated newspaper, and finally delivering
his profound decision: "This thing means mischief
— it is too darkly, too suspiciously inoffensive —
suppress it!   Warn the publisher that we cannot
have this sort of thing: put the editor in prison!"

The newspaper business has its inconveniences in
Constantinople.   Two Greek papers and one French
one were suppressed here within a few days of each
other.   No victories of the Cretans are allowed to be
printed.   From time to time the Grand Vizier sends
a notice to the various editors that the Cretan insur-
rection is entirely suppressed, and although that
editor knows better, he still has to print the notice.
The *Levant Herald* is too fond of speaking praise-
fully of Americans to be popular with the Sultan,
who does not relish our sympathy with the Cretans,
and therefore that paper has to be particularly cir-
cumspect in order to keep out of trouble.   Once the
editor, forgetting the official notice in his paper that
the Cretans were crushed out, printed a letter of a
very different tenor, from the American Consul in

G**

Crete, and was fined two hundred and fifty dollars for it. Shortly he printed another from the same source and was imprisoned three months for his pains. I think I could get the assistant editorship of the *Levant Herald*, but I am going to try to worry along without it.

To suppress a paper here involves the ruin of the publisher, almost. But in Naples I think they speculate on misfortunes of that kind. Papers are suppressed there every day, and spring up the next day under a new name. During the ten days or a fortnight we stayed there one paper was murdered and resurrected twice. The newsboys are smart there, just as they are elsewhere. They take advantage of popular weaknesses. When they find they are not likely to sell out, they approach a citizen mysteriously, and say in a low voice — "Last copy, sir: double price; paper just been suppressed!" The man buys it, of course, and finds nothing in it. They do say — I do not vouch for it — but they do say that men sometimes print a vast edition of a paper, with a ferociously seditious article in it, distribute it quickly among the newsboys, and clear out till the Government's indignation cools. It pays well. Confiscation don't amount to anything. The type and presses are not worth taking care of.

There is only one English newspaper in Naples. It has seventy subscribers. The publisher is getting rich very deliberately — very deliberately indeed.

I shall never want another Turkish lunch. The

cooking apparatus was in a little lunch-room, near the bazaar, and it was all open to the street. The cook was slovenly, and so was the table, and it had no cloth on it. The fellow took a mass of sausage-meat and coated it round a wire and laid it on a charcoal fire to cook. When it was done, he laid it aside and a dog walked sadly in and nipped it. He smelt it first, and probably recognized the remains of a friend. The cook took it away from him and laid it before us. Jack said, "I pass"— he plays euchre sometimes — and we all passed in turn. Then the cook baked a broad, flat, wheaten cake, greased it well with the sausage, and started towards us with it. It dropped in the dirt, and he picked it up and polished it on his breeches, and laid it before us. Jack said, ' I pass." We all passed. He put some eggs in a frying-pan, and stood pensively prying slabs of meat from between his teeth with a fork. Then he used the fork to turn the eggs with — and brought them along. Jack said " Pass again." All followed suit. We did not know what to do, and so we ordered a new ration of sausage. The cook got out his wire, apportioned a proper amount of sausage-meat, spat on his hands, and fell to work! This time, with one accord, we all passed out. We paid and left. That is all I learned about Turkish lunches. A Turkish lunch is good, no doubt, but it has its little drawbacks.

When I think how I have been swindled by books of Oriental travel, I want a tourist for breakfast. For years and years I have dreamed of the wonders of the Turkish bath; for years and years I have promised myself that I would yet enjoy one. Many and many a time, in fancy, I have lain in the marble bath, and breathed the slumbrous fragrance of Eastern spices that filled the air; then passed through a weird and complicated system of pulling and hauling and drenching and scrubbing, by a gang of naked savages who loomed vast and vaguely through the steaming mists, like demons; then rested for a while on a divan fit for a king; then passed through another complex ordeal, and one more fearful than the first; and, finally, swathed in soft fabrics, been conveyed to a princely saloon and laid on a bed of eiderdown, where eunuchs, gorgeous of costume, fanned me while I drowsed and dreamed, or contentedly gazed at the rich hangings of the apartment, the soft carpets, the sumptuous furniture, the pictures, and drank delicious coffee, smoked the soothing narghili, and dropped, at the last, into tranquil repose, lulled by sensuous odors from unseen censers, by the gentle influence of the narghili's Persian tobacco, and by the music of fountains that counterfeited the pattering of summer rain.

That was the picture, just as I got it from incendiary books of travel. It was a poor, miserable imposture. The reality is no more like it than the Five Points are like the Garden of Eden. They received me in a great court, paved with marble slabs; around it were broad galleries, one above another, carpeted with seedy matting, railed with unpainted balustrades, and furnished with huge rickety chairs, cushioned with rusty old mattresses, indented with impressions left by the forms of nine successive generations of men who had reposed upon them. The place was vast, naked, dreary; its court a barn, its galleries stalls for human horses. The cadaverous, half-nude varlets that served in the establishment had nothing of poetry in their appearance, nothing of romance, nothing of Oriental splendor. They shed no entrancing odors — just the contrary. Their hungry eyes and their lank forms continually suggested one glaring, unsentimental fact — they wanted what they term in California "a square meal."

I went into one of the racks and undressed. An unclean starveling wrapped a gaudy tablecloth about his loins, and hung a white rag over my shoulders. If I had had a tub then, it would have come natural to me to take in washing. I was then conducted down stairs into the wet, slippery court, and the first things that attracted my attention were my heels. My fall excited no comment. They expected it, no doubt. It belonged in the list of softening, sensuous influences peculiar to this home of Eastern luxury. It was softening enough, certainly, but its application was not happy. They now gave me a pair of wooden clogs — benches in miniature, with leather straps over them to confine my feet (which they would have done, only I do not wear No. 13s). These things dangled uncomfortably by the straps when I lifted up my feet, and came down in awkward and unexpected places when I put them on the floor again, and sometimes turned sideways and wrenched my ankles out of joint.   However, it was all Oriental luxury, and I did what I could to enjoy it.

They put me in another part of the barn and laid me on a stuffy sort of pallet, which was not made of cloth of gold, or Persian shawls, but was merely the unpretending sort of thing I have seen in the negro quarters of Arkansas.   There was nothing whatever in this dim marble prison but five more of these biers.   It was a very solemn place.   I expected that the spiced odors of Araby were going to steal over my senses now, but they did not.   A copper-colored skeleton, with a rag around him, brought me a glass decanter of water, with a lighted tobacco pipe in the top of it, and a pliant stem a yard long, with a brass mouth-piece to it.

It was the famous " narghili " of the East — the thing the Grand Turk smokes in the pictures.   This began to look like luxury.   I took one blast at it, and it was sufficient; the smoke went in a great volume down into my stomach, my lungs, even into the uttermost parts of my frame.   I exploded one mighty cough, and it was as if Vesuvius had let go.   For the next five minutes I smoked at every pore, like a frame house that is on fire on the inside.   Not any more narghili for me.   The smoke had a vile taste, and the taste of a thousand infidel tongues that remained on that brass mouthpiece was viler still.   I was getting discouraged. Whenever, hereafter, I see the cross-legged Grand Turk smoking his narghili, in pretended bliss, on the outside of a paper of Connecticut tobacco, I shall know him for the shameless humbug he is.

This prison was filled with hot air. When I had got warmed up sufficiently to prepare me for a still warmer temperature, they took me where it was — into a marble room, wet, slippery, and steamy, and laid me out on a raised platform in the center. It was very warm. Presently my man sat me down by a tank of hot water, drenched me well, gloved his hand with a coarse mitten, and began to polish me all over with it. I began to smell disagreeably. The more he polished the worse I smelt. It was alarming. I said to him:

"I perceive that I am pretty far gone. It is plain that I ought to be buried without any unnecessary delay. Perhaps you had better go after my friends at once, because the weather is warm, and I cannot 'keep' long."

He went on scrubbing, and paid no attention. I soon saw that he was reducing my size. He bore hard on his mitten, and from under it rolled little cylinders, like macaroni. It could not be dirt, for it was too white. He pared me down in this way for a long time. Finally I said:

"It is a tedious process. It will take hours to trim me to the size you want me; I will wait; go and borrow a jack-plane."

He paid no attention at all.

After a while he brought a basin, some soap, and something that seemed to be the tail of a horse. He made up a prodigious quantity of soapsuds, deluged me with them from head to foot, without warning me to shut my eyes, and then swabbed me viciously with the horse-tail. Then he left me there, a snowy statue of lather, and went away. When I got tired of waiting I went and hunted him up. He was propped against the wall, in another room, asleep. I woke him. He was not disconcerted. He took me back and flooded me with hot water, then turbaned my head, swathed me with dry tablecloths, and conducted me to a latticed chicken-coop in one of the galleries, and pointed to one of those Arkansas beds. I mounted it, and vaguely expected the odors of Araby again. They did not come.

The blank, unornamented coop had nothing about it of that oriental voluptuousness one reads of so much. It was more suggestive of the county hospital than anything else. The skinny servitor brought a narghili, and I got him to take it out again without wasting any time about it. Then he brought the world-renowned Turkish coffee that poets have sung so rapturously for many generations, and I seized upon it as the last hope that was left of my old dreams of Eastern luxury. It was another fraud. Of all the unchristian beverages that ever passed my lips, Turkish coffee is the worst. The cup is small, it is smeared with grounds; the coffee is black, thick, unsavory of smell, and execrable in taste. The bottom of the cup has a muddy sediment in it half an inch deep. This goes down your throat, and portions of it lodge by the way, and produce a tickling aggravation that keeps you barking and coughing for an hour.

Here endeth my experience of the celebrated Turkish bath, and here also endeth my dream of the bliss the mortal revels in who passes through it. It is a malignant swindle. The man who enjoys it is qualified to enjoy anything that is repulsive to sight or sense, and he that can invest it with a charm of poetry is able to do the same with anything else in the world that is tedious, and wretched, and dismal, and nasty.

CHAPTER VIII.

WE left a dozen passengers in Constantinople, and sailed through the beautiful Bosporus and far up into the Black Sea. We left them in the clutches of the celebrated Turkish guide, "FAR-AWAY MOSES," who will seduce them into buying a shipload of ottar of roses, splendid Turkish vestments, and all manner of curious things they can never have any use for. Murray's invaluable guidebooks have mentioned Far-away Moses' name, and he is a made man. He rejoices daily in the fact that he is a recognized celebrity. However, we cannot alter our established customs to please the whims of guides; we cannot show partialities this late in the day. Therefore, ignoring this fellow's brilliant fame, and ignoring the fanciful name he takes such pride in, we called him Ferguson, just as we had done with all other guides. It has kept him in a state of smothered exasperation all the time. Yet we meant him no harm. After he has gotten himself up regardless of expense, in showy, baggy trowsers, yellow, pointed slippers, fiery fez, silken jacket of blue, voluminous waist-sash of fancy

Persian stuff filled with a battery of silver-mounted horse-pistols, and has strapped on his terrible scimeter, he considers it an unspeakable humiliation to be called Ferguson. It cannot be helped. All guides are Ferguson to us. We cannot master their dreadful foreign names.

Sebastopol is probably the worst battered town in Russia or anywhere else. But we ought to be pleased with it, nevertheless, for we have been in no country yet where we have been so kindly received, and where we felt that to be Americans was a sufficient *visé* for our passports. The moment the anchor was down, the Governor of the town immediately dispatched an officer on board to inquire if he could be of any assistance to us, and to invite us to make ourselves at home in Sebastopol! If you know Russia, you know that this was a wild stretch of hospitality. They are usually so suspicious of strangers that they worry them excessively with the delays and aggravations incident to a complicated passport system. Had we come from any other country we could not have had permission to enter Sebastopol and leave again under three days — but as it was, we were at liberty to go and come when and where we pleased. Everybody in Constantinople warned us to be very careful about our passports, see that they were strictly *en regle*, and never to mislay them for a moment: and they told us of numerous instances of Englishmen and others who were delayed days, weeks, and even months, in Sebastopol, on account of trifling informalities in their passports, and for which they were not to blame. I had lost my passport, and was traveling under my room-mate's, who stayed behind in Constantinople to await our return. To read the description of him in that passport and then look at me, any man could see that I was no more like him than I am like Hercules. So I went into the harbor of Sebastopol with fear and trembling — full of a vague, horrible apprehension that I was going to be found out and hanged. But all that time my true passport had been floating gallantly overhead — and behold it was only our flag. They never asked us for any other.

We have had a great many Russian and English gentlemen and ladies on board to-day, and the time has passed cheerfully away. They were all happy-spirited people, and I never heard our mother tongue sound so pleasantly as it did when it fell from those English lips in this far-off land. I talked to the Russians a good deal, just to be friendly, and they talked to me from the same motive; I am sure that both enjoyed the conversation, but never a word of it either of us understood. I did most of my talking to those English people though, and I am sorry we cannot carry some of them along with us.

We have gone whithersoever we chose, to-day, and have met with nothing but the kindest attentions. Nobody inquired whether we had any passports or not.

Several of the officers of the government have

suggested that we take the ship to a little watering-place thirty miles from here, and pay the Emperor of Russia a visit. He is rusticating there. These officers said they would take it upon themselves to insure us a cordial reception. They said if we would go, they would not only telegraph the Emperor, but send a special courier overland to announce our coming. Our time is so short, though, and more especially our coal is so nearly out, that we judged it best to forego the rare pleasure of holding social intercourse with an Emperor.

Ruined Pompeii is in good condition compared to Sebastopol. Here, you may look in whatsoever direction you please, and your eye encounters scarcely anything but ruin, ruin, ruin! — fragments of houses, crumbled walls, torn and ragged hills, devastation everywhere! It is as if a mighty earthquake had spent all its terrible forces upon this one little spot. For eighteen long months the storms of war beat upon the helpless town, and left it at last the saddest wreck that ever the sun has looked upon. Not one solitary house escaped unscathed — not one remained habitable, even. Such utter and complete ruin one could hardly conceive of. The houses had all been solid, dressed-stone structures; most of them were plowed through and through by cannon-balls — unroofed and sliced down from eaves to foundation — and now a row of them, half a mile long, looks merely like an endless procession of battered chimneys. No semblance of a house re-

8**

mains in such as these. Some of the larger buildings had corners knocked off; pillars cut in two;
cornices smashed; holes driven straight through the
walls. Many of these holes are as round and as
cleanly cut as if they had been made with an auger.
Others are half pierced through, and the clean impression is there in the rock, as smooth and as
shapely as if it were done in putty. Here and there
a ball still sticks in a wall, and from it iron tears
trickle down and discolor the stone.

The battle-fields were pretty close together. The
Malakoff tower is on a hill which is right in the edge
of the town. The Redan was within rifle-shot of
the Malakoff; Inkerman was a mile away; and
Balaklava removed but an hour's ride. The French
trenches, by which they approached and invested
the Malakoff, were carried so close under its sloping
sides that one might have stood by the Russian guns
and tossed a stone into them. Repeatedly, during
three terrible days, they swarmed up the little
Malakoff hill, and were beaten back with terrible
slaughter. Finally, they captured the place, and
drove the Russians out, who then tried to retreat
into the town, but the English had taken the Redan,
and shut them off with a wall of flame; there was
nothing for them to do but go back and retake the
Malakoff or die under its guns. They did go back;
they took the Malakoff and retook it two or three
times, but their desperate valor could not avail, and
they had to give up at last.

These fearful fields, where such tempests of death used to rage, are peaceful enough now; no sound is heard, hardly a living thing moves about them, they are lonely and silent — their desolation is complete.

There was nothing else to do, and so everybody went to hunting relics. They have stocked the ship with them. They brought them from the Malakoff, from the Redan, Inkerman, Balaklava — everywhere. They have brought cannon-balls, broken ramrods, fragments of shell — iron enough to freight a sloop. Some have even brought bones — brought them laboriously from great distances, and were grieved to hear the surgeon pronounce them only bones of mules and oxen. I knew Blucher would not lose an opportunity like this. He brought a sack full on board and was going for another. I prevailed upon him not to go. He has already turned his state-room into a museum of worthless trumpery, which he has gathered up in his travels. He is labeling his trophies, now. I picked up one a while ago, and found it marked " Fragment of a Russian General." I carried it out to get a better light upon it — it was nothing but a couple of teeth and part of the jaw-bone of a horse. I said with some asperity:

" Fragment of a Russian General! This is absurd. Are you never going to learn any sense?"

He only said: " Go slow — the old woman won't know any different." [His aunt.]

This person gathers mementoes with a perfect recklessness, nowadays; mixes them all up together.

8**

and then serenely labels them without any regard to truth, propriety, or even plausibility. I have found him breaking a stone in two, and labeling half of it "Chunk busted from the pulpit of Demosthenes," and the other half "Darnick from the Tomb of Abelard and Heloise." I have known him to gather up a handful of pebbles by the roadside, and bring them on board ship and label them as coming from twenty celebrated localities five hundred miles apart. I remonstrate against these outrages upon reason and truth, of course, but it does no good. I get the same tranquil, unanswerable reply every time:

"It don't signify — the old woman won't know any different."

Ever since we three or four fortunate ones made the midnight trip to Athens, it has afforded him genuine satisfaction to give everybody in the ship a pebble from the Mars Hill where St. Paul preached. He got all those pebbles on the seashore, abreast the ship, but professes to have gathered them from one of our party. However, it is not of any use for me to expose the deception — it affords him pleasure, and does no harm to anybody. He says he never expects to run out of mementoes of St. Paul as long as he is in reach of a sand bank. Well, he is no worse than others. I notice that all travelers supply deficiencies in their collections in the same way. I shall never have any confidence in such things again while I live.

CHAPTER IX.

WE have got so far East now — a hundred and fifty-five degrees of longitude from San Francisco — that my watch cannot "keep the hang" of the time any more. It has grown discouraged, and stopped. I think it did a wise thing. The difference in time between Sebastopol and the Pacific coast is enormous. When it is six o'clock in the morning here, it is somewhere about week before last in California. We are excusable for getting a little tangled as to time. These distractions and distresses about the time have worried me so much that I was afraid my mind was so much affected that I never would have any appreciation of time again; but when I noticed how handy I was yet about comprehending when it was dinner-time, a blessed tranquillity settled down upon me, and I am tortured with doubts and fears no more.

Odessa is about twenty hours' run from Sebastopol, and is the most northerly port in the Black Sea. We came here to get coal, principally. The city has a population of one hundred and thirty-three thousand, and is growing faster than any other small

H**

city out of America. It is a free port, and is the
great grain mart of this particular part of the world.
Its roadstead is full of ships. Engineers are at
work, now, turning the open roadstead into a
spacious artificial harbor. It is to be almost inclosed by massive stone piers, one of which will
extend into the sea over three thousand feet in a
straight line.

I have not felt so much at home for a long time
as I did when I " raised the hill " and stood in
Odessa for the first time. It looked just like an
American city; fine, broad streets, and straight as
well; low houses (two or three stories), wide, neat,
and free from any quaintness of architectural ornamentation; locust trees bordering the sidewalks
(they call them acacias); a stirring, business-look
about the streets and the stores; fast walkers; a
familiar *new* look about the houses and everything;
yea, and a driving and smothering cloud of dust that
was so like a message from our own dear native
land that we could hardly refrain from shedding a
few grateful tears and execrations in the old time-
honored American way. Look up the street or
down the street, this way or that way, we saw only
America! There was not one thing to remind us
that we were in Russia. We walked for some little
distance, reveling in this home vision, and then we
came upon a church and a hack-driver, and presto!
the illusion vanished! The church had a slender-
spired dome that rounded inward at its base, and

looked like a turnip turned upside down, and the
hackman seemed to be dressed in a long petticoat
without any hoops. These things were essentially
foreign, and so were the carriages — but everybody
knows about these things, and there is no occasion
for my describing them.

We were only to stay here a day and a night and
take in coal; we consulted the guide-books and were
rejoiced to know that there were no sights in Odessa
to see; and so we had one good, untrammeled
holiday on our hands, with nothing to do but idle
about the city and enjoy ourselves. We sauntered
through the markets and criticised the fearful and
wonderful costumes from the back country; examined the populace as far as eyes could do it; and
closed the entertainment with an ice-cream debauch.
We do not get ice-cream everywhere, and so, when
we do, we are apt to dissipate to excess. We
never cared anything about ice-cream at home, but
we look upon it with a sort of idolatry now that it is
so scarce in these red-hot climates of the East.

We only found two pieces of statuary, and this
was another blessing. One was a bronze image of
the Duc de Richelieu, grandnephew of the splendid
Cardinal. It stood in a spacious, handsome prom-
enade, overlooking the sea, and from its base a vast
flight of stone steps led down to the harbor — two
hundred of them, fifty feet long, and a wide landing
at the bottom of every twenty. It is a noble staircase, and from a distance the people toiling up it

looked like insects. I mention this statue and this stairway because they have their story. Richelieu founded Odessa — watched over it with paternal care — labored with a fertile brain and a wise understanding for its best interests — spent his fortune freely to the same end — endowed it with a sound prosperity, and one which will yet make it one of the great cities of the Old World — built this noble stairway with money from his own private purse — and —— Well, the people for whom he had done so much let him walk down these same steps, one day, unattended, old, poor, without a second coat to his back; and when, years afterward, he died in Sebastopol in poverty and neglect, they called a meeting, subscribed liberally, and immediately erected this tasteful monument to his memory, and named a great street after him. It reminds me of what Robert Burns' mother said when they erected a stately monument to his memory: "Ah, Robbie, ye asked them for bread and they hae gi'en ye a stane."

The people of Odessa have warmly recommended us to go and call on the Emperor, as did the Sebastopolians. They have telegraphed his Majesty, and he has signified his willingness to grant us an audience. So we are getting up the anchors and preparing to sail to his watering-place. What a scratching around there will be now! what a holding of important meetings and appointing of solemn committees! — and what a furbishing up of claw-hammer coats and white silk neckties! As this fearful ordeal we are about to pass through pictures itself to my fancy in all its dread sublimity, I begin to feel my fierce desire to converse with a genuine Emperor cooling down and passing away. What am I to do with my hands? What am I to do with my feet? What in the world am I to do with myself?

CHAPTER X.

WE anchored here at Yalta, Russia, two or three days ago. To me the place was a vision of the Sierras. The tall, gray mountains that back it, their sides bristling with pines — cloven with ravines — here and there a hoary rock towering into view — long, straight streaks sweeping down from the summit to the sea, marking the passage of some avalanche of former times — all these were as like what one sees in the Sierras as if the one were a portrait of the other. The little village of Yalta nestles at the foot of an amphitheater which slopes backward and upward to the wall of hills, and looks as if it might have sunk quietly down to its present position from a higher elevation. This depression is covered with the great parks and gardens of noblemen, and through the mass of green foliage the bright colors of their palaces bud out here and there like flowers. It is a beautiful spot.

We had the United States consul on board — the Odessa consul. We assembled in the cabin and commanded him to tell us what we must do to be saved, and tell us quickly. He made a speech.

The first thing he said fell like a blight on every
hopeful spirit; he had never seen a court reception.
(Three groans for the consul.)   But he said he had
seen receptions at the Governor-General's in Odessa,
and had often listened to people's experiences of
receptions at the Russian and other courts, and believed he knew very well what sort of ordeal we were
about to essay.   (Hope budded again.)   He said
we were many; the summer-palace was small — a
mere mansion; doubtless we should be received in
summer fashion — in the garden; we would stand in
a row, all the gentlemen in swallow-tail coats, white
kids, and white neckties, and the ladies in light-
colored silks, or something of that kind; at the
proper moment — 12 meridian — the Emperor, attended by his suite arrayed in splendid uniforms,
would appear and walk slowly along the line, bowing
to some, and saying two or three words to others.
At the moment his Majesty appeared, a universal,
delighted, enthusiastic smile ought to break out like
a rash among the passengers — a smile of love, of
gratification, of admiration — and with one accord,
the party must begin to bow — not obsequiously,
but respectfully, and with dignity; at the end of
fifteen minutes the Emperor would go in the house,
and we could run along home again.   We felt im-
mensely relieved.   It seemed, in a manner, easy.
There was not a man in the party but believed that
with a little practice he could stand in a row, especially if there were others along; there was not a man

but believed he could bow without tripping on his coat-tail and breaking his neck; in a word, we came to believe we were equal to any item in the performance except that complicated smile. The consul also said we ought to draft a little address to the Emperor, and present it to one of his aids-de-camp, who would forward it to him at the proper time. Therefore, five gentlemen were appointed to prepare the document, and the fifty others went sadly smiling about the ship — practicing. During the next twelve hours we had the general appearance, somehow, of being at a funeral, where everybody was sorry the death had occurred, but glad it was over — where everybody was smiling, and yet broken-hearted.

A committee went ashore to wait on his Excellency, the Governor-General, and learn our fate. At the end of three hours of boding suspense, they came back and said the Emperor would receive us at noon the next day — would send carriages for us — would hear the address in person. The Grand Duke Michael had sent to invite us to his palace also. Any man could see that there was an intention here to show that Russia's friendship for America was so genuine as to render even her private citizens objects worthy of kindly attentions.

At the appointed hour we drove out three miles, and assembled in the handsome garden in front of the Emperor's palace.

We formed a circle under the trees before the

door, for there was no one room in the house able to accommodate our threescore persons comfortably, and in a few minutes the imperial family came out bowing and smiling, and stood in our midst. A number of great dignitaries of the empire, in undress uniforms, came with them. With every bow, His Majesty said a word of welcome. I copy these speeches. There is character in them — Russian character — which is politeness itself, and the genuine article. The French are polite, but it is often mere ceremonious politeness. A Russian imbues his polite things with a heartiness, both of phrase and expression, that compels belief in their sincerity. As I was saying, the Czar punctuated his speeches with bows:

" Good morning — I am glad to see you — I am gratified — I am delighted — I am happy to receive you !"

All took off their hats, and the consul inflicted the address on him. He bore it with unflinching fortitude ; then took the rusty-looking document and handed it to some great officer or other, to be filed away among the archives of Russia — in the stove. He thanked us for the address, and said he was very much pleased to see us, especially as such friendly relations existed between Russia and the United States. The Empress said the Americans were favorites in Russia, and she hoped the Russians were similarly regarded in America. These were all the speeches that were made, and I recommend them to

parties who present policemen with gold watches, as
models of brevity and point. After this the Empress went and talked sociably (for an Empress)
with various ladies around the circle; several gentlemen entered into a disjointed general conversation
with the Emperor; the Dukes and Princes, Admirals
and Maids of Honor dropped into free-and-easy
chat with first one and then another of our party,
and whoever chose stepped forward and spoke with
the modest little Grand Duchess Marie, the Czar's
daughter. She is fourteen years old, light-haired,
blue-eyed, unassuming, and pretty. Everybody talks
English.

The Emperor wore a cap, frock-coat, and pantaloons, all of some kind of plain white drilling —
cotton or linen — and sported no jewelry or any
insignia whatever of rank. No costume could be
less ostentatious. He is very tall and spare, and a
determined-looking man, though a very pleasant-
looking one, nevertheless. It is easy to see that he
is kind and affectionate. There is something very
noble in his expression when his cap is off. There
is none of that cunning in his eye that all of us
noticed in Louis Napoleon's.

The Empress and the little Grand Duchess wore
simple suits of foulard (or foulard silk, I don't know
which is proper), with a small blue spot in it; the
dresses were trimmed with blue; both ladies wore
broad blue sashes about their waists; linen collars
and clerical ties of muslin; low-crowned straw-hats

trimmed with blue velvet; parasols and flesh-colored
gloves.   The Grand Duchess had no heels on her
shoes.   I do not know this of my own knowledge,
but one of our ladies told me so.   I was not looking
at her shoes.   I was glad to observe that she wore
her own hair, plaited in thick braids against the back
of her head, instead of the uncomely thing they call
a waterfall, which is about as much like a waterfall
as a canvas-covered ham is like a cataract.   Taking
the kind expression that is in the Emperor's face
and the gentleness that is in his young daughter's
into consideration, I wondered if it would not tax
the Czar's firmness to the utmost to condemn a sup-
plicating wretch to misery in the wastes of Siberia
if she pleaded for him.   Every time their eyes met,
I saw more and more what a tremendous power that
weak, diffident schoolgirl could wield if she chose
to do it.   Many and many a time she might rule the
Autocrat of Russia, whose lightest word is law to
seventy millions of human beings!   She was only a
girl, and she looked like a thousand others I have
seen, but never a girl provoked such a novel and
peculiar interest in me before.   A strange, new
sensation is a rare thing in this humdrum life, and
I had it here.   There was nothing stale or worn out
about the thoughts and feelings the situation and
the circumstances created.   It seemed strange —
stranger than I can tell — to think that the central
figure in the cluster of men and women, chatting
here under the trees like the most ordinary individual

in the land, was a man who could open his lips and
ships would fly through the waves, locomotives
would speed over the plains, couriers would hurry
from village to village, a hundred telegraphs would
flash the word to the four corners of an empire that
stretches its vast proportions over a seventh part of
the habitable globe, and a countless multitude of
men would spring to do his bidding. I had a sort
of vague desire to examine his hands and see if they
were of flesh and blood, like other men's. Here
was a man who could do this wonderful thing, and
yet if I chose I could knock him down. The case
was plain, but it seemed preposterous, nevertheless
— as preposterous as trying to knock down a mountain or wipe out a continent. If this man sprained
his ankle, a million miles of telegraph would carry
the news over mountains — valleys — uninhabited
deserts — under the trackless sea — and ten thousand newspapers would prate of it; if he were
grievously ill, all the nations would know it before
the sun rose again; if he dropped lifeless where he
stood, his fall might shake the thrones of half a
world! If I could have stolen his coat, I would
have done it. When I meet a man like that, I want
something to remember him by.

As a general thing, we have been shown through
palaces by some plush-legged, filigreed flunkey or
other, who charged a franc for it; but after talking
with the company half an hour, the Emperor of
Russia and his family conducted us all through their

mansion themselves. They made no charge. They seemed to take a real pleasure in it.

We spent half an hour idling through the palace, admiring the cosy apartments and the rich but eminently home-like appointments of the place, and then the imperial family bade our party a kind goodbye, and proceeded to count the spoons.

An invitation was extended to us to visit the palace of the eldest son, the Crown Prince of Russia, which was near at hand. The young man was absent, but the Dukes and Countesses and Princes went over the premises with us as leisurely as was the case at the Emperor's, and conversation continued as lively as ever.

It was a little after one o'clock now. We drove to the Grand Duke Michael's, a mile away, in response to his invitation, previously given.

We arrived in twenty minutes from the Emperor's. It is a lovely place. The beautiful palace nestles among the grand old groves of the park, the park sits in the lap of the picturesque crags and hills, and both look out upon the breezy ocean. In the park are rustic seats, here and there, in secluded nooks that are dark with shade; there are rivulets of crystal water; there are lakelets, with inviting, grassy banks; there are glimpses of sparkling cascades through openings in the wilderness of foliage; there are streams of clear water gushing from mimic knots on the trunks of forest trees; there are miniature marble temples perched upon gray old

9**

crags; there are airy lookouts whence one may gaze
upon a broad expanse of landscape and ocean.
The palace is modeled after the choicest forms of
Grecian architecture, and its wide colonnades surround a central court that is banked with rare
flowers that fill the place with their fragrance, and in
their midst springs a fountain that cools the summer
air, and may possibly breed mosquitoes, but I do
not think it does.

The Grand Duke and his Duchess came out, and
the presentation ceremonies were as simple as they
had been at the Emperor's. In a few minutes,
conversation was under way, as before. The Empress appeared in the veranda, and the little Grand
Duchess came out into the crowd. They had beaten
us there. In a few minutes, the Emperor came
himself on horseback. It was very pleasant. You
can appreciate it if you have ever visited royalty
and felt occasionally that possibly you might be
wearing out your welcome — though as a general
thing, I believe, royalty is not scrupulous about
discharging you when it is done with you.

The Grand Duke is the third brother of the Emperor, is about thirty-seven years old, perhaps, and
is the princeliest figure in Russia. He is even taller
than the Czar, as straight as an Indian, and bears
himself like one of those gorgeous knights we read
about in romances of the Crusades. He looks like
a great-hearted fellow who would pitch an enemy
into the river in a moment, and then jump in and

risk his life fishing him out again. The stories they tell of him show him to be of a brave and generous nature. He must have been desirous of proving that Americans were welcome guests in the imperial palaces of Russia, because he rode all the way to Yalta and escorted our procession to the Emperor's himself, and kept his aids scurrying about, clearing the road and offering assistance wherever it could be needed. We were rather familiar with him then, because we did not know who he was. We recognized him now, and appreciated the friendly spirit that prompted him to do us a favor that any other Grand Duke in the world would have doubtless declined to do. He had plenty of servitors whom he could have sent, but he chose to attend to the matter himself.

The Grand Duke was dressed in the handsome and showy uniform of a Cossack officer. The Grand Duchess had on a white alpaca robe, with the seams and gores trimmed with black barb lace, and a little gray hat with a feather of the same color. She is young, rather pretty, modest and unpretending, and full of winning politeness.

Our party walked all through the house, and then the nobility escorted them all over the grounds, and finally brought them back to the palace about half-past two o'clock to breakfast. They called it breakfast, but we would have called it luncheon. It consisted of two kinds of wine; tea, bread, cheese, and cold meats, and was served on the center-tables in

9**

the reception-room and the verandas — anywhere
that was convenient; there was no ceremony. It
was a sort of picnic. I had heard before that we
were to breakfast there, but Blucher said he believed
Baker's boy had suggested it to his Imperial High-
ness. I think not — though it would be like him.
Baker's boy is the famine-breeder of the ship. He
is always hungry. They say he goes about the
staterooms when the passengers are out, and eats up
all the soap. And they say he eats oakum. They
say he will eat anything he can get between meals,
but he prefers oakum. He does not like oakum for
dinner, but he likes it for a lunch, at odd hours, or
anything that way. It makes him very disagreeable,
because it makes his breath bad, and keeps his teeth
all stuck up with tar. Baker's boy may have suggested the breakfast, but I hope he did not. It
went off well, anyhow. The illustrious host moved
about from place to place, and helped to destroy the
provisions and keep the conversation lively, and the
Grand Duchess talked with the veranda parties and
such as had satisfied their appetites and straggled
out from the reception-room.

The Grand Duke's tea was delicious. They give
one a lemon to squeeze into it, or iced milk, if he
prefers it. The former is best. This tea is brought
overland from China. It injures the article to
transport it by sea.

When it was time to go, we bade our distinguished
hosts good-bye, and they retired happy and

contented to their apartments to count *their*
spoons.

We had spent the best part of half a day in the
home of royalty, and had been as cheerful and comfortable all the time as we could have been in the
ship. I would as soon have thought of being cheerful in Abraham's bosom as in the palace of an
Emperor. I supposed that Emperors were terrible
people. I thought they never did anything but wear
magnificent crowns and red velvet dressing-gowns
with dabs of wool sewed on them in spots, and sit
on thrones and scowl at the flunkies and the people
in the parquette, and order Dukes and Duchesses
off to execution. I find, however, that when one is
so fortunate as to get behind the scenes and see them
at home and in the privacy of their firesides, they
are strangely like common mortals. They are
pleasanter to look upon then than they are in their
theatrical aspect. It seems to come as natural to
them to dress and act like other people as it is to
put a friend's cedar pencil in your pocket when you
are done using it. But I can never have any confidence in the tinsel kings of the theater after this.
It will be a great loss. I used to take such a thrilling pleasure in them. But, hereafter, I will turn
me sadly away and say:

"This does not answer — this isn't the style of
king that *I* am acquainted with."

When they swagger around the stage in jeweled
crowns and splendid robes, I shall feel bound to ob-

I **

serve that all the Emperors that ever *I* was personally acquainted with wore the commonest sort of clothes, and did not swagger. And when they come on the stage attended by a vast body-guard of supes in helmets and tin breastplates, it will be my duty as well as my pleasure to inform the ignorant that no crowned head of my acquaintance has a soldier anywhere about his house or his person.

Possibly it may be thought that our party tarried too long, or did other improper things, but such was not the case. The company felt that they were occupying an unusually responsible position — they were representing the people of America, not the government — and therefore they were careful to do their best to perform their high mission with credit.

On the other hand, the Imperial families, no doubt, considered that in entertaining us they were more especially entertaining the people of America than they could by showering attentions on a whole platoon of ministers plenipotentiary; and therefore they gave to the event its fullest significance, as an expression of good will and friendly feeling toward the entire country. We took the kindnesses we received as attentions thus directed, of course, and not to ourselves as a party. That we felt a personal pride in being received as the representatives of a nation, we do not deny; that we felt a national pride in the warm cordiality of that reception, cannot be doubted.

Our poet has been rigidly suppressed, from the time we let go the anchor. When it was announced that we were going to visit the Emperor of Russia, the fountains of his great deep were broken up, and he rained ineffable bosh for four-and-twenty hours. Our original anxiety as to what we were going to do with ourselves, was suddenly transformed into anxiety about what we were going to do with our poet. The problem was solved at last. Two alternatives were offered him — he must either swear a dreadful oath that he would not issue a line of his poetry while he was in the Czar's dominions, or else remain under guard on board the ship until we were safe at Constantinople again. He fought the dilemma long, but yielded at last. It was a great deliverance. Perhaps the savage reader would like a specimen of his style. I do not mean this term to be offensive. I only use it because "the gentle reader" has been used so often that any change from it cannot but be refreshing:

> "Save us and sanctify us, and finally, then,
>   See good provisions we enjoy while we journey to
>   Jerusa*lem*.
>   For so man proposes, which it is most true,
>   And time will wait for none, nor for us too."

The sea has been unusually rough all day. However, we have had a lively time of it, anyhow. We have had quite a run of visitors. The Governor-General came, and we received him with a salute of nine guns. He brought his family with him. I

observed that carpets were spread from the pier-head
to his carriage for him to walk on, though I have seen
him walk there without any carpet when he was not
on business. I thought may be he had what the
accidental insurance people might call an extra-hazardous polish (" policy " — joke, but not above
mediocrity) on his boots, and wished to protect
them, but I examined and could not see that they
were blacked any better than usual. It may have
been that he had forgotten his carpet before, but he
did not have it with him, anyhow. He was an exceedingly pleasant old gentleman; we all liked him,
especially Blucher. When he went away, Blucher
invited him to come again and fetch his carpet
along.

Prince Dolgorouki and a Grand Admiral or two,
whom we had seen yesterday at the reception, came
on board also. I was a little distant with these
parties, at first, because when I have been visiting
Emperors I do not like to be too familiar with people
I only know by reputation, and whose moral characters and standing in society I cannot be thoroughly
acquainted with. I judged it best to be a little
offish, at first. I said to myself, Princes and Counts
and Grand Admirals are very well, but they are not
Emperors, and one cannot be too particular about
whom he associates with.

Baron Wrangel came, also. He used to be a Russian Ambassador at Washington. I told him I had
an uncle who fell down a shaft and broke himself in

two, as much as a year before that. That was a falsehood, but then I was not going to let any man eclipse me on surprising adventures, merely for the want of a little invention. The Baron is a fine man, and is said to stand high in the Emperor's confidence and esteem.

Baron Ungern-Sternberg, a boisterous, whole-souled old nobleman, came with the rest. He is a man of progress and enterprise — a representative man of the age. He is the Chief Director of the railway system of Russia — a sort of railroad king. In his line he is making things move along in this country. He has traveled extensively in America. He says he has tried convict labor on his railroads, and with perfect success. He says the convicts work well, and are quiet and peaceable. He observed that he employs nearly ten thousand of them now. This appeared to be another call on my resources. I was equal to the emergency. I said we had eighty thousand convicts employed on the railways in America — all of them under sentence of death for murder in the first degree. That closed *him* out. We had General Todleben (the famous defender of Sebastopol, during the siege), and many inferior army and also navy officers, and a number of un-official Russian ladies and gentlemen. Naturally, a champagne luncheon was in order, and was accom-plished without loss of life. Toasts and jokes were discharged freely, but no speeches were made save one thanking the Emperor and the Grand Duke,

through the Governor-General, for our hospitable
reception, and one by the Governor-General in reply,
in which he returned the Emperor's thanks for
the speech, etc.

CHAPTER XI.

WE returned to Constantinople, and after a day or two spent in exhausting marches about the city and voyages up the Golden Horn in *caïques*, we steamed away again. We passed through the Sea of Marmora and the Dardanelles, and steered for a new land — a new one to us, at least — Asia. We had as yet only acquired a bowing acquaintance with it, through pleasure excursions to Scutari and the regions round about.

We passed between Lemnos and Mytilene, and saw them as we had seen Elba and the Balearic Isles — mere bulky shapes, with the softening mists of distance upon them — whales in a fog, as it were. Then we held our course southward, and began to "read up" celebrated Smyrna.

At all hours of the day and night the sailors in the forecastle amused themselves and aggravated us by burlesquing our visit to royalty. The opening paragraph of our Address to the Emperor was framed as follows:

"We are a handful of private citizens of America, traveling simply for recreation — and unostentatiously, as becomes our unofficial state — and, there-fore, we have no excuse to tender for presenting ourselves before Your Majesty, save the desire of offering our grateful acknowledgments to the lord of a realm, which, through good and through evil re-port, has been the steadfast friend of the land we love so well."

The third cook, crowned with a resplendent tin basin and wrapped royally in a tablecloth mottled with grease-spots and coffee-stains, and bearing a scepter that looked strangely like a belaying pin, walked upon a dilapidated carpet and perched himself on the capstan, careless of the flying spray; his tarred and weather-beaten Chamberlains, Dukes, and Lord High Admirals surrounded him, arrayed in all the pomp that spare tarpaulins and remnants of old sails could furnish. Then the visiting " watch be-low," transformed into graceless ladies and uncouth pilgrims, by rude travesties upon waterfalls, hoop-skirts, white kid gloves, and swallow-tail coats, moved solemnly up the companion-way, and bowing low, began a system of complicated and extraordinary smiling which few monarchs could look upon and live. Then the mock consul, a slush-plastered deck-sweep, drew out a soiled fragment of paper and pro-ceeded to read, laboriously:

" To His Imperial Majesty, Alexander II., Em-peror of Russia:

" We are a handful of private citizens of America, traveling simply for recreation — and unostenta-

tiously, as becomes our unofficial state — and therefore, we have no excuse to tender for presenting
ourselves before your Majesty — ''

The Emperor — '' Then what the devil did you
come for ? ''

— '' Save the desire of offering our grateful acknowledgments to the lord of a realm which — ''

The Emperor — '' Oh, d—n the Address ! — read
it to the police.   Chamberlain, take these people
over to my brother, the Grand Duke's, and give
them a square meal.   Adieu !   I am happy — I am
gratified — I am delighted — I am bored.   Adieu,
adieu — vamose the ranch !   The First Groom of the
Palace will proceed to count the portable articles of
value belonging to the premises.''

The farce then closed, to be repeated again with
every change of the watches, and embellished with
new and still more extravagant inventions of pomp
and conversation.

At all times of the day and night the phraseology
of that tiresome address fell upon our ears.   Grimy
sailors came down out of the foretop placidly announcing themselves as '' a handful of private citizens of America, *traveling simply for recreation* and
unostentatiously,'' etc.;   the coal-passers moved to
their duties in the profound depths of the ship, ex-
plaining the blackness of their faces and their un-
couthness of dress, with the reminder that *they* were
'' a handful of private citizens, traveling simply for
recreation,'' etc., and when the cry rang through

the vessel at midnight: "EIGHT BELLS!—LAR-
BOARD WATCH, TURN OUT!" the larboard watch
came gaping and stretching out of their den, with the
everlasting formula: "Aye, aye, sir! We are a
handful of private citizens of America, traveling
simply for recreation, and unostentatiously, as becomes our unofficial state!"

As I was a member of the committee, and helped
to frame the Address, these sarcasms came home to
me. I never heard a sailor proclaiming himself as a
handful of American citizens traveling for recreation,
but I wished he might trip and fall overboard, and
so reduce his handful by one individual, at least. I
never was so tired of any one phrase as the sailors
made me of the opening sentence of the Address to
the Emperor of Russia.

This seaport of Smyrna, our first notable acquaintance in Asia, is a closely-packed city of one hundred
and thirty thousand inhabitants, and, like Constantinople, it has no outskirts. It is as closely packed at
its outer edges as it is in the center, and then the
habitations leave suddenly off and the plain beyond
seems houseless. It is just like any other Oriental
city. That is to say, its Moslem houses are heavy
and dark, and as comfortless as so many tombs; its
streets are crooked, rudely and roughly paved, and
as narrow as an ordinary staircase; the streets uni-
formly carry a man to any other place than the one
he wants to go to, and surprise him by landing him
in the most unexpected localities; business is chiefly

carried on in great covered bazaars, celled like a honeycomb with innumerable shops no larger than a common closet, and the whole hive cut up into a maze of alleys about wide enough to accommodate a laden camel, and well calculated to confuse a stranger and eventually lose him; everywhere there is dirt, everywhere there are fleas, everywhere there are lean, broken-hearted dogs; every alley is thronged with people; wherever you look, your eye rests upon a wild masquerade of extravagant costumes; the workshops are all open to the streets, and the workmen visible; all manner of sounds assail the ear, and over them all rings out the muezzin's cry from some tall minaret, calling the faithful vagabonds to prayer; and superior to the call to prayer, the noises in the streets, the interest of the costumes — superior to everything, and claiming the bulk of attention first, last, and all the time — is a combination of Mohammedan stenches, to which the smell of even a Chinese quarter would be as pleasant as the roasting odors of the fatted calf to the nostrils of the returning Prodigal. Such is Oriental luxury — such is Oriental splendor! We read about it all our days, but we comprehend it not until we see it. Smyrna is a very old city. Its name occurs several times in the Bible, one or two of the disciples of Christ visited it, and here was located one of the original seven apocalyptic churches spoken of in Revelations. These churches were symbolized in the Scriptures as candlesticks, and on certain conditions there was a

sort of implied promise that Smyrna should be endowed with a "crown of life." She was to "be
faithful unto death"—those were the terms. She
has not kept up her faith straight along, but the pilgrims that wander hither consider that she has come
near enough to it to save her, and so they point to
the fact that Smyrna to-day wears her crown of life,
and is a great city, with a great commerce and full
of energy, while the cities wherein were located the
other six churches, and to which no crown of life
was promised, have vanished from the earth. So
Smyrna really still possesses her crown of life, in
a business point of view. Her career, for eighteen
centuries, has been a chequered one, and she has
been under the rule of princes of many creeds, yet
there has been no season during all that time, as far
as we know (and during such seasons as she was inhabited at all), that she has been without her little
community of Christians "faithful unto death."
Hers was the only church against which no threats
were implied in the Revelation, and the only one
which survived.

With Ephesus, forty miles from here, where was
located another of the seven churches, the case was
different. The "candlestick" has been removed
from Ephesus. Her light has been put out. Pilgrims, always prone to find prophecies in the Bible,
and often where none exist, speak cheerfully and
complacently of poor, ruined Ephesus as the victim
of prophecy. And yet there is no sentence that

promises, without due qualification, the destruction of the city.   The words are:

> "Remember, therefore, from whence thou art fallen, and repent, and do the first works; or else I will come unto thee quickly, and will remove thy candlestick out of his place, except thou repent."

That is all; the other verses are singularly *complimentary* to Ephesus.   The threat is qualified.   There is no history to show that she did not repent.   But the cruelest habit the modern prophecy-savans have, is that one of coolly and arbitrarily fitting the prophetic shirt on to the wrong man.   They do it without regard to rhyme or reason.   Both the cases I have just mentioned are instances in point.   Those "prophecies" are distinctly leveled at the "*churches* of Ephesus, Smyrna,*" etc., and yet the pilgrims invariably make them refer to the *cities* instead.   No crown of life is promised to the town of Smyrna and its commerce, but to the handful of Christians who formed its "church."   If *they* were "faithful unto death," they have their crown now — but no amount of faithfulness and legal shrewdness combined could legitimately drag the *city* into a participation in the promises of the prophecy.   The stately language of the Bible refers to a crown of life whose luster will reflect the day-beams of the endless ages of eternity, not the butterfly existence of a city built by men's hands, which must pass to dust with the builders and be forgotten even in the mere handful of centuries vouchsafed to the solid world itself between its cradle and its grave.

10**

The fashion of delving out fulfillments of prophecy where that prophecy consists of mere " ifs," trenches upon the absurd. Suppose, a thousand years from now, a malarious swamp builds itself up in the shallow harbor of Smyrna, or something else kills the town; and suppose, also, that within that time the swamp that has filled the renowned harbor of Ephesus and rendered her ancient site deadly and uninhabitable to-day, becomes hard and healthy ground; suppose the natural consequence ensues, to wit: that Smyrna becomes a melancholy ruin, and Ephesus is rebuilt. What would the prophecy savans say? They would coolly skip over our age of the world, and say: " Smyrna was not faithful unto death, and so her crown of life was denied her; Ephesus repented, and lo! her candlestick was not removed. Behold these evidences! How wonderful is prophecy!"

Smyrna has been utterly destroyed six times. If her crown of life had been an insurance policy, she would have had an opportunity to collect on it the first time she fell. But she holds it on sufferance and by a complimentary construction of language which does not refer to her. Six different times, however, I suppose some infatuated prophecy-enthusiast blundered along and said, to the infinite disgust of Smyrna and the Smyrniotes: " In sooth, here is astounding fulfillment of prophecy! Smyrna hath not been faithful unto death, and behold her crown of life is vanished from her head. Verily, these things be astonishing!"

Such things have a bad influence. They provoke worldly men into using light conversation concerning sacred subjects. Thick-headed commentators upon the Bible, and stupid preachers and teachers, work more damage to religion than sensible, cool-brained clergymen can fight away again, toil as they may. It is not good judgment to fit a crown of life upon a city which has been destroyed six times. That other class of wiseacres who twist prophecy in such a manner as to make it promise the destruction and desolation of the same city, use judgment just as bad, since the city is in a very flourishing condition now, unhappily for them. These things put arguments into the mouth of infidelity.

A portion of the city is pretty exclusively Turkish; the Jews have a quarter to themselves; the Franks another quarter; so, also, with the Armenians. The Armenians, of course, are Christians. Their houses are large, clean, airy, handsomely paved with black and white squares of marble, and in the center of many of them is a square court, which has in it a luxuriant flower-garden and a sparkling fountain; the doors of all the rooms open on this. A very wide hall leads to the street door, and in this the women sit, the most of the day. In the cool of the evening they dress up in their best raiment and show themselves at the door. They are all comely of countenance, and exceedingly neat and cleanly; they look as if they were just out of a band-box. Some of the young ladies — many of them, I

10**

may say — are even very beautiful; they average a shade better than American girls — which treasonable words I pray may be forgiven me. They are very sociable, and will smile back when a stranger smiles at them, bow back when he bows, and talk back if he speaks to them. No introduction is required. An hour's chat at the door with a pretty girl one never saw before, is easily obtained, and is very pleasant. I have tried it. I could not talk anything but English, and the girl knew nothing but Greek, or Armenian, or some such barbarous tongue, but we got along very well. I find that in cases like these, the fact that you cannot comprehend each other isn't much of a drawback. In that Russian town of Yalta I danced an astonishing sort of dance an hour long, and one I had not heard of before, with a very pretty girl, and we talked incessantly, and laughed exhaustingly, and neither one ever knew what the other was driving at. But it was splendid. There were twenty people in the set, and the dance was very lively and complicated. It was complicated enough without me — with me it was more so. I threw in a figure now and then that surprised those Russians. But I have never ceased to think of that girl. I have written to her, but I cannot direct the epistle because her name is one of those nine-jointed Russian affairs, and there are not letters enough in our alphabet to hold out. I am not reckless enough to try to pronounce it when I am awake, but I make a stagger at it in my dreams, and get up with the lockjaw in the morning. I am fading. I do not take my meals now, with any sort of regularity. Her dear name haunts me still in my dreams. It is awful on teeth. It never comes out of my mouth but it fetches an old snag along with it. And then the lockjaw closes down and nips off a couple of the last syllables — but they taste good.

Coming through the Dardanelles, we saw camel trains on shore with the glasses, but we were never close to one till we got to Smyrna. These camels are very much larger than the scrawny specimens one sees in the menagerie. They stride along these streets, in single file, a dozen in a train, with heavy loads on their backs, and a fancy-looking negro in Turkish costume, or an Arab, preceding them on a little donkey and completely overshadowed and rendered insignificant by the huge beasts. To see a camel train laden with the spices of Arabia and the rare fabrics of Persia come marching through the narrow alleys of the bazaar, among porters with their burdens, money-changers, lamp-merchants, Alnaschars in the glassware business, portly cross-legged Turks smoking the famous narghili, and the crowds drifting to and fro in the fanciful costumes of the East, is a genuine revelation of the Orient. The picture lacks nothing. It casts you back at once into your forgotten boyhood, and again you dream over the wonders of the Arabian Nights; again your companions are princes, your lord is the

Caliph Haroun Al Raschid, and your servants are
terrific giants and genii that come with smoke and
lightning and thunder, and go as a storm goes when
they depart!

CHAPTER XII.

WE inquired, and learned that the lions of Smyrna consisted of the ruins of the ancient citadel, whose broken and prodigious battlements frown upon the city from a lofty hill just in the edge of the town — the Mount Pagus of Scripture, they call it; the site of that one of the seven apocalyptic churches of Asia which was located here in the first century of the Christian era; and the grave and the place of martyrdom of the venerable Polycarp, who suffered in Smyrna for his religion some eighteen hundred years ago.

We took little donkeys and started. We saw Polycarp's tomb, and then hurried on.

The "Seven Churches"—thus they abbreviate it — came next on the list. We rode there — about a mile and a half in the sweltering sun — and visited a little Greek church which they said was built upon the ancient site; and we paid a small fee, and the holy attendant gave each of us a little wax candle as a remembrancer of the place, and I put mine in my hat and the sun melted it and the grease all ran down the back of my neck; and so now I have not

anything left but the wick, and it is a sorry and
wilted-looking wick at that.

Several of us argued as well as we could that the
" church " mentioned in the Bible meant a party of
Christians, and not a building; that the Bible spoke
of them as being very poor — so poor, I thought,
and so subject to persecution (as per Polycarp's
martyrdom) that in the first place they probably
could not have afforded a church edifice, and in the
second would not have dared to build it in the open
light of day if they could; and finally, that if they
had had the privilege of building it, common judgment would have suggested that they build it somewhere near the town. But the elders of the ship's
family ruled us down and scouted our evidences.
However, retribution came to them afterward. They
found that they had been led astray and had gone to
the wrong place; they discovered that the accepted
site is in the city.

Riding through the town, we could see marks of
the six Smyrnas that have existed here and been
burned up by fire or knocked down by earthquakes.
The hills and the rocks are rent asunder in places,
excavations expose great blocks of building-stone
that have lain buried for ages, and all the mean
houses and walls of modern Smyrna along the way
are spotted white with broken pillars, capitals, and
fragments of sculptured marble that once adorned
the lordly palaces that were the glory of the city in
the olden time.

The ascent of the hill of the citadel is very steep, and we proceeded rather slowly. But there were matters of interest about us. In one place, five hundred feet above the sea, the perpendicular bank on the upper side of the road was ten or fifteen feet high, and the cut exposed three veins of oyster-shells, just as we have seen quartz veins exposed in the cutting of a road in Nevada or Montana. The veins were about eighteen inches thick and two or three feet apart, and they slanted along downward for a distance of thirty feet or more, and then disappeared where the cut joined the road. Heaven only knows how far a man might trace them by "stripping." They were clean, nice oyster-shells, large, and just like any other oyster-shells. They were thickly massed together, and none were scattered above or below the veins. Each one was a well-defined lead by itself, and without a spur. My first instinct was to set up the usual —

NOTICE:

"We, the undersigned, claim five claims of two hundred feet each (and one for discovery) on this ledge or lode of oyster-shells, with all its dips, spurs, angles, variations, and sinuosities, and fifty feet on each side of the same, to work it, etc., etc., according to the mining laws of Smyrna."

They were such perfectly natural-looking leads that I could hardly keep from "taking them up." Among the oyster-shells were mixed many fragments of ancient, broken crockeryware. Now how did those masses of oyster-shells get there? I cannot

determine.   Broken crockery and oyster-shells are
suggestive of restaurants — but then they could have
had no such places away up there on that mountain-
side in our time, because nobody has lived up there.
A restaurant would not pay in such a stony, forbidding, desolate place.   And besides, there were no
champagne corks among the shells.   If there ever
was a restaurant there, it must have been in Smyrna's
palmy days, when the hills were covered with palaces.
I could believe in one restaurant, on those terms;
but then how about the three?   Did they have restaurants there at three different periods of the
world? — because there are two or three feet of
solid earth between the oyster leads.   Evidently,
the restaurant solution will not answer.

The hill might have been the bottom of the sea,
once, and been lifted up, with its oyster-beds, by an
earthquake — but, then, how about the crockery?
And, moreover, how about *three* oyster-beds, one
above another, and thick strata of good honest
earth between?

That theory will not do.   It is just possible that
this hill is Mount Ararat, and that Noah's Ark rested
here, and he ate oysters and threw the shells overboard.   But that will not do, either.   There are the
three layers again and the solid earth between —
and, besides, there were only eight in Noah's family,
and they could not have eaten all these oysters in the
two or three months they stayed on top of that
mountain.   The beasts — however, it is simply ab-

surd to suppose he did not know any more than to feed the beasts on oyster suppers.

It is painful — it is even humiliating — but I am reduced at last to one slender theory: that the oysters climbed up there of their own accord. But what object could they have had in view? — what did they want up there? What could any oyster want to climb a hill for? To climb a hill must necessarily be fatiguing and annoying exercise for an oyster. The most natural conclusion would be that the oysters climbed up there to look at the scenery. Yet when one comes to reflect upon the nature of an oyster, it seems plain that he does not care for scenery. An oyster has no taste for such things; he cares nothing for the beautiful. An oyster is of a retiring disposition, and not lively — not even cheerful above the average, and never enterprising. But, above all, an oyster does not take any interest in scenery — he scorns it. What have I arrived at now? Simply at the point I started from, namely, *those oyster shells are there*, in regular layers, five hundred feet above the sea, and no man knows how they got there. I have hunted up the guide-books, and the gist of what they say is this: "They are there, but how they got there is a mystery."

Twenty-five years ago, a multitude of people in America put on their ascension robes, took a tearful leave of their friends, and made ready to fly up into heaven at the first blast of the trumpet. But the

angel did not blow it.   Miller's resurrection day was
a failure.   The Millerites were disgusted.   I did not
suspect that there were Millers in Asia Minor, but a
gentleman tells me that they had it all set for the
world to come to an end in Smyrna one day about
three years ago.   There was much buzzing and
preparation for a long time previously, and it culminated in a wild excitement at the appointed time.
A vast number of the populace ascended the citadel
hill early in the morning, to get out of the way of
the general destruction, and many of the infatuated
closed up their shops and retired from all earthly
business.   But the strange part of it was that about
three in the afternoon, while this gentleman and his
friends were at dinner in the hotel, a terrific storm
of rain, accompanied by thunder and lightning,
broke forth and continued with dire fury for two or
three hours.   It was a thing unprecedented in
Smyrna at that time of the year, and scared some
of the most skeptical.   The streets ran rivers and
the hotel floor was flooded with water.   The dinner
had to be suspended.   When the storm finished and
left everybody drenched through and through, and
melancholy and half-drowned, the ascensionists came
down from the mountain as dry as so many charity-
sermons!   They had been looking down upon the
fearful storm going on below, and really believed
that their proposed destruction of the world was
proving a grand success.

A railway here in Asia — in the dreamy realm of

the Orient — in the fabled land of the Arabian
Nights — is a strange thing to think of.   And yet
they have one already, and are building another.
The present one is well built and well conducted, by
an English Company, but is not doing an immense
amount of business.   The first year it carried a good
many passengers, but its freight list only comprised
eight hundred pounds of figs!

It runs almost to the very gates of Ephesus — a
town great in all ages of the world — a city familiar
to readers of the Bible, and one which was as old as
the very hills when the disciples of Christ preached
in its streets.   It dates back to the shadowy ages of
tradition, and was the birthplace of gods renowned
in Grecian mythology.   The idea of a locomotive
tearing through such a place as this, and waking the
phantoms of its old days of romance out of their
dreams of dead and gone centuries, is curious
enough.

We journey thither to-morrow to see the celebrated ruins.

CHAPTER XIII.

THIS has been a stirring day. The superinten-
dent of the railway put a train at our disposal,
and did us the further kindness of accompanying us
to Ephesus and giving to us his watchful care. We
brought sixty scarcely perceptible donkeys in the
freight cars, for we had much ground to go over.
We have seen some of the most grotesque costumes,
along the line of the railroad, that can be imagined.
I am glad that no possible combination of words
could describe them, for I might then be foolish
enough to attempt it.

At ancient Ayassalook, in the midst of a forbidding desert, we came upon long lines of ruined
aqueducts, and other remnants of architectural
grandeur, that told us plainly enough we were nearing what had been a metropolis once. We left the
train and mounted the donkeys, along with our
invited guests — pleasant young gentlemen from the
officers' list of an American man-of-war.

The little donkeys had saddles upon them which
were made very high in order that the rider's feet
might not drag the ground. The preventative did

not work well in the cases of our tallest pilgrims, however. There were no bridles — nothing but a single rope, tied to the bit. It was purely ornamental, for the donkey cared nothing for it. If he were drifting to starboard, you might put your helm down hard the other way, if it were any satisfaction to you to do it, but he would continue to drift to starboard all the same. There was only one process which could be depended on, and that was to get down and lift his rear around until his head pointed in the right direction, or take him under your arm and carry him to a part of the road which he could not get out of without climbing. The sun flamed down as hot as a furnace, and neck-scarfs, veils, and umbrellas seemed hardly any protection; they served only to make the long procession look more than ever fantastic — for be it known the ladies were all riding astride because they could not stay on the shapeless saddles sidewise, the men were perspiring and out of temper, their feet were banging against the rocks, the donkeys were capering in every direction but the right one and being belabored with clubs for it, and every now and then a broad umbrella would suddenly go down out of the cavalcade, announcing to all that one more pilgrim had bitten the dust. It was a wilder picture than those solitudes had seen for many a day. No donkeys ever existed that were as hard to navigate as these, I think, or that had so many vile, exasperating instincts. Occasionally, we grew so tired and breathless with fighting them that we had to desist,— and immediately the donkey would come down to a deliberate walk. This, with the fatigue, and the sun, would put a man asleep; and as soon as the man was asleep, the donkey would lie down. My donkey shall never see his boyhood's home again. He has lain down once too often. He must die.

We all stood in the vast theater of ancient Ephesus,— the stone-benched amphitheater, I mean — and had our picture taken. We looked as proper there as we would look anywhere, I suppose. We do not embellish the general desolation of a desert much. We add what dignity we can to a stately ruin with our green umbrellas and jackasses, but it is little. However, we mean well.

I wish to say a brief word of the aspect of Ephesus.

On a high, steep hill, toward the sea, is a gray ruin of ponderous blocks of marble, wherein, tradition says, St. Paul was imprisoned eighteen centuries ago. From these old walls you have the finest view of the desolate scene where once stood Ephesus, the proudest city of ancient times, and whose Temple of Diana was so noble in design and so exquisite of workmanship, that it ranked high in the list of the Seven Wonders of the World.

Behind you is the sea; in front is a level green valley (a marsh, in fact), extending far away among the mountains; to the right of the front view is the old citadel of Ayassalook, on a high hill; the ruined mosque of the Sultan Selim stands near it in the plain (this is built over the grave of St. John, and was formerly a Christian church); further toward you is the hill of Prion, around whose front is clustered all that remains of the ruins of Ephesus that still stand; divided from it by a narrow valley is the long, rocky, rugged mountain of Coressus. The scene is a pretty one, and yet desolate — for in that wide plain no man can live, and in it is no human habitation. But for the crumbling arches and monstrous piers and broken walls that rise from the foot of the hill of Prion, one could not believe that in this place once stood a city whose renown is older than tradition itself. It is incredible to reflect that things as familiar all over the world to-day as household words belong in the history and in the shadowy legends of this silent, mournful solitude. We speak of Apollo and of Diana — they were born here; of the metamorphosis of Syrinx into a reed — it was done here; of the great god Pan — he dwelt in the caves of this hill of Coressus; of the Amazons — this was their best-prized home; of Bacchus and Hercules — both fought the warlike women here; of the Cyclops — they laid the ponderous marble blocks of some of the ruins yonder; of Homer — this was one of his many birthplaces; of Cimon of Athens; of Alcibiades, Lysander, Agesilaus — they visited here; so did Alexander the Great; so did Hannibal and Antiochus, Scipio, Lucullus, and Sylla; Brutus, Cassius, Pompey,

11**

Cicero, and Augustus; Antony was a judge in this place, and left his seat in the open court, while the advocates were speaking, to run after Cleopatra, who passed the door; from this city these two sailed on pleasure excursions, in galleys with silver oars and perfumed sails, and with companies of beautiful girls to serve them, and actors and musicians to amuse them; in days that seem almost modern, so remote are they from the early history of this city, Paul the Apostle preached the new religion here, and so did John, and here it is supposed the former was pitted against wild beasts, for in I Corinthians, xv. 32, he says:

"If after the manner of men I have fought with beasts at Ephesus," etc.

when many men still lived who had seen the Christ; here Mary Magdalen died, and here the Virgin Mary ended her days with John, albeit Rome has since judged it best to locate her grave elsewhere; six or seven hundred years ago — almost yesterday, as it were — troops of mail-clad Crusaders thronged the streets; and to come down to trifles, we speak of meandering streams, and find a new interest in a common word when we discover that the crooked river Meander, in yonder valley, gave it to our dictionary. It makes me feel as old as these dreary hills to look down upon these moss-hung ruins, this historic desolation. One may read the Scriptures and believe, but he cannot go and stand yonder in the ruined theater and in imagination people it

again with the vanished multitudes who mobbed
Paul's comrades there and shouted, with one voice,
" Great is Diana of the Ephesians ! " The idea of
a shout in such a solitude as this almost makes one
shudder.

It was a wonderful city, this Ephesus. Go where
you will about these broad plains, you find the most
exquisitely-sculptured marble fragments scattered
thick among the dust and weeds; and protruding
from the ground, or lying prone upon it, are beautiful fluted columns of porphyry and all precious
marbles; and at every step you find elegantly-carved
capitals and massive bases, and polished tablets
engraved with Greek inscriptions. It is a world of
precious relics, a wilderness of marred and mutilated
gems. And yet what are these things to the wonders that lie buried here under the ground? At
Constantinople, at Pisa, in the cities of Spain, are
great mosques and cathedrals, whose grandest columns came from the temples and palaces of Ephesus,
and yet one has only to scratch the ground here to
match them. We shall never know what magnificence is, until this imperial city is laid bare to the
sun.

The finest piece of sculpture we have yet seen
and the one that impressed us most (for we do not
know much about art and cannot easily work up
ourselves into ecstasies over it), is one that lies in
this old theater of Ephesus which St. Paul's riot
has made so celebrated. It is only the headless
11**

body of a man, clad in a coat of mail, with a Medusa head upon the breast-plate, but we feel persuaded that such dignity and such majesty were never thrown into a form of stone before.

What builders they were, these men of antiquity! The massive arches of some of these ruins rest upon piers that are fifteen feet square and built entirely of solid blocks of marble, some of which are as large as a Saratoga trunk, and some the size of a boarding-house sofa. They are not shells or shafts of stone filled inside with rubbish, but the whole pier is a mass of solid masonry. Vast arches, that may have been the gates of the city, are built in the same way. They have braved the storms and sieges of three thousand years, and have been shaken by many an earthquake, but still they stand. When they dig alongside of them, they find ranges of ponderous masonry that are as perfect in every detail as they were the day those old Cyclopean giants finished them. An English company is going to excavate Ephesus — and then!

And now am I reminded of —

THE LEGEND OF THE SEVEN SLEEPERS.

In the Mount of Prion, yonder, is the Cave of the Seven Sleepers. Once upon a time, about fifteen hundred years ago, seven young men lived near each other in Ephesus, who belonged to the despised sect of the Christians. It came to pass that the good King Maximilianus (I am telling this story for nice

little boys and girls), it came to pass, I say, that
the good King Maximilianus fell to persecuting the
Christians, and as time rolled on he made it very
warm for them.   So the seven young men said one to
the other, Let us get up and travel.   And they got
up and traveled.   They tarried not to bid their
fathers and mothers good-bye, or any friend they
knew.   They only took certain moneys which their
parents had, and garments that belonged unto their
friends, whereby they might remember them when
far away; and they took also the dog Ketmehr,
which was the property of their neighbor Malchus,
because the beast did run his head into a noose which
one of the young men was carrying carelessly, and
they had not time to release him; and they took also
certain chickens that seemed lonely in the neighboring coops, and likewise some bottles of curious
liquors that stood near the grocer's window; and
then they departed from the city.   By-and-by they
came to a marvelous cave in the Hill of Prion and
entered into it and feasted, and presently they
hurried on again.   But they forgot the bottles of
curious liquors, and left them behind.   They
traveled in many lands, and had many strange
adventures.   They were virtuous young men, and
lost no opportunity that fell in their way to make
their livelihood.   Their motto was in these words,
namely, "Procrastination is the thief of time."   And
so, whenever they did come upon a man who was
alone, they said, Behold, this person hath the where-

K**

withal — let us go through him. And they went through him. At the end of five years they had waxed tired of travel and adventure, and longed to revisit their old home again and hear the voices and see the faces that were dear unto their youth. Therefore they went through such parties as fell in their way where they sojourned at that time, and journeyed back toward Ephesus again. For the good King Maximilianus was become converted unto the new faith, and the Christians rejoiced because they were no longer persecuted. One day as the sun went down, they came to the cave in the Mount of Prion, and they said, each to his fellow, Let us sleep here, and go and feast and make merry with our friends when the morning cometh. And each of the seven lifted up his voice and said, It is a whiz. So they went in, and lo, where they had put them, there lay the bottles of strange liquors, and they judged that age had not impaired their excellence. Wherein the wanderers were right, and the heads of the same were level. So each of the young men drank six bottles, and behold they felt very tired, then, and lay down and slept soundly.

When they awoke, one of them, Johannes — surnamed Smithianus — said, We are naked. And it was so. Their raiment was all gone, and the money which they had gotten from a stranger whom they had proceeded through as they approached the city, was lying upon the ground, corroded and rusted and defaced. Likewise the dog Ketmehr was gone, and nothing save the brass that was upon his collar remained.   They wondered much at these things. But they took the money, and they wrapped about their bodies some leaves, and came up to the top of the hill.   Then were they perplexed.   The wonderful temple of Diana was gone; many grand edifices they had never seen before stood in the city; men in strange garbs moved about the streets, and every thing was changed.

Johannes said, It hardly seems like Ephesus.   Yet here is the great gymnasium; here is the mighty theater, wherein I have seen seventy thousand men assembled; here is the Agora; there is the font where the sainted John the Baptist immersed the converts; yonder is the prison of the good St. Paul, where we all did use to go to touch the ancient chains that bound him and be cured of our distempers; I see the tomb of the disciple Luke, and afar off is the church wherein repose the ashes of the holy John, where the Christians of Ephesus go twice a year to gather the dust from the tomb, which is able to make bodies whole again that are corrupted by disease, and cleanse the soul from sin; but see how the wharves encroach upon the sea, and what multitudes of ships are anchored in the bay; see, also, how the city hath stretched abroad, far over the valley behind Prion, and even unto the walls of Ayassalook; and lo, all the hills are white with palaces and ribbed with colonnades of marble.   How mighty is Ephesus become!

And wondering at what their eyes had seen, they went down into the city and purchased garments and clothed themselves. And when they would have passed on, the merchant bit the coins which they had given him, with his teeth, and turned them about and looked curiously upon them, and cast them upon his counter, and listened if they rang; and then he said, These be bogus. And they said, Depart thou to Hades, and went their way. When they were come to their houses, they recognized them, albeit they seemed old and mean; and they rejoiced, and were glad. They ran to the doors, and knocked, and strangers opened, and looked inquiringly upon them. And they said, with great excitement, while their hearts beat high, and the color in their faces came and went, Where is my father? Where is my mother? Where are Dionysius and Serapion, and Pericles, and Decius? And the strangers that opened said, We know not these. The Seven said, How, you know them not? How long have ye dwelt here, and whither are they gone that dwelt here before ye? And the strangers said, Ye play upon us with a jest, young men; we and our fathers have sojourned under these roofs these six generations; the names ye utter rot upon the tombs, and they that bore them have run their brief race, have laughed and sung, have borne the sorrows and the weariness that were allotted them, and are at rest; for nine-score years the summers have come and gone, and the autumn leaves have fallen, since the

roses faded out of their cheeks and they laid them
to sleep with the dead.

Then the seven young men turned them away from
their homes, and the strangers shut the doors upon
them.   The wanderers marveled greatly, and looked
into the faces of all they met, as hoping to find one
that they knew; but all were strange, and passed them
by and spake no friendly word.   They were sore distressed and sad.   Presently they spake unto a citizen
and said, Who is King in Ephesus?   And the citizen
answered and said, Whence come ye that ye know
not that great Laertius reigns in Ephesus?   They
looked one at the other, greatly perplexed, and presently asked again, Where, then, is the good King
Maximilianus?   The citizen moved him apart, as one
who is afraid, and said, Verily these men be mad,
and dream dreams, else would they know that the
King whereof they speak is dead above two hundred
years agone.

Then the scales fell from the eyes of the Seven,
and one said, Alas, that we drank of the curious
liquors.   They have made us weary, and in dream-
less sleep these two long centuries have we lain.   Our
homes are desolate, our friends are dead.   Behold,
the jig is up — let us die.   And that same day went
they forth and laid them down and died.   And in
that selfsame day, likewise, the Seven-up did cease
in Ephesus, for that the Seven that were up were
down again, and departed and dead withal.   And
the names that be upon their tombs, even unto this

time, are Johannes Smithianus, Trumps, Gift, High, and Low, Jack, and The Game. And with the sleepers lie also the bottles wherein were once the curious liquors; and upon them is writ, in ancient letters, such words as these — names of heathen gods of olden time, perchance: Rumpunch, Jinsling, Eggnog.

Such is the story of the Seven Sleepers (with slight variations), and I know it is true, because I have seen the cave myself.

Really, so firm a faith had the ancients in this legend, that as late as eight or nine hundred years ago, learned travelers held it in superstitious fear.

Two of them record that they ventured into it, but ran quickly out again, not daring to tarry lest they should fall asleep and outlive their great-grand-children a century or so. Even at this day the ignorant denizens of the neighboring country prefer not to sleep in it.

CHAPTER XIV.

WHEN I last made a memorandum, we were at Ephesus. We are in Syria, now, encamped in the mountains of Lebanon. The interregnum has been long, both as to time and distance. We brought not a relic from Ephesus! After gathering up fragments of sculptured marbles and breaking ornaments from the interior work of the mosques; and after bringing them, at a cost of infinite trouble and fatigue, five miles on muleback to the railway depot, a government officer compelled all who had such things to disgorge! He had an order from Constantinople to *look out for our party*, and see that we carried nothing off. It was a wise, a just, and a well-deserved rebuke, but it created a sensation. I never resist a temptation to plunder a stranger's premises without feeling insufferably vain about it. This time I felt proud beyond expression. I was serene in the midst of the scoldings that were heaped upon the Ottoman government for its affront offered to a pleasuring party of entirely respectable gentlemen and ladies. I said, "We that have free souls, it touches us not." The shoe not only pinched our

(169)

party, but it pinched hard; a principal sufferer dis·
covered that the imperial order was inclosed in an
envelope bearing the seal of the British Embassy at
Constantinople, and therefore must have been inspired by the representative of the Queen.   This was
bad — very bad.   Coming solely from the Ottomans,
it might have signified only Ottoman hatred of
Christians, and a vulgar ignorance as to genteel methods of expressing it; but coming from the Chris-
tianized, educated, politic British legation, it simply
intimated that we were a sort of gentlemen and ladies
who would bear watching!   So the party regarded
it, and were incensed accordingly.   The truth doubtless was, that the same precautions would have been
taken against *any* travelers, because the English
Company who have acquired the right to excavate
Ephesus, and have paid a great sum for that right,
need to be protected, and deserve to be.   They cannot afford to run the risk of having their hospitality
abused by travelers, especially since travelers are
such notorious scorners of honest behavior.

We sailed from Smyrna, in the wildest spirit of
expectancy, for the chief feature, the grand goal of
the expedition, was near at hand — we were approaching the Holy Land!   Such a burrowing into
the hold for trunks that had lain buried for weeks,
yes, for months; such a hurrying to and fro above
decks and below; such a riotous system of packing
and unpacking; such a littering up of the cabins
with shirts and skirts, and indescribable and unclass·

able odds and ends; such a making up of bundles, and setting apart of umbrellas, green spectacles, and thick veils; such a critical inspection of saddles and bridles that had never yet touched horses; such a cleaning and loading of revolvers and examining of bowie-knives; such a half-soling of the seats of pantaloons with serviceable buckskin; then such a poring over ancient maps; such a reading up of Bibles and Palestine travels; such a marking out of routes; such exasperating efforts to divide up the company into little bands of congenial spirits who might make the long and arduous journey without quarreling; and morning, noon, and night, such mass-meetings in the cabins, such speech-making, such sage suggesting, such worrying and quarreling, and such a general raising of the very mischief, was never seen in the ship before!

But it is all over now. We are cut up into parties of six or eight, and by this time are scattered far and wide. Ours is the only one, however, that is venturing on what is called " the long trip "— that is, out into Syria, by Baalbec to Damascus, and thence down through the full length of Palestine. It would be a tedious, and also a too risky journey, at this hot season of the year, for any but strong, healthy men, accustomed somewhat to fatigue and rough life in the open air. The other parties will take shorter journeys.

For the last two months we have been in a worry about one portion of this Holy Land pilgrimage. I

refer to transportation service. We knew very well
that Palestine was a country which did not do a large
passenger business, and every man we came across
who knew anything about it gave us to understand
that not half of our party would be able to get dragomen and animals. At Constantinople everybody fell
to telegraphing the American consuls at Alexandria
and Beirout to give notice that we wanted dragomen
and transportation. We were desperate — would
take horses, jackasses, camelopards, kangaroos —
anything. At Smyrna, more telegraphing was done,
to the same end. Also, fearing for the worst, we
telegraphed for a large number of seats in the diligence for Damascus, and horses for the ruins of
Baalbec.

As might have been expected, a notion got
abroad in Syria and Egypt that the whole population
of the Province of America (the Turks consider us a
trifling little province in some unvisited corner of the
world) were coming to the Holy Land — and so,
when we got to Beirout yesterday, we found the
place full of dragomen and their outfits. We had
all intended to go by diligence to Damascus, and
switch off to Baalbec as we went along — because we
expected to rejoin the ship, go to Mount Carmel,
and take to the woods from there. However, when
our own private party of eight found that it was possible, and proper enough, to make the "long trip,"
we adopted that program. We have never been
much trouble to a consul before, but we have been

a fearful nuisance to our consul at Beirout. I mention this because I cannot help admiring his patience, his industry, and his accommodating spirit. I mention it, also, because I think some of our ship's company did not give him as full credit for his excellent services as he deserved.

Well, out of our eight, three were selected to attend to all business connected with the expedition. The rest of us had nothing to do but look at the beautiful city of Beirout, with its bright, new houses nestled among a wilderness of green shrubbery spread abroad over an upland that sloped gently down to the sea; and also at the mountains of Lebanon that environ it; and likewise to bathe in the transparent blue water that rolled its billows about the ship (we did not know there were sharks there). We had also to range up and down through the town and look at the costumes. These are picturesque and fanciful, but not so varied as at Constantinople and Smyrna; the women of Beirout add an agony — in the two former cities the sex wear a thin veil which one can see through (and they often expose their ankles), but at Beirout they cover their entire faces with dark-colored or black veils, so that they look like mummies, and then expose their breasts to the public. A young gentleman (I believe he was a Greek) volunteered to show us around the city, and said it would afford him great pleasure, because he was studying English and wanted practice in that language. When we had finished the rounds, however, he called for remuneration — said he hoped the gentlemen would give him a trifle in the way of a few piasters (equivalent to a few five-cent pieces). We did so. The consul was surprised when he heard it, and said he knew the young fellow's family very well, and that they were an old and highly respectable family and worth a hundred and fifty thousand dollars! Some people, so situated, would have been ashamed of the berth he had with us and his manner of crawling into it.

At the appointed time our business committee reported, and said all things were in readiness — that we were to start to-day, with horses, pack animals, and tents, and go to Baalbec, Damascus, the Sea of Tiberias, and thence southward by the way of the scene of Jacob's Dream and other notable Bible localities to Jerusalem — from thence probably to the Dead Sea, but possibly not — and then strike for the ocean and rejoin the ship three or four weeks hence at Joppa; terms, five dollars a day apiece, in gold, and everything to be furnished by the dragoman. They said we would live as well as at a hotel. I had read something like that before, and did not shame my judgment by believing a word of it. I said nothing, however, but packed up a blanket and a shawl to sleep in, pipes and tobacco, two or three woolen shirts, a portfolio, a guide-book, and a Bible. I also took along a towel and a cake of soap, to inspire respect in the Arabs, who would take me for a king in disguise.

We were to select our horses at 3 P.M.   At that hour Abraham, the dragoman, marshaled them before us.   With all solemnity I set it down here, that those horses were the hardest lot I ever did come across, and their accoutrements were in exquisite keeping with their style.   One brute had an eye out; another had his tail sawed off close, like a rabbit, and was proud of it; another had a bony ridge running from his neck to his tail, like one of those ruined aqueducts one sees about Rome, and had a neck on him like a bowsprit; they all limped, and had sore backs, and likewise raw places and old scales scattered about their persons like brass nails in a hair trunk; their gaits were marvelous to contemplate, and replete with variety — under way the procession looked like a fleet in a storm.   It was fearful.   Blucher shook his head and said:

"That dragon is going to get himself into trouble fetching these old crates out of the hospital the way they are, unless he has got a permit."

I said nothing.   The display was exactly according to the guide-book, and were we not traveling by the guide-book ?   I selected a certain horse because I thought I saw him shy, and I thought that a horse that had spirit enough to shy was not to be despised.

At 6 o'clock P. M. we came to a halt here on the breezy summit of a shapely mountain overlooking the sea, and the handsome valley where dwelt some of those enterprising Phœnicians of ancient times we read so much about; all around us are what were

12**

once the dominions of Hiram, King of Tyre, who
furnished timber from the cedars of these Lebanon
hills to build portions of King Solomon's Temple
with.

Shortly after six, our pack-train arrived. I had
not seen it before, and a good right I had to be
astonished. We had nineteen serving men and
twenty-six pack mules! It was a perfect caravan.
It looked like one, too, as it wound among the
rocks. I wondered what in the very mischief we
wanted with such a vast turnout as that, for eight
men. I wondered awhile, but soon I began to long
for a tin plate, and some bacon and beans. I had
camped out many and many a time before, and
knew just what was coming. I went off, without
waiting for serving men, and unsaddled my horse,
and washed such portions of his ribs and his spine
as projected through his hide, and when I came
back, behold five stately circus-tents were up — tents
that were brilliant, within, with blue and gold and
crimson, and all manner of splendid adornment! I
was speechless. Then they brought eight little iron
bedsteads, and set them up in the tents; they put a
soft mattress and pillows and good blankets and two
snow-white sheets on each bed. Next, they rigged
a table about the center-pole, and on it placed
pewter pitchers, basins, soap, and the whitest of
towels — one set for each man; they pointed to
pockets in the tent, and said we could put our small
trifles in them for convenience, and if we needed

pins or such things, they were sticking everywhere.
Then came the finishing touch — they spread carpets
on the floor! I simply said, "If you call this
camping out, all right — but it isn't the style *I* am
used to; my little baggage that I brought along is
at a discount."

It grew dark, and they put candles on the tables
— candles set in bright, new, brazen candlesticks.
And soon the bell — a genuine, simon-pure bell —
rang, and we were invited to "the saloon." I had
thought before that we had a tent or so too many,
but now here was one, at least, provided for; it
was to be used for nothing but an eating saloon.
Like the others, it was high enough for a family of
giraffes to live in, and was very handsome and clean
and bright-colored within. It was a gem of a place.
A table for eight, and eight canvas chairs; a tablecloth and napkins whose whiteness and whose fine-
ness laughed to scorn the things we were used to in
the great excursion steamer; knives and forks, soup-
plates, dinner-plates — everything, in the handsomest kind of style. It was wonderful! And they
call *this* camping out. Those stately fellows in
baggy trowsers and turbaned fezes brought in a
dinner which consisted of roast mutton, roast
chicken, roast goose, potatoes, bread, tea, pudding,
apples, and delicious grapes; the viands were better
cooked than any we had eaten for weeks, and the
table made a finer appearance, with its large German
silver candlesticks and other finery, than any table

12 **

we had sat down to for a good while, and yet that polite dragoman, Abraham, came bowing in and apologizing for the whole affair, on account of the unavoidable confusion of getting under way for a very long trip, and promising to do a great deal better in future!

It is midnight now, and we break camp at six in the morning.

They call this camping out. At this rate it is a glorious privilege to be a pilgrim to the Holy Land.

CHAPTER XV.

WE are camped near *Temnin-el-Foka* — a name which the boys have simplified a good deal, for the sake of convenience in spelling. They call it Jacksonville. It sounds a little strangely, here in the Valley of Lebanon, but it has the merit of being easier to remember than the Arabic name.

> "COME LIKE SPIRITS, SO DEPART."
> "The night shall be filled with music,
>   And the cares that infest the day
> Shall fold their tents like the Arabs,
>   And as silently steal away."

I slept very soundly last night, yet when the dragoman's bell rang at half-past five this morning and the cry went abroad of "Ten minutes to dress for breakfast!" I heard both. It surprised me, because I have not heard the breakfast gong in the ship for a month, and whenever we have had occasion to fire a salute at daylight, I have only found it out in the course of conversation afterward. However, camping out, even though it be in a gorgeous tent, makes one fresh and lively in the morning — especially if the air you are breathing is the cool, fresh air of the mountains.

L**   (179)

I was dressed within the ten minutes, and came out. The saloon tent had been stripped of its sides, and had nothing left but its roof; so when we sat down to table we could look out over a noble panorama of mountain, sea, and hazy valley. And sitting thus, the sun rose slowly up and suffused the picture with a world of rich coloring.

Hot mutton-chops, fried chicken, omelettes, fried potatoes, and coffee — all excellent. This was the bill of fare. It was sauced with a savage appetite purchased by hard riding the day before, and re-freshing sleep in a pure atmosphere. As I called for a second cup of coffee, I glanced over my shoulder, and behold, our white village was gone — the splendid tents had vanished like magic! It was wonderful how quickly those Arabs had "folded their tents"; and it was wonderful, also, how quickly they had gathered the thousand odds and ends of the camp together and disappeared with them.

By half-past six we were under way, and all the Syrian world seemed to be under way also. The road was filled with mule trains and long processions of camels. This reminds me that we have been trying for some time to think what a camel looks like, and now we have made it out. When he is down on all his knees, flat on his breast to receive his load, he looks something like a goose swimming; and when he is upright he looks like an ostrich with an extra set of legs. Camels are not beautiful, and

their long under lip gives them an exceedingly
" gallus "* expression. They have immense flat,
forked cushions of feet, that make a track in the
dust like a pie with a slice cut out of it. They are
not particular about their diet. They would eat a
tombstone if they could bite it. A thistle grows
about here which has needles on it that would pierce
through leather, I think; if one touches you, you
can find relief in nothing but profanity. The camels
eat these. They show by their actions that they
enjoy them. I suppose it would be a real treat to a
camel to have a keg of nails for supper.

While I am speaking of animals, I will mention
that I have a horse now by the name of " Jericho."
He is a mare. I have seen remarkable horses before, but none so remarkable as this. I wanted a
horse that could shy, and this one fills the bill. I
had an idea that shying indicated spirit. If I was
correct, I have got the most spirited horse on earth.
He shies at everything he comes across, with the
utmost impartiality. He appears to have a mortal
dread of telegraph poles, especially; and it is fortunate that these are on both sides of the road, because
as it is now, I never fall off twice in succession on
the same side. If I fell on the same side always, it
would get to be monotonous after a while. This
creature has scared at everything he has seen to-
day, except a haystack. He walked up to that with

---

* Excuse the slang — no other word will describe it.

an intrepidity and a recklessness that were astonishing. And it would fill any one with admiration to see how he preserves his self-possession in the presence of a barley-sack. This dare-devil bravery will be the death of this horse some day.

He is not particularly fast, but I think he will get me through the Holy Land. He has only one fault. His tail has been chopped off or else he has sat down on it too hard, some time or other, and he has to fight the flies with his heels. This is all very well, but when he tries to kick a fly off the top of his head with his hind foot, it is too much variety. He is going to get himself into trouble that way some day. He reaches around and bites my legs, too. I do not care particularly about that, only I do not like to see a horse too sociable.

I think the owner of this prize had a wrong opinion about him. He had an idea that he was one of those fiery, untamed steeds, but he is not of that character. I know the Arab had this idea, because when he brought the horse out for inspection in Beirout, he kept jerking at the bridle and shouting in Arabic, "Whoa! will you? Do you want to run away, you ferocious beast, and break your neck?" when all the time the horse was not doing anything in the world, and only looked like he wanted to lean up against something and think. Whenever he is not shying at things, or reaching after a fly, he wants to do that yet. How it would surprise his owner to know this.

We have been in a historical section of country all day. At noon we camped three hours and took luncheon at Mekseh, near the junction of the Lebanon Mountains and the Jebel el Kuneiyiseh, and looked down into the immense, level, garden-like Valley of Lebanon. To-night we are camping near the same valley, and have a very wide sweep of it in view. We can see the long, whale-backed ridge of Mount Hermon projecting above the eastern hills. The " dews of Hermon " are falling upon us now, and the tents are almost soaked with them.

Over the way from us, and higher up the valley, we can discern, through the glasses, the faint out-lines of the wonderful ruins of Baalbec, the sup-posed Baal-Gad of Scripture. Joshua and another person were the two spies who were sent into this land of Canaan by the children of Israel to report upon its character — I mean they were the spies who reported favorably. They took back with them some specimens of the grapes of this country, and in the children's picture-books they are always represented as bearing one monstrous bunch swung to a pole between them, a respectable load for a pack-train. The Sunday-school books exaggerated it a little. The grapes are most excellent to this day, but the bunches are not as large as those in the pictures. I was surprised and hurt when I saw them, because those colossal bunches of grapes were one of my most cherished juvenile traditions.

Joshua reported favorably, and the children of

Israel journeyed on, with Moses at the head of the
general government, and Joshua in command of the
army of six hundred thousand fighting men. Of
women and children and civilians there was a countless swarm. Of all that mighty host, none but the
two faithful spies ever lived to set their feet in the
Promised Land. They and their descendants wandered forty years in the desert, and then Moses, the
gifted warrior, poet, statesman, and philosopher,
went up into Pisgah and met his mysterious fate.
Where he was buried no man knows — for

> ". . . no man dug that sepulchre,
> And no man saw it e'er —
> For the sons of God upturned the sod
> And laid the dead man there!"

Then Joshua began his terrible raid, and from
Jericho clear to this Baal-Gad, he swept the land
like the Genius of Destruction. He slaughtered the
people, laid waste their soil, and razed their cities to
the ground. He wasted thirty-one kings also. One
may call it that, though really it can hardly be
called wasting them, because there were always
plenty of kings in those days, and to spare. At
any rate, he destroyed thirty-one kings, and divided
up their realms among his Israelites. He divided
up this valley stretched out here before us, and so
it was once Jewish territory. The Jews have long
since disappeared from it, however.

Back yonder, an hour's journey from here, we
passed through an Arab village of stone dry-goods

boxes (they look like that), where Noah's tomb lies under lock and key. [Noah built the ark.] Over these old hills and valleys the ark that contained all that was left of a vanished world once floated.

I make no apology for detailing the above information. It will be news to some of my readers, at any rate.

Noah's tomb is built of stone, and is covered with a long stone building. Bucksheesh let us in. The building had to be long, because the grave of the honored old navigator is two hundred and ten feet long itself! It is only about four feet high, though. He must have cast a shadow like a lightning-rod. The proof that this is the genuine spot where Noah was buried can only be doubted by uncommonly incredulous people. The evidence is pretty straight. Shem, the son of Noah, was present at the burial, and showed the place to his descendants, who transmitted the knowledge to their descendants, and the lineal descendants of these introduced themselves to us to-day. It was pleasant to make the acquaintance of members of so respectable a family. It was a thing to be proud of. It was the next thing to being acquainted with Noah himself.

Noah's memorable voyage will always possess a living interest for me, henceforward.

If ever an oppressed race existed, it is this one we see fettered around us under the inhuman tyranny of the Ottoman empire. I wish Europe would let Russia annihilate Turkey a little — not much, but enough to make it difficult to find the place again without a divining-rod or a diving-bell. The Syrians are very poor, and yet they are ground down by a system of taxation that would drive any other nation frantic. Last year their taxes were heavy enough, in all conscience — but this year they have been increased by the addition of taxes that were forgiven them in times of famine in former years. On top of this the government has levied a tax of *one-tenth* of the whole proceeds of the land. This is only half the story. The Pacha of a Pachalic does not trouble himself with appointing tax-collectors. He figures up what all these taxes ought to amount to in a certain district. Then he farms the collection out. He calls the rich men together, the highest bidder gets the speculation, pays the Pacha on the spot, and then sells out to smaller fry, who sell in turn to a piratical horde of still smaller fry. These latter compel the peasant to bring his little trifle of grain to the village, at his own cost. It must be weighed, the various taxes set apart, and the remainder returned to the producer. But the collector delays this duty day after day, while the producer's family are perishing for bread; at last the poor wretch, who cannot but understand the game, says, "Take a quarter — take half — take two-thirds if you will, and let me go!" It is a most outrageous state of things.

These people are naturally good-hearted and intelligent, and, with education and liberty, would be a happy and contented race. They often appeal to the stranger to know if the great world will not some day come to their relief and save them. The Sultan has been lavishing money like water in England and Paris, but his subjects are suffering for it now.

This fashion of camping out bewilders me. We have bootjacks and a bathtub now, and yet all the mysteries the pack-mules carry are not revealed. What next?

CHAPTER XVI.

WE had a tedious ride of about five hours, in the sun, across the Valley of Lebanon. It proved to be not quite so much of a garden as it had seemed from the hillsides. It was a desert, weed-grown waste, littered thickly with stones the size of a man's fist. Here and there the natives had scratched the ground and reared a sickly crop of grain, but for the most part the valley was given up to a handful of shepherds, whose flocks were doing what they honestly could to get a living, but the chances were against them. We saw rude piles of stones standing near the roadside, at intervals, and recognized the custom of marking boundaries which obtained in Jacob's time. There were no walls, no fences, no hedges — nothing to secure a man's pos-sessions but these random heaps of stones. The Israelites held them sacred in the old patriarchal times, and these other Arabs, their lineal descend-ants, do so likewise. An American, of ordinary intelligence, would soon widely extend his property, at an outlay of mere manual labor, performed at night, under so loose a system of fencing as this.

The plows these people use are simply a sharpened stick, such as Abraham plowed with, and they
still winnow their wheat as he did — they pile it on
the house top, and then toss it by shovelfuls into
the air until the wind has blown all the chaff away.
They never invent anything, never learn anything.

We had a fine race, of a mile, with an Arab
perched on a camel. Some of the horses were fast,
and made very good time, but the camel scampered
by them without any very great effort. The yelling
and shouting, and whipping and galloping, of all
parties interested, made it an exhilarating, exciting,
and particularly boisterous race.

At eleven o'clock, our eyes fell upon the walls
and columns of Baalbec, a noble ruin whose history
is a sealed book. It has stood there for thousands
of years, the wonder and admiration of travelers;
but who built it, or when it was built, are questions
that may never be answered. One thing is very
sure, though. Such grandeur of design, and such
grace of execution, as one sees in the temples of
Baalbec, have not been equaled or even approached
in any work of men's hands that has been built
within twenty centuries past.

The great Temple of the Sun, the Temple of
Jupiter, and several smaller temples, are clustered
together in the midst of one of these miserable
Syrian villages, and look strangely enough in such
plebeian company. These temples are built upon
massive substructions that might support a world,

almost; the materials used are blocks of stone as large as an omnibus — very few, if any, of them are smaller than a carpenter's tool chest — and these substructions are traversed by tunnels of masonry through which a train of cars might pass. With such foundations as these, it is little wonder that Baalbec has lasted so long. The Temple of the Sun is nearly three hundred feet long and one hundred and sixty feet wide. It had fifty-four columns around it, but only six are standing now — the others lie broken at its base, a confused and picturesque heap. The six columns are perfect, as also are their bases, Corinthian capitals and entablature — and six more shapely columns do not exist. The columns and the entablature together are ninety feet high — a prodigious altitude for shafts of stone to reach, truly — and yet one only thinks of their beauty and symmetry when looking at them; the pillars look slender and delicate, the entablature, with its elaborate sculpture, looks like rich stucco-work. But when you have gazed aloft till your eyes are weary, you glance at the great fragments of pillars among which you are standing, and find that they are eight feet through; and with them lie beautiful capitals apparently as large as a small cottage; and also single slabs of stone, superbly sculptured, that are four or five feet thick, and would completely cover the floor of any ordinary parlor. You wonder where these monstrous things came from, and it takes some little time to satisfy yourself that the airy and graceful fabric that towers above your head is made up of their mates. It seems too preposterous.

The Temple of Jupiter is a smaller ruin than the one I have been speaking of, and yet is immense. It is in a tolerable state of preservation. One row of nine columns stands almost uninjured. They are sixty-five feet high and support a sort of porch or roof, which connects them with the roof of the building. This porch-roof is composed of tremendous slabs of stone, which are so finely sculptured on the under side that the work looks like a fresco from below. One or two of these slabs had fallen, and again I wondered if the gigantic masses of carved stone that lay about me were no larger than those above my head. Within the temple, the ornamentation was elaborate and colossal. What a wonder of architectural beauty and grandeur this edifice must have been when it was new! And what a noble picture it and its statelier companion, with the chaos of mighty fragments scattered about them, yet makes in the moonlight!

I cannot conceive how those immense blocks of stone were ever hauled from the quarries, or how they were ever raised to the dizzy heights they occupy in the temples. And yet these sculptured blocks are trifles in size compared with the rough-hewn blocks that form the wide veranda or platform which surrounds the Great Temple. One stretch of that platform, two hundred feet long, is composed of
13**

blocks of stone as large and some of them larger,
than a street-car. They surmount a wall about ten
or twelve feet high. I thought those were large
rocks, but they sank into insignificance compared
with those which formed another section of the
platform. These were three in number, and I
thought that each of them was about as long as
three street cars placed end to end, though, of
course, they are a third wider and a third higher
than a street car. Perhaps two railway freight cars
of the largest pattern, placed end to end, might
better represent their size. In combined length
these three stones stretch nearly two hundred feet;
they are thirteen feet square; two of them are sixty-
four feet long each, and the third is sixty-nine.
They are built into the massive wall some twenty
feet above the ground. They are there, but how
they got there is the question. I have seen the hull
of a steamboat that was smaller than one of those
stones. All these great walls are as exact and
shapely as the flimsy things we build of bricks in
these days. A race of gods or of giants must have
inhabited Baalbec many a century ago. Men like
the men of our day could hardly rear such temples
as these.

We went to the quarry from whence the stones of
Baalbec were taken. It was about a quarter of a
mile off, and down hill. In a great pit lay the mate
of the largest stone in the ruins. It lay there just
as the giants of that old forgotten time had left it

when they were called hence — just as they had left it, to remain for thousands of years, an eloquent rebuke unto such as are prone to think slightingly of the men who lived before them. This enormous block lies there, squared and ready for the builders' hands — a solid mass fourteen feet by seventeen, and but a few inches less than seventy feet long! Two buggies could be driven abreast of each other, on its surface, from one end of it to the other, and leave room enough for a man or two to walk on either side.

One might swear that, all the John Smiths and George Wilkinsons, and all the other pitiful nobodies between Kingdom Come and Baalbec would inscribe their poor little names upon the walls of Baalbec's magnificent ruins, and would add the town, the county, and the state they came from — and, swearing thus, be infallibly correct. It is a pity some great ruin does not fall in and flatten out some of these reptiles, and scare their kind out of ever giving their names to fame upon any walls or monuments again, forever.

Properly, with the sorry relics we bestrode, it was a three-days journey to Damascus. It was necessary that we should do it in less than two. It was necessary because our three pilgrims would not travel on the Sabbath day. We were all perfectly willing to keep the Sabbath day, but there are times when to keep the *letter* of a sacred law whose spirit is righteous, becomes a sin, and this was a case in

13**

point. We pleaded for the tired, ill-treated horses, and tried to show that their faithful service deserved kindness in return, and their hard lot compassion. But when did ever self-righteousness know the sentiment of pity? What were a few long hours added to the hardships of some overtaxed brutes when weighed against the peril of those human souls? It was not the most promising party to travel with and hope to gain a higher veneration for religion through the example of its devotees. We said the Saviour, who pitied dumb beasts and taught that the ox must be rescued from the mire even on the Sabbath day, would not have counseled a forced march like this. We said the " long trip " was exhausting and therefore dangerous in the blistering heats of summer, even when the ordinary days' stages were traversed, and if we persisted in this hard march, some of us might be stricken down with the fevers of the country in consequence of it. Nothing could move the pilgrims. They *must* press on. Men might die, horses might die, but they must enter upon holy soil next week, with no Sabbath-breaking stain upon them. Thus they were willing to commit a sin against the spirit of religious law, in order that they might preserve the letter of it. It was not worth while to tell them " the letter kills." I am talking now about personal friends; men whom I like; men who are good citizens; who are honorable, upright, conscientious: but whose idea of the Saviour's religion seems to me distorted. They

lecture our shortcomings unsparingly, and every
night they call us together and read to us chapters
from the Testament that are full of gentleness, of
charity, and of tender mercy; and then all the next
day they stick to their saddles clear up to the sum-
mits of these rugged mountains, and clear down
again. Apply the Testament's gentleness, and
charity, and tender mercy to a toiling, worn, and
weary horse? Nonsense — these are for God's
human creatures, not His dumb ones. What the
pilgrims choose to do, respect for their almost
sacred character demands that I should allow to pass
— but I would so like to catch any other member of
the party riding his horse up one of these exhausting hills once!

We have given the pilgrims a good many examples that might benefit them, but it is virtue thrown
away. They have never heard a cross word out of
our lips toward each other — but *they* have quarreled
once or twice. We love to hear them at it, after
they have been lecturing us. The very first thing
they did, coming ashore at Beirout, was to quarrel
in the boat. I have said I like them, and I do like
them — but every time they read me a scorcher of a
lecture I mean to talk back in print.

Not content with doubling the legitimate stages,
they switched off the main road and went away out
of the way to visit an absurd fountain called Figia,
because Balaam's ass had drank there once. So we
journeyed on, through the terrible hills and deserts

M **

and the roasting sun, and then far into the night, seeking the honored pool of Balaam's ass, the patron saint of all pilgrims like us. I find no entry but this in my note-book:

"Rode to-day, altogether, thirteen hours, through deserts, partly, and partly over barren, unsightly hills, and latterly through wild, rocky scenery, and camped at about eleven o'clock at night on the banks of a limpid stream, near a Syrian village. Do not know its name — do not wish to know it — want to go to bed. Two horses lame (mine and Jack's) and the others worn out. Jack and I walked three or four miles, over the hills, and led the horses. Fun — but of a mild type."

Twelve or thirteen hours in the saddle, even in a Christian land and a Christian climate, and on a good horse, is a tiresome journey; but in an oven like Syria, in a ragged spoon of a saddle that slips fore-and-aft, and "thort-ships," and every way, and on a horse that is tired and lame, and yet must be whipped and spurred with hardly a moment's cessation all day long, till the blood comes from his side, and your conscience hurts you every time you strike, if you are half a man, — it is a journey to be remembered in bitterness of spirit and execrated with emphasis for a liberal division of a man's lifetime.

CHAPTER XVII.

THE next day was an outrage upon men and horses both. It was another thirteen-hour stretch (including an hour's "nooning"). It was over the barrenest chalk-hills and through the baldest cañons that even Syria can show. The heat quivered in the air everywhere. In the cañons we almost smothered in the baking atmosphere. On high ground, the reflection from the chalk-hills was blinding. It was cruel to urge the crippled horses, but it had to be done in order to make Damascus Saturday night. We saw ancient tombs and temples of fanciful architecture carved out of the solid rock high up in the face of precipices above our heads, but we had neither time nor strength to climb up there and examine them. The terse language of my note-book will answer for the rest of this day's experiences:

Broke camp at 7 A. M., and made a ghastly trip through the Zeb Dana valley and the rough mountains — horses limping and that Arab screech-owl that does most of the singing and carries the water-skins, always a thousand miles ahead of course, and no water to drink — will he *never* die? Beautiful stream in a chasm, lined thick with pomegranate, fig, olive, and quince orchards, and nooned an hour at the

(197)

celebrated Balaam's Ass Fountain of Figia, second in size in Syria, and the coldest water out of Siberia — guide-books do not say Balaam's ass ever drank there — somebody been imposing on the pilgrims, may be. Bathed in it — Jack and I. Only a second — ice water. It is the principal source of the Abana river — only one-half mile down to where it joins. Beautiful place — giant trees all around — *so* shady and cool, if one could keep awake — vast stream gushes straight out from under the mountain in a torrent. Over it is a very ancient ruin, with no known history — supposed to have been for the worship of the deity of the fountain or Balaam's ass or somebody. Wretched nest of human vermin about the fountain — rags, dirt, sunken cheeks, pallor of sickness, sores, projecting bones, dull, aching misery in their eyes and ravenous hunger speaking from every eloquent fiber and muscle from head to foot. How they sprang upon a bone, how they crunched the bread we gave them! Such as these to swarm about one and watch every bite he takes with greedy looks, and swallow unconsciously every time he swallows, as if they half fancied the precious morsel went down their own throats — hurry up the caravan! — I never shall enjoy a meal in this distressful country. To think of eating three times every day under *such* circumstances for three weeks yet — it is worse punishment than riding all day in the sun. There are sixteen starving babies from one to six years old in the party, and their legs are no larger than broom handles. Left the fountain at 1 P. M. (the fountain took us at least two hours out of our way), and reached Mahomet's lookout perch, over Damascus, in time to get a good long look before it was necessary to move on. Tired? Ask of the winds that far away with fragments strewed the sea.

As the glare of day mellowed into twilight, we looked down upon a picture which is celebrated all over the world. I think I have read about four hundred times that when Mahomet was a simple camel-driver he reached this point and looked down upon Damascus for the first time, and then made a certain renowned remark. He said man could enter only one paradise; he preferred to go to the one above. So he sat down there and feasted his eyes upon the earthly paradise of Damascus, and then went away without entering its gates. They have erected a tower on the hill to mark the spot where he stood.

Damascus *is* beautiful from the mountain. It is beautiful even to foreigners accustomed to luxuriant vegetation, and I can easily understand how unspeakably beautiful it must be to eyes that are only used to the God-forsaken barrenness and desolation of Syria. I should think a Syrian would go wild with ecstasy when such a picture bursts upon him for the first time.

From his high perch, one sees before him and below him a wall of dreary mountains, shorn of vegetation, glaring fiercely in the sun; it fences in a level desert of yellow sand, smooth as velvet and threaded far away with fine lines that stand for roads, and dotted with creeping mites we know are camel trains and journeying men; right in the midst of the desert is spread a billowy expanse of green foliage; and nestling in its heart sits the great white city, like an island of pearls and opals gleaming out of a sea of emeralds. This is the picture you see spread far below you, with distance to soften it, the sun to glorify it, strong contrasts to heighten the effects, and over it and about it a drowsing air of repose to spiritualize it and make it seem rather a beautiful estray from the mysterious worlds we visit in dreams than a substantial tenant of our coarse, dull globe. And when you think of the leagues of blighted, blasted, sandy, rocky, sunburnt, ugly, dreary, infamous country you have ridden over to get here, you think it is the most beautiful, beautiful picture that ever human eyes rested upon in all the broad universe! If I were to go to Damascus again, I would camp on Mahomet's hill about a week, and then go away. There is no need to go inside the walls. The Prophet was wise without knowing it when he decided not to go down into the paradise of Damascus.

There is an honored old tradition that the immense garden which Damascus stands in was the Garden of Eden, and modern writers have gathered up many chapters of evidence tending to show that it really was the Garden of Eden, and that the rivers Pharpar and Abana are the "two rivers" that watered Adam's Paradise. It may be so, but it is not paradise now, and one would be as happy outside of it as he would be likely to be within. It is so crooked and cramped and dirty that one cannot realize that he is in the splendid city he saw from the hilltop. The gardens are hidden by high mud-walls, and the paradise is become a very sink of pollution and uncomeliness. Damascus has plenty of clear, pure water in it, though, and this is enough, of itself, to make an Arab think it beautiful and blessed. Water is scarce in blistered Syria. We run railways by our large cities in America; in Syria they curve the roads so as to make them run by the meager little puddles they call "fountains," and which are not found oftener on a journey than every four hours.

But the " rivers " of Pharpar and Abana of Scripture (mere creeks) run through Damascus, and so
every house and every garden have their sparkling
fountains and rivulets of water. With her forest of
foliage and her abundance of water, Damascus must
be a wonder of wonders to the Bedouin from the
deserts. Damascus is simply an oasis — that is
what it is. For four thousand years its waters have
not gone dry or its fertility failed. Now we can
understand why the city has existed so long. It
could not die. So long as its waters remain to it
away out there in the midst of that howling desert,
so long will Damascus live to bless the sight of the
tired and thirsty wayfarer.

"Though old as history itself, thou art fresh as the breath of spring,
blooming as thine own rose-bud, and fragrant as thine own orange
flower, O Damascus, pearl of the East!"

Damascus dates back anterior to the days of
Abraham, and is the oldest city in the world. It
was founded by Uz, the grandson of Noah. "The
early history of Damascus is shrouded in the mists
of a hoary antiquity." Leave the matters written
of in the first eleven chapters of the Old Testament
out, and no recorded event has occurred in the world
but Damascus was in existence to receive the news
of it. Go back as far as you will into the vague
past, there was always a Damascus. In the writings
of every century for more than four thousand years,
its name has been mentioned and its praises sung.
To Damascus, years are only moments, decades are

only flitting trifles of time. She measures time, not by days and months and years, but by the empires she has seen rise and prosper and crumble to ruin. She is a type of immortality. She saw the foundations of Baalbec, and Thebes, and Ephesus laid; she saw these villages grow into mighty cities, and amaze the world with their grandeur — and she has lived to see them desolate, deserted, and given over to the owls and the bats. She saw the Israelitish empire exalted, and she saw it annihilated. She saw Greece rise, and flourish two thousand years, and die. In her old age she saw Rome built; she saw it overshadow the world with its power; she saw it perish. The few hundreds of years of Genoese and Venetian might and splendor were, to grave old Damascus, only a trifling scintillation hardly worth remembering. Damascus has seen all that has ever occurred on earth, and still she lives. She has looked upon the dry bones of a thousand empires, and will see the tombs of a thousand more before she dies. Though another claims the name, old Damascus is by right the Eternal City.

We reached the city gates just at sundown. They do say that one can get into any walled city of Syria, after night, for bucksheesh, except Damascus. But Damascus, with its four thousand years of respectability in the world, has many old fogy notions. There are no street lamps there, and the law compels all who go abroad at night to carry lanterns, just as was the case in old days, when heroes and heroines of the Arabian Nights walked the streets of Damascus, or flew away toward Bagdad on enchanted carpets.

It was fairly dark a few minutes after we got within the wall, and we rode long distances through wonderfully crooked streets, eight to ten feet wide, and shut in on either side by the high mud walls of the gardens. At last we got to where lanterns could be seen flitting about here and there, and knew we were in the midst of the curious old city. In a little narrow street, crowded with our pack-mules and with a swarm of uncouth Arabs, we alighted, and through a kind of a hole in the wall entered the hotel. We stood in a great flagged court, with flowers and citron trees about us, and a huge tank in the center that was receiving the waters of many pipes. We crossed the court and entered the rooms prepared to receive four of us. In a large marble-paved recess between the two rooms was a tank of clear, cool water, which was kept running over all the time by the streams that were pouring into it from half a dozen pipes. Nothing, in this scorching, desolate land could look so refreshing as this pure water flashing in the lamplight; nothing could look so beautiful, nothing could sound so delicious as this mimic rain to ears long unaccustomed to sounds of such a nature. Our rooms were large, comfortably furnished, and even had their floors clothed with soft, cheerful-tinted carpets. It was a pleasant thing to see a carpet again, for if there is anything drearier than the tomb-like, stone-paved parlors and bedrooms of Europe and Asia, I do not know what it is. They make one think of the grave all the time. A very broad, gaily capari-soned divan, some twelve or fourteen feet long, extended across one side of each room, and opposite were single beds with spring mattresses. There were great looking-glasses and marble-top tables. All this luxury was as grateful to systems and senses worn out with an exhausting day's travel, as it was unexpected — for one cannot tell what to expect in a Turkish city of even a quarter of a million inhabitants.

I do not know, but I think they used that tank between the rooms to draw drinking water from; that did not occur to me, however, until I had dipped my baking head far down into its cool depths. I thought of it then, and, superb as the bath was, I was sorry I had taken it, and was about to go and explain to the landlord. But a finely curled and scented poodle dog frisked up and nipped the calf of my leg just then, and before I had time to think I had soused him to the bottom of the tank, and when I saw a servant coming with a pitcher I went off and left the pup trying to climb out and not succeeding very well. Satisfied revenge was all I needed to make me perfectly happy, and when I walked in to supper that first night in Damascus I was in that condition. We lay on those divans a long time, after supper, smoking narghilis and long-stemmed chibouks, and talking about the dreadful ride of the day, and I knew then what I had sometimes known before — that it is worth while to get tired out, because one so enjoys resting afterward.

In the morning we sent for donkeys. It is worthy of note that we had to *send* for these things. I said Damascus was an old fossil, and she is. Anywhere else we would have been assailed by a clamorous army of donkey-drivers, guides, peddlers, and beggars — but in Damascus they so hate the very sight of a foreign Christian that they want no intercourse whatever with him; only a year or two ago, his person was not always safe in Damascus streets. It is the most fanatical Mohammedan purgatory out of Arabia. Where you see one green turban of a Hadji elsewhere (the honored sign that my lord has made the pilgrimage to Mecca), I think you will see a dozen in Damascus. The Damascenes are the ugliest, wickedest looking villains we have seen. All the veiled women we had seen yet, nearly, left their eyes exposed, but numbers of these in Damascus completely hid the face under a close-drawn black veil that made the woman look like a mummy. If ever we caught an eye exposed it was quickly hidden from our contaminating Christian vision; the beggars actually passed us by without demanding bucksheesh; the merchants in the bazaars did not hold up their goods and cry out eagerly, " Hey, John!" or " Look this, Howajji!" On the contrary, they only scowled at us and said never a word.

The narrow streets swarmed like a hive with men and women in strange Oriental costumes, and our small donkeys knocked them right and left as we plowed through them, urged on by the merciless donkey-boys. These persecutors run after the animals, shouting and goading them for hours together; they keep the donkey in a gallop always, yet never get tired themselves or fall behind. The donkeys fell down and spilt us over their heads occasionally, but there was nothing for it but to mount and hurry on again. We were banged against sharp corners, loaded porters, camels, and citizens generally; and we were so taken up with looking out for collisions and casualties that we had no chance to look about us at all. We rode half through the city and through the famous " street which is called Straight " without seeing anything, hardly. Our bones were nearly knocked out of joint, we were wild with excitement, and our sides ached with the jolting we had suffered. I do not like riding in the Damascus street cars.

We were on our way to the reputed houses of Judas and Ananias. About eighteen or nineteen hundred years ago, Saul, a native of Tarsus, was particularly bitter against the new sect called Christians, and he left Jerusalem and started across the country on a furious crusade against them. He went forth " breathing threatenings and slaughter against the disciples of the Lord."

"And as he journeyed, he came near Damascus, and suddenly there shined round about him a light from heaven:

"And he fell to the earth and heard a voice saying unto him, 'Saul, Saul, why persecutest thou me?'

"And when he knew that it was Jesus that spoke to him he trembled, and was astonished, and said, 'Lord, what wilt thou have me to do?'"

He was told to arise and go into the ancient city and one would tell him what to do. In the meantime his soldiers stood speechless and awe-stricken, for they heard the mysterious voice but saw no man. Saul rose up and found that that fierce supernatural light had destroyed his sight, and he was blind, so "they led him by the hand and brought him to Damascus." He was converted.

Paul lay three days blind, in the house of Judas, and during that time he neither ate nor drank.

There came a voice to a citizen of Damascus, named Ananias, saying, "Arise, and go into the street which is called Straight, and inquire at the house of Judas, for one called Saul, of Tarsus; for behold, he prayeth."

Ananias did not wish to go at first, for he had heard of Saul before, and he had his doubts about that style of a "chosen vessel" to preach the gospel of peace. However, in obedience to orders, he went into the "street called Straight" (how he ever found his way into it, and after he did, how he ever found his way out of it again, are mysteries only to be accounted for by the fact that he was acting under Divine inspiration). He found Paul and restored him, and ordained him a preacher; and from this old house we had hunted up in the street which is

14**

miscalled Straight, he had started out on that bold missionary career which he prosecuted till his death.

It was not the house of the disciple who sold the Master for thirty pieces of silver. I make this explanation in justice to Judas, who was a far different sort of man from the person just referred to. A very different style of man, and lived in a very good house. It is a pity we do not know more about him.

I have given, in the above paragraphs, some more information for people who will not read Bible history until they are defrauded into it by some such method as this. I hope that no friend of progress and education will obstruct or interfere with my peculiar mission.

The street called Straight is straighter than a corkscrew, but not as straight as a rainbow. St. Luke is careful not to commit himself; he does not say it is the street which *is* straight, but the " street which is *called* Straight." It is a fine piece of irony; it is the only facetious remark in the Bible, I believe. We traversed the street called Straight a good way, and then turned off and called at the reputed house of Ananias. There is small question that a part of the original house is there still; it is an old room twelve or fifteen feet under ground, and its masonry is evidently ancient. If Ananias did not live there in St. Paul's time, somebody else did, which is just as well. I took a drink out of Ananias' well, and, singularly enough, the water was just as fresh as if the well had been dug yesterday.

We went out toward the north end of the city to
see the place where the disciples let Paul down over
the Damascus wall at dead of night — for he preached
Christ so fearlessly in Damascus that the people
sought to kill him, just as they would to-day for the
same offense, and he had to escape and flee to
Jerusalem.

Then we called at the tomb of Mahomet's children
and at a tomb which purported to be that of St.
George who killed the dragon, and so on out to the
hollow place under a rock where Paul hid during his
flight till his pursuers gave him up; and to the
mausoleum of the five thousand Christians who were
massacred in Damascus in 1861 by the Turks.   They
say those narrow streets ran blood for several days,
and that men, women, and children were butchered
indiscriminately and left to rot by hundreds all
through the Christian quarter; they say, further,
that the stench was dreadful.   All the Christians
who could get away fled from the city, and the
Mohammedans would not defile their hands by bury-
ing the " infidel dogs."   The thirst for blood extended to the high lands of Hermon and Anti-Leba-
non, and in a short time twenty-five thousand more
Christians were massacred and their possessions laid
waste.   How they hate a Christian in Damascus! —
and pretty much all over Turkeydom as well.   And
how they will pay for it when Russia turns her guns
upon them again!

It is soothing to the heart to abuse England and
14**

France for interposing to save the Ottoman Empire from the destruction it has so richly deserved for a thousand years. It hurts my vanity to see these pagans refuse to eat of food that has been cooked for us; or to eat from a dish we have eaten from; or to drink from a goatskin which we have polluted with our Christian lips, except by filtering the water through a rag which they put over the mouth of it or through a sponge! I never disliked a Chinaman as I do these degraded Turks and Arabs, and, when Russia is ready to war with them again, I hope England and France will not find it good breeding or good judgment to interfere.

In Damascus they think there are no such rivers in all the world as their little Abana and Pharpar. The Damascenes have always thought that way. In 2 Kings, chapter v, Naaman boasts extravagantly about them. That was three thousand years ago. He says: "Are not Abana and Pharpar, rivers of Damascus, better than all the waters of Israel? May I not wash in them and be clean?" But some of my readers have forgotten who Naaman was, long ago. Naaman was the commander of the Syrian armies. He was the favorite of the king and lived in great state. "He was a mighty man of valor, but he was a leper." Strangely enough, the house they point out to you now as his has been turned into a leper hospital, and the inmates expose their horrid deformities and hold up their hands and beg for backsheesh when a stranger enters.

One cannot appreciate the horror of this disease until he looks upon it in all its ghastliness, in Naaman's ancient dwelling in Damascus. Bones all twisted out of shape, great knots protruding from face and body, joints decaying and dropping away — horrible!

CHAPTER XVIII.

THE last twenty-four hours we stayed in Damascus I lay prostrate with a violent attack of cholera, or cholera morbus, and therefore had a good chance and a good excuse to lie there on that wide divan and take an honest rest. I had nothing to do but listen to the pattering of the fountains and take medicine and throw it up again. It was dangerous recreation, but it was pleasanter than traveling in Syria. I had plenty of snow from Mount Hermon, and, as it would not stay on my stomach, there was nothing to interfere with my eating it — there was always room for more. I enjoyed myself very well. Syrian travel has its interesting features, like travel in any other part of the world, and yet to break your leg or have the cholera adds a welcome variety to it.

We left Damascus at noon and rode across the plain a couple of hours, and then the party stopped a while in the shade of some fig-trees to give me a chance to rest. It was the hottest day we had seen yet — the sun-flames shot down like the shafts of fire that stream out before a blowpipe; the rays seemed

OUR PARTY OF EIGHT

to fall in a steady deluge on the head and pass downward like rain from a roof. I imagined I could distinguish between the floods of rays — I thought I could tell when each flood struck my head, when it reached my shoulders, and when the next one came. It was terrible. All the desert glared so fiercely that my eyes were swimming in tears all the time. The boys had white umbrellas heavily lined with dark green. They were a priceless blessing. I thanked fortune that I had one, too, notwithstanding it was packed up with the baggage and was ten miles ahead. It is madness to travel in Syria without an umbrella. They told me in Beirout (these people who always gorge you with advice) that it was madness to travel in Syria without an umbrella. It was on this account that I got one.

But, honestly, I think an umbrella is a nuisance anywhere when its business is to keep the sun off. No Arab wears a brim to his fez, or uses an umbrella, or anything to shade his eyes or his face, and he always looks comfortable and proper in the sun. But of all the ridiculous sights I ever have seen, our party of eight is the most so — they do cut such an outlandish figure. They travel single file; they all wear the endless white rag of Constantinople wrapped round and round their hats and dangling down their backs; they all wear thick green spectacles, with side-glasses to them; they all hold white umbrellas, lined with green, over their heads; without exception their stirrups are too short — they are the very worst gang of horsemen on earth; their animals to a horse trot fearfully hard — and when they get strung out one after the other, glaring straight ahead and breathless; bouncing high and out of turn, all along the line; knees well up and stiff, elbows flapping like a rooster's that is going to crow, and the long file of umbrellas popping convulsively up and down — when one sees this outrageous picture exposed to the light of day, he is amazed that the gods don't get out their thunderbolts and destroy them off the face of the earth! I do — I wonder at it. I wouldn't let any such caravan go through a country of mine.

And when the sun drops below the horizon and the boys close their umbrellas and put them under their arms, it is only a variation of the picture, not a modification of its absurdity.

But maybe you cannot see the wild extravagance of my panorama. You could if you were here. Here, you feel all the time just as if you were living about the year 1200 before Christ — or back to the patriarchs — or forward to the New Era. The scenery of the Bible is about you — the customs of the patriarchs are around you — the same people, in the same flowing robes, and in sandals, cross your path — the same long trains of stately camels go and come — the same impressive religious solemnity and silence rest upon the desert and the mountains that were upon them in the remote ages of antiquity, and behold, intruding upon a scene like this, comes this fantastic mob of green-spectacled Yanks, with their flapping elbows and bobbing umbrellas! It is Daniel in the lion's den with a green cotton umbrella under his arm, all over again.

My umbrella is with the baggage, and so are my green spectacles — and there they shall stay. I will not use them. I will show some respect for the eternal fitness of things. It will be bad enough to get sunstruck, without looking ridiculous into the bargain. If I fall, let me fall bearing about me the semblance of a Christian, at least.

Three or four hours out from Damascus we passed the spot where Saul was so abruptly converted, and from this place we looked back over the scorching desert, and had our last glimpse of beautiful Damascus, decked in its robes of shining green. After nightfall we reached our tents, just outside of the nasty Arab village of Jonesborough. Of course the real name of the place is El something or other, but the boys still refuse to recognize the Arab names or try to pronounce them. When I say that that village is of the usual style, I mean to insinuate that all Syrian villages within fifty miles of Damascus are alike — so much alike that it would require more than human intelligence to tell wherein one differed from another. A Syrian village is a hive of huts one story high (the height of a man), and as square as a drygoods box; it is mud-plastered all over, flat roof and all, and generally whitewashed after a fashion. The same roof often extends over half the town, covering many of the *streets*, which are generally about a yard wide. When you ride through one of these villages at noonday, you first meet a melancholy dog, that looks up at you and silently begs that you won't run over him, but he does not offer to get out of the way; next you meet a young boy without any clothes on, and he holds out his hand and says "Bucksheesh!" — he don't really expect a cent, but then he learned to say that before he learned to say mother, and now he cannot break himself of it; next you meet a woman with a black veil drawn closely over her face, and her bust exposed; finally, you come to several sore-eyed children and children in all stages of mutilation and decay; and sitting humbly in the dust, and all fringed with filthy rags, is a poor devil whose arms and legs are gnarled and twisted like grapevines. These are all the people you are likely to see. The balance of the population are asleep within doors, or abroad tending goats in the plains and on the hillsides. The village is built on some consumptive little water-course, and about it is a little fresh-looking vegetation. Beyond this charmed circle, for miles on every side, stretches a weary desert of sand and gravel, which produces a gray bunchy shrub like sage brush. A Syrian village is the sorriest sight in the world, and its surroundings are eminently in keeping with it.

I would not have gone into this dissertation upon Syrian villages but for the fact that Nimrod, the Mighty Hunter of Scriptural notoriety, is buried in

Jonesborough, and I wished the public to know about how he is located. Like Homer, he is said to be buried in many other places, but this is the only true and genuine place his ashes inhabit.

When the original tribes were dispersed, more than four thousand years ago, Nimrod and a large party traveled three or four hundred miles, and settled where the great city of Babylon afterwards stood. Nimrod built that city. He also began to build the famous Tower of Babel, but circumstances over which he had no control put it out of his power to finish it. He ran it up eight stories high, however, and two of them still stand at this day, a colossal mass of brickwork, rent down the center by earthquakes, and seared and vitrified by the lightnings of an angry God. But the vast ruin will still stand for ages, to shame the puny labors of these modern generations of men. Its huge compartments are tenanted by owls and lions, and old Nimrod lies neglected in this wretched village, far from the scene of his grand enterprise.

We left Jonesborough very early in the morning, and rode forever and forever and forever, it seemed to me, over parched deserts and rocky hills, hungry, and with no water to drink. We had drained the goat-skins dry in a little while. At noon we halted before the wretched Arab town of El Yuba Dam, perched on the side of a mountain, but the dragoman said if we applied there for water we would be attacked by the whole tribe, for they did not love Christians.

We had to journey on. Two hours later we reached the foot of a tall isolated mountain, which is crowned by the crumbling castle of Banias, the stateliest ruin of that kind on earth, no doubt. It is a thousand feet long and two hundred wide, all of the most symmetrical, and at the same time the most ponderous, masonry. The massive towers and bastions are more than thirty feet high, and have been sixty. From the mountain's peak its broken turrets rise above the groves of ancient oaks and olives, and look wonderfully picturesque. It is of such high antiquity that no man knows who built it or when it was built. It is utterly inaccessible, except in one place, where a bridle-path winds upward among the solid rocks to the old portcullis. The horses' hoofs have bored holes in these rocks to the depth of six inches during the hundreds and hundreds of years that the castle was garrisoned. We wandered for three hours among the chambers and crypts and dungeons of the fortress, and trod where the mailed heels of many a knightly Crusader had rang, and where Phœnician heroes had walked ages before them.

We wondered how such a solid mass of masonry could be affected even by an earthquake, and could not understand what agency had made Banias a ruin; but we found the destroyer, after a while, and then our wonder was increased tenfold. Seeds had fallen in crevices in the vast walls; the seeds had sprouted; the tender, insignificant sprouts had hardened; they grew larger and larger, and by a steady, imperceptible pressure forced the great stones apart, and now are bringing sure destruction upon a giant work that has even mocked the earthquakes to scorn! Gnarled and twisted trees spring from the old walls everywhere, and beautify and overshadow the gray battlements with a wild luxuriance of foliage.

From these old towers we looked down upon a broad, far-reaching green plain, glittering with the pools and rivulets which are the sources of the sacred river Jordan. It was a grateful vision, after so much desert.

And as the evening drew near, we clambered down the mountain, through groves of the Biblical oaks of Bashan (for we were just stepping over the border and entering the long-sought Holy Land), and at its extreme foot, toward the wide valley, we entered this little execrable village of Banias and camped in a great grove of olive trees near a torrent of sparkling water whose banks are arrayed in fig-trees, pomegranates, and oleanders in full leaf. Barring the proximity of the village, it is a sort of paradise.

The very first thing one feels like doing when he gets into camp, all burning up and dusty, is to hunt up a bath. We followed the stream up to where it gushes out of the mountain side, three hundred yards from the tents, and took a bath that was so icy that if I did not know this was the main source of the sacred river, I would expect harm to come of it. It was bathing at noonday in the chilly source of the Abana, "River of Damascus," that gave me the cholera, so Dr. B. said. However, it generally does give me the cholera to take a bath.

The incorrigible pilgrims have come in with their pockets full of specimens broken from the ruins. I wish this vandalism could be stopped. They broke off fragments from Noah's tomb; from the exquisite sculptures of the temples of Baalbec; from the houses of Judas and Ananias, in Damascus; from the tomb of Nimrod the Mighty Hunter in Jonesborough; from the worn Greek and Roman inscriptions set in the hoary walls of the castle of Banias; and now they have been hacking and chipping these old arches here that Jesus looked upon in the flesh. Heaven protect the Sepulchre when this tribe invades Jerusalem!

The ruins here are not very interesting. There are the massive walls of a great square building that was once the citadel; there are many ponderous old arches that are so smothered with débris that they barely project above the ground; there are heavy walled sewers through which the crystal brook of which Jordan is born still runs; in the hillside are the substructions of a costly marble temple that Herod the Great built here — patches of its handsome mosaic floors still remain; there is a quaint old stone bridge that was here before Herod's time, may be; scattered everywhere, in the paths and in the woods, are Corinthian capitals, broken porphyry pillars, and little fragments of sculpture; and up yonder in the precipice where the fountain gushes out, are well-worn Greek inscriptions over niches in the rock where in ancient times the Greeks, and after them the Romans, worshiped the sylvan god Pan.   But trees and bushes grow above many of these ruins now; the miserable huts of a little crew of filthy Arabs are perched upon the broken masonry of antiquity, the whole place has a sleepy, stupid, rural look about it, and one can hardly bring himself to believe that a busy, substantially built city once existed here, even two thousand years ago.   The place was nevertheless the scene of an event whose effects have added page after page and volume after volume to the world's history.   For in this place Christ stood when He said to Peter:

"Thou art Peter; and upon this rock will I build my church, and the gates of hell shall not prevail against it.   And I will give unto thee the keys of the Kingdom of Heaven; and whatsoever thou shalt bind on earth shall be bound in heaven, and whatsoever thou shalt loose on earth shall be loosed in heaven."

On these little sentences have been built up the mighty edifice of the Church of Rome; in them lie the authority for the imperial power of the Popes over temporal affairs, and their godlike power to curse a soul or wash it white from sin.   To sustain the position of "the only true Church," which Rome claims was thus conferred upon her, she has fought and labored and struggled for many a century, and will continue to keep herself busy in the same work to the end of time.   The memorable words I have quoted give to this ruined city about all the interest it possesses to people of the present day.

It seems curious enough to us to be standing on ground that was once actually pressed by the feet of the Saviour. The situation is suggestive of a reality and a tangibility that seem at variance with the vagueness and mystery and ghostliness that one naturally attaches to the character of a god. I cannot comprehend yet that I am sitting where a god has stood, and looking upon the brook and the mountains which that god looked upon, and am surrounded by dusky men and women whose ancestors saw him, and even talked with him, face to face, and carelessly, just as they would have done with any other stranger. I cannot comprehend this; the gods of my understanding have been always hidden in clouds and very far away.

This morning, during breakfast, the usual assemblage of squalid humanity sat patiently without the charmed circle of the camp and waited for such crumbs as pity might bestow upon their misery. There were old and young, brown-skinned and yellow. Some of the men were tall and stalwart (for one hardly sees anywhere such splendid looking men as here in the East), but all the women and children looked worn and sad, and distressed with hunger. They reminded me much of Indians, did these people. They had but little clothing, but such as they had was fanciful in character and fantastic in its arrangement. Any little absurd gewgaw or gimcrack they had they disposed in such a way as to make it attract attention most readily. They sat in silence, and with tireless patience watched our every motion with that vile, uncomplaining impoliteness which is so truly Indian, and which makes a white man so nervous and uncomfortable and savage that he wants to exterminate the whole tribe.

These people about us had other peculiarities, which I have noticed in the noble red man, too: they were infested with vermin, and the dirt had caked on them till it amounted to bark.

The little children were in a pitiable condition — they all had sore eyes, and were otherwise afflicted in various ways. They say that hardly a native child in all the East is free from sore eyes, and that thousands of them go blind of one eye or both every year. I think this must be so, for I see plenty of blind people every day, and I do not remember seeing any children that hadn't sore eyes. And, would you suppose that an American mother could sit for an hour, with her child in her arms, and let a hundred flies roost upon its eyes all that time undisturbed? I see that every day. It makes my flesh creep. Yesterday we met a woman riding on a little jackass, and she had a little child in her arms; honestly, I thought the child had goggles on as we approached, and I wondered how its mother could afford so much style. But when we drew near, we saw that the goggles were nothing but a camp meeting of flies assembled around each of the child's eyes, and at the same time there was a detachment prospecting its nose. The flies were happy, the child

15**

was contented, and so the mother did not interfere.

As soon as the tribe found out that we had a
doctor in our party, they began to flock in from all
quarters. Dr. B., in the charity of his nature, had
taken a child from a woman who sat near by, and
put some sort of a wash upon its diseased eyes.
That woman went off and started the whole nation,
and it was a sight to see them swarm! The lame,
the halt, the blind, the leprous — all the distempers
that are bred of indolence, dirt, and iniquity — were
represented in the congress in ten minutes, and still
they came! Every woman that had a sick baby
brought it along, and every woman that hadn't,
borrowed one. What reverent and what worshiping
looks they bent upon that dread, mysterious power,
the Doctor! They watched him take his phials out;
they watched him measure the particles of white
powder; they watched him add drops of one precious
liquid, and drops of another; they lost not the
slightest movement; their eyes were riveted upon
him with a fascination that nothing could distract.
I believe they thought he was gifted like a god.
When each individual got his portion of medicine,
his eyes were radiant with joy — notwithstanding by
nature they are a thankless and impassive race —
and upon his face was written the unquestioning
faith that nothing on earth could prevent the patient
from getting well now.

Christ knew how to preach to these simple,

superstitious, disease-tortured creatures: He healed
the sick. They flocked to our poor human doctor
this morning when the fame of what he had done to
the sick child went abroad in the land, and they
worshiped him with their eyes while they did not
know as yet whether there was virtue in his simples
or not. The ancestors of these — people precisely
like them in color, dress, manners, customs, simplicity — flocked in vast multitudes after Christ, and
when they saw Him make the afflicted whole with a
word, it is no wonder they worshiped Him. No
wonder His deeds were the talk of the nation. No
wonder the multitude that followed Him was so
great that at one time — thirty miles from here —
they had to let a sick man down through the roof
because no approach could be made to the door;
no wonder His audiences were so great at Galilee
that He had to preach from a ship removed a little
distance from the shore; no wonder that even in the
desert places about Bethsaida, five thousand invaded
His solitude, and He had to feed them by a miracle
or else see them suffer for their confiding faith and
devotion; no wonder when there was a great commotion in a city in those days, one neighbor explained it to another in words to this effect: "They
say that Jesus of Nazareth is come!"

Well, as I was saying, the doctor distributed
medicine as long as he had any to distribute, and
his reputation is mighty in Galilee this day. Among
his patients was the child of the Sheik's daughter —

15**

for even this poor, ragged handful of sores and sin has its royal Sheik — a poor old mummy that looked as if he would be more at home in a poor-house than in the Chief Magistracy of this tribe of hopeless, shirtless savages. The princess — I mean the Sheik's daughter — was only thirteen or fourteen years old, and had a very sweet face and a pretty one. She was the only Syrian female we have seen yet who was not so sinfully ugly that she couldn't smile after ten o'clock Saturday night without breaking the Sabbath. Her child was a hard speci-men, though — there wasn't enough of it to make a pie, and the poor little thing looked so pleadingly up at all who came near it (as if it had an idea that now was its chance or never) that we were filled with compassion which was genuine and not put on.

But this last new horse I have got is trying to break his neck over the tent-ropes, and I shall have to go out and anchor him. Jericho and I have parted company. The new horse is not much to boast of, I think. One of his hind legs bends the wrong way, and the other one is as straight and stiff as a tent-pole. Most of his teeth are gone, and he is as blind as a bat. His nose has been broken at some time or other, and is arched like a culvert now. His under lip hangs down like a camel's, and his ears are chopped off close to his head. I had some trouble at first to find a name for him, but I finally concluded to call him Baalbec, because he is such a magnificent ruin. I cannot keep from talking about my horses, because I have a very long and tedious journey before me, and they naturally occupy my thoughts about as much as matters of apparently much greater importance.

We satisfied our pilgrims by making those hard rides from Baalbec to Damascus, but Dan's horse and Jack's were so crippled we had to leave them behind and get fresh animals for them. The dragoman says Jack's horse died. I swapped horses with Mohammed, the kingly-looking Egyptian who is our Ferguson's lieutenant. By Ferguson I mean our dragoman Abraham, of course. I did not take this horse on account of his personal appearance, but because I have not seen his back. I do not wish to see it. I have seen the backs of all the other horses, and found most of them covered with dreadful saddle-boils which I know have not been washed or doctored for years. The idea of riding all day long over such ghastly inquisitions of torture is sickening. My horse must be like the others, but I have at least the consolation of not knowing it to be so.

I hope that in future I may be spared any more sentimental praises of the Arab's idolatry of his horse. In boyhood I longed to be an Arab of the desert and have a beautiful mare, and call her Selim or Benjamin or Mohammed, and feed her with my own hands, and let her come into the tent, and teach her to caress me and look fondly upon me with her great tender eyes; and I wished that a stranger might come at such a time and offer me a

O**

hundred thousand dollars for her, so that I could do like the other Arabs — hesitate, yearn for the money, but, overcome by my love for my mare, at last say, "Part with thee, my beautiful one! Never with my life! Away, tempter, I scorn thy gold!" and then bound into the saddle and speed over the desert like the wind!

But I recall those aspirations. If these Arabs be like the other Arabs, their love for their beautiful mares is a fraud. These of my acquaintance have no love for their horses, no sentiment of pity for them, and no knowledge of how to treat them or care for them. The Syrian saddle-blanket is a quilted mattress two or three inches thick. It is never removed from the horse, day or night. It gets full of dirt and hair, and becomes soaked with sweat. It is bound to breed sores. These pirates never think of washing a horse's back. They do not shelter the horses in the tents, either; they must stay out and take the weather as it comes. Look at poor cropped and dilapidated "Baalbec," and weep for the sentiment that has been wasted upon the Selims of romance.

CHAPTER XIX.

ABOUT an hour's ride over a rough, rocky road, half flooded with water, and through a forest of oaks of Bashan, brought us to Dan.

From a little mound here in the plain issues a broad stream of limpid water and forms a large shallow pool, and then rushes furiously onward, augmented in volume. This puddle is an important source of the Jordan. Its banks, and those of the brook, are respectably adorned with blooming oleanders, but the unutterable beauty of the spot will not throw a well-balanced man into convulsions, as the Syrian books of travel would lead one to suppose.

From the spot I am speaking of, a cannon-ball would carry beyond the confines of Holy Land and light upon profane ground three miles away. We were only one little hour's travel within the borders of Holy Land — we had hardly begun to appreciate yet that we were standing upon any different sort of earth than that we had always been used to, and yet see how the historic names began already to cluster! Dan — Bashan — Lake Huleh — the Sources of Jordan — the Sea of Galilee. They were all in sight but the last, and it was not far away. The little township of Bashan was once the kingdom so famous in Scripture for its bulls and its oaks. Lake Huleh is the Biblical " Waters of Merom." Dan was the northern and Beersheba the southern limit of Palestine — hence the expression " from Dan to Beersheba." It is equivalent to our phrases " from Maine to Texas."— " from Baltimore to San Francisco." Our expression and that of the Israelites both mean the same — great distance. With their slow camels and asses, it was about a seven-days journey from Dan to Beersheba — say a hundred and fifty or sixty miles — it was the entire length of their country, and was not to be undertaken without great preparation and much ceremony. When the prodigal traveled to " a far country," it is not likely that he went more than eighty or ninety miles. Palestine is only from forty to sixty miles wide. The state of Missouri could be split into three Palestines, and there would then be enough material left for part of another — possibly a whole one. From Baltimore to San Francisco is several thousand miles, but it will be only a seven-days journey in the cars when I am two or three years older.* If I live I shall necessarily have to go across the continent every now and then in those cars, but one journey from Dan to Beersheba will be sufficient, no doubt. It

---

* The railroad has been completed since the above was written.

must be the most trying of the two. Therefore, if we chance to discover that from Dan to Beersheba seemed a mighty stretch of country to the Israelites, let us not be airy with them, but reflect that it *was* and *is* a mighty stretch when one cannot traverse it by rail.

The small mound I have mentioned a while ago was once occupied by the Phœnician city of Laish. A party of filibusters from Zorah and Eshcol captured the place, and lived there in a free and easy way, worshiping gods of their own manufacture and stealing idols from their neighbors whenever they wore their own out. Jeroboam set up a golden calf here to fascinate his people and keep them from making dangerous trips to Jerusalem to worship, which might result in a return to their rightful allegiance. With all respect for those ancient Israelites, I cannot overlook the fact that they were not always virtuous enough to withstand the seductions of a golden calf. Human nature has not changed much since then.

Some forty centuries ago the city of Sodom was pillaged by the Arab princes of Mesopotamia, and among other prisoners they seized upon the patriarch Lot and brought him here on their way to their own possessions. They brought him to Dan, and father Abraham, who was pursuing them, crept softly in at dead of night, among the whispering oleanders and under the shadows of the stately oaks, and fell upon the slumbering victors and startled them from their dreams with the clash of steel. He recaptured Lot and all the other plunder.

We moved on. We were now in a green valley, five or six miles wide and fifteen long. The streams which are called the sources of the Jordan flow through it to Lake Huleh, a shallow pond three miles in diameter, and from the southern extremity of the lake the concentrated Jordan flows out. The lake is surrounded by a broad marsh, grown with reeds. Between the marsh and the mountains which wall the valley is a respectable strip of fertile land; at the end of the valley, toward Dan, as much as half the land is solid and fertile, and watered by Jordan's sources. There is enough of it to make a farm. It almost warrants the enthusiasm of the spies of that rabble of adventurers who captured Dan. They said: "We have seen the land, and behold it is very good. . . . A place where there is no want of anything that is in the earth."

Their enthusiasm was at least warranted by the fact that they had never seen a country as good as this. There was enough of it for the ample support of their six hundred men and their families, too.

When we got fairly down on the level part of the Danite farm, we came to places where we could actually run our horses. It was a notable circumstance.

We had been painfully clambering over interminable hills and rocks for days together, and when we suddenly came upon this astonishing piece of rockless plain, every man drove the spurs into his horse and sped away with a velocity he could surely enjoy to the utmost, but could never hope to comprehend in Syria.

Here were evidences of cultivation — a rare sight in this country — an acre or two of rich soil studded with last season's dead cornstalks of the thickness of your thumb and very wide apart. But in such a land it was a thrilling spectacle. Close to it was a stream, and on its banks a great herd of curious-looking Syrian goats and sheep were gratefully eating gravel. I do not state this as a petrified fact — I only *suppose* they were eating gravel, because there did not appear to be anything else for them to eat. The shepherds that tended them were the very pictures of Joseph and his brethren, I have no doubt in the world. They were tall, muscular, and very dark-skinned Bedouins, with inky black beards. They had firm lips, unquailing eyes, and a kingly stateliness of bearing. They wore the parti-colored half bonnet, half hood, with fringed ends falling upon their shoulders, and the full, flowing robe barred with broad black stripes — the dress one sees in all pictures of the swarthy sons of the desert. These chaps would sell their younger brothers if they had a chance, I think. They have the manners, the customs, the dress, the occupation, and the loose principles of the ancient stock. [They attacked our camp last night, and I bear them no good will.] They had with them the pigmy jackasses one sees all over Syria and remembers in all pictures of the "Flight into Egypt," where Mary and the Young Child are riding and Joseph is walking alongside, towering high above the little donkey's shoulders.

But, really, here the man rides and carries the child, as a general thing, and the woman walks. The customs have not changed since Joseph's time. We would not have in our houses a picture representing Joseph riding and Mary walking; we would see profanation in it, but a Syrian Christian would not. I know that hereafter the picture I first spoke of will look odd to me.

We could not stop to rest two or three hours out from our camp, of course, albeit the brook was beside us. So we went on an hour longer. We saw water then, but nowhere in all the waste around was there a foot of shade, and we were scorching to death. "Like unto the shadow of a great rock in a weary land." Nothing in the Bible is more beautiful than that, and surely there is no place we have wandered to that is able to give it such touching expression as this blistering, naked, treeless land.

Here you do not stop just when you please, but when you can. We found water, but no shade. We traveled on and found a tree at last, but no water. We rested and lunched, and came on to this place, Ain Mellahah (the boys call it Baldwinsville). It was a very short day's run, but the dragoman does not want to go further, and has invented a plausible lie about the country beyond this being infested by ferocious Arabs, who would make sleeping in their midst a dangerous pastime. Well, they ought to be dangerous. They carry a rusty old weather-beaten flintlock gun, with a barrel that is longer than themselves; it has no sights on it; it will not carry farther than a brickbat, and is not half so certain. And the great sash they wear in many a fold around their waists has two or three absurd old horse pistols in it that are rusty from eternal disuse — weapons that would hang fire just about long enough for you to walk out of range, and then burst and blow the Arab's head off. Exceedingly dangerous these sons of the desert are.

It used to make my blood run cold to read Wm. C. Grimes' hairbreadth escapes from Bedouins, but I think I could read them now without a tremor. He never said he was attacked by Bedouins, I believe, or was ever treated uncivilly, but then in about every other chapter he discovered them approaching, anyhow, and he had a blood-curdling fashion of working up the peril; and of wondering how his relations far away would feel could they see their poor wandering boy, with his weary feet and his dim eyes, in such fearful danger; and of thinking for the last time of the old homestead, and the dear old church, and the cow, and those things; and of finally straightening his form to its utmost height in the saddle, drawing his trusty revolver, and then dashing the spurs into "Mohammed" and sweeping down upon the ferocious enemy determined to sell his life as dearly as possible.   True, the Bedouins never did anything to him when he arrived, and never had any intention of doing anything to him in the first place, and wondered what in the mischief he was making all that to-do about; but still I could not divest myself of the idea, somehow, that a frightful peril had been escaped through that man's dare-devil bravery, and so I never could read about Wm. C. Grimes' Bedouins and sleep comfortably afterward.   But I believe the Bedouins to be a fraud, now.   I have seen the monster, and I can outrun him.   I shall never be afraid of his daring to stand behind his own gun and discharge it.

About fifteen hundred years before Christ, this campground of ours by the Waters of Merom was the scene of one of Joshua's exterminating battles. Jabin, King of Hazor (up yonder above Dan), called all the sheiks about him together, with their hosts, to make ready for Israel's terrible General who was approaching.

"And when all these Kings were met together, they came and pitched together by the Waters of Merom, to fight against Israel.

"And they went out, they and all their hosts with them, much people, even as the sand that is upon the seashore for multitude," etc.

But Joshua fell upon them and utterly destroyed them, root and branch.   That was his usual policy in war.   He never left any chance for newspaper controversies about who won the battle.   He made this valley, so quiet now, a reeking slaughter-pen.

Somewhere in this part of the country — I do not

know exactly where — Israel fought another bloody battle a hundred years later. Deborah, the prophetess, told Barak to take ten thousand men and sally forth against another King Jabin who had been doing something. Barak came down from Mount Tabor, twenty or twenty-five miles from here, and gave battle to Jabin's forces, who were in command of Sisera. Barak won the fight, and while he was making the victory complete by the usual method of exterminating the remnant of the defeated host, Sisera fled away on foot, and when he was nearly exhausted by fatigue and thirst, one Jael, a woman he seems to have been acquainted with, invited him to come into her tent and rest himself. The weary soldier acceded readily enough, and Jael put him to bed. He said he was very thirsty, and asked his generous preserver to get him a cup of water. She brought him some milk, and he drank of it gratefully and lay down again, to forget in pleasant dreams his lost battle and his humbled pride. Presently when he was asleep she came softly in with a hammer and drove a hideous tent-pin down through his brain!

"For he was fast asleep and weary. So he died." Such is the touching language of the Bible. "The Song of Deborah and Barak" praises Jael for the memorable service she had rendered, in an exultant strain:

"Blessed above women shall Jael the wife of Heber the Kenite be, blessed shall she be above women in the tent.

" He asked for water, and she gave him milk; she brought forth butter in a lordly dish.

" She put her hand to the nail, and her right hand to the workman's hammer; and with the hammer she smote Sisera, she smote off his head when she had pierced and stricken through his temples.

"At her feet he bowed, he fell, he lay down: at her feet he bowed, he fell; where he bowed, there he fell down dead."

Stirring scenes like these occur in this valley no more. There is not a solitary village throughout its whole extent — not for thirty miles in either direction. There are two or three small clusters of Bedouin tents, but not a single permanent habitation. One may ride ten miles, hereabouts, and not see ten human beings.

To this region one of the prophecies is applied:

"I will bring the land into desolation; and your enemies which dwell therein shall be astonished at it. And I will scatter you among the heathen, and I will draw out a sword after you; and your land shall be desolate and your cities waste."

No man can stand here by deserted Ain Mellahah and say the prophecy has not been fulfilled.

In a verse from the Bible which I have quoted above, occurs the phrase " all these kings." It attracted my attention in a moment, because it carries to my mind such a vastly different significance from what it always did at home. I can see easily enough that if I wish to profit by this tour and come to a correct understanding of the matters of interest connected with it, I must studiously and faithfully unlearn a great many things I have somehow absorbed concerning Palestine. I must begin a system

of reduction.   Like my grapes which the spies bore
out of the Promised Land, I have got everything in
Palestine on too large a scale.   Some of my ideas
were wild enough.   The word Palestine always
brought to my mind a vague suggestion of a
country as large as the United States.   I do not
know why, but such was the case.   I suppose it was
because I could not conceive of a small country
having so large a history.   I think I was a little
surprised to find that the grand Sultan of Turkey
was a man of only ordinary size.   I must try to
reduce my ideas of Palestine to a more reasonable
shape.   One gets large impressions in boyhood,
sometimes, which he has to fight against all his life.
"All these kings."   When I used to read that in
Sunday-school, it suggested to me the several kings
of such countries as England, France, Spain, Ger-
many, Russia, etc., arrayed in splendid robes ablaze
with jewels, marching in grave procession, with
scepters of gold in their hands and flashing crowns
upon their heads.   But here in Ain Mellahah, after
coming through Syria, and after giving serious study
to the character and customs of the country, the
phrase "all these kings" loses its grandeur.   It
suggests only a parcel of petty chiefs — ill-clad and
ill-conditioned savages much like our Indians, who
lived in full sight of each other and whose "kingdoms" were large when they were five miles square
and contained two thousand souls.   The combined
monarchies of the thirty "kings" destroyed by
16**

Joshua on one of his famous campaigns, only covered an area about equal to four of our counties of ordinary size. The poor old sheik we saw at Cesarea Philippi, with his ragged band of a hundred followers, would have been called a "king" in those ancient times.

It is seven in the morning, and as we are in the country, the grass ought to be sparkling with dew, the flowers enriching the air with their fragrance, and the birds singing in the trees. But, alas! there is no dew here, nor flowers, nor birds, nor trees. There is a plain and an unshaded lake, and beyond them some barren mountains. The tents are tumbling, the Arabs are quarreling like dogs and cats, as usual, the campground is strewn with packages and bundles, the labor of packing them upon the backs of the mules is progressing with great activity, the horses are saddled, the umbrellas are out, and in ten minutes we shall mount and the long procession will move again. The white city of the Mellahah, resurrected for a moment out of the dead centuries, will have disappeared again and left no sign.

CHAPTER XX.

WE traversed some miles of desolate country whose soil is rich enough, but is given over wholly to weeds — a silent, mournful expanse, wherein we saw only three persons — Arabs, with nothing on but a long coarse shirt like the "tow-linen" shirts which used to form the only summer garment of little negro boys on Southern plantations. Shepherds they were, and they charmed their flocks with the traditional shepherd's pipe — a reed instrument that made music as exquisitely infernal as these same Arabs create when they sing.

In their pipes lingered no echo of the wonderful music the shepherd forefathers heard in the Plains of Bethlehem what time the angels sang " Peace on earth, good will to men."

Part of the ground we came over was not ground at all, but rocks — cream-colored rocks, worn smooth, as if by water; with seldom an edge or a corner on them, but scooped out, honey-combed, bored out with eye-holes, and thus wrought into all manner of quaint shapes, among which the uncouth imitation of skulls was frequent. Over this part of

16 **   (241)

the route were occasional remains of an old Roman
road like the Appian Way, whose paving stones still
clung to their places with Roman tenacity.

Gray lizards, those heirs of ruin, of sepulchres
and desolation, glided in and out among the rocks
or lay still and sunned themselves. Where prosperity has reigned, and fallen; where glory has
flamed, and gone out; where beauty has dwelt, and
passed away; where gladness was, and sorrow is;
where the pomp of life has been, and silence and
death brood in its high places, there this reptile
makes his home, and mocks at human vanity. His
coat is the color of ashes; and ashes are the symbol of
hopes that have perished, of aspirations that came to
naught, of loves that are buried. If he could speak,
he would say, Build temples: I will lord it in their
ruins; build palaces: I will inhabit them; erect
empires: I will inherit them; bury your beautiful:
I will watch the worms at their work; and you, who
stand here and moralize over me: I will crawl over
your corpse at the last.

A few ants were in this desert place, but merely
to spend the summer. They brought their provisions from Ain Mellahah — eleven miles.

Jack is not very well to-day, it is easy to see; but,
boy as he is, he is too much of a man to speak of
it. He exposed himself to the sun too much yesterday, but since it came of his earnest desire to learn,
and to make this journey as useful as the oppor-
tunities will allow, no one seeks to discourage him

by fault-finding. We missed him an hour from the camp, and then found him some distance away, by the edge of a brook, and with no umbrella to protect him from the fierce sun. If he had been used to going without his umbrella, it would have been well enough, of course; but he was not. He was just in the act of throwing a clod at a mud-turtle which was sunning itself on a small log in the brook. We said:

"Don't do that, Jack. What do you want to harm him for? What has he done?"

"Well, then, I won't kill him, but I ought to, because he is a fraud."

We asked him why, but he said it was no matter. We asked him why, once or twice, as we walked back to the camp, but he still said it was no matter. But late at night, when he was sitting in a thoughtful mood on the bed, we asked him again and he said:

"Well, it don't matter; I don't mind it now, but I did not like it to-day, you know, because *I* don't tell anything that isn't so, and I don't think the Colonel ought to, either. But he did; he told us at prayers in the Pilgrims' tent, last night, and he seemed as if he was reading it out of the Bible, too, about this country flowing with milk and honey, and about the voice of the turtle being heard in the land. I thought that was drawing it a little strong, about the turtles, anyhow, but I asked Mr. Church if it was so, and he said it was, and what Mr.

P**

Church tells me, I believe. But I sat there and watched that turtle nearly an hour to-day, and I almost burned up in the sun; but I never heard him sing. I believe I sweated a double handful of sweat — I *know* I did — because it got in my eyes, and it was running down over my nose all the time; and you know my pants are tighter than anybody else's — Paris foolishness — and the buckskin seat of them got wet with sweat, and then got dry again and began to draw up and pinch and tear loose — it was awful — but I never heard him sing. Finally I said, This is a fraud — that is what it is, it is a fraud — and if I had had any sense I might have known a cursed mud-turtle couldn't sing. And then I said, I don't wish to be hard on this fellow, and I will just give him ten minutes to commence; ten minutes — and then if he don't, down goes his building. But he *didn't* commence, you know. I had stayed there all that time, thinking maybe he might, pretty soon, because he kept on raising his head up and letting it down, and drawing the skin over his eyes for a minute and then opening them out again, as if he was trying to study up something to sing, but just as the ten minutes were up and I was all beat out and blistered, he laid his blamed head down on a knot and went fast asleep.''

'' It *was* a little hard, after you had waited so long.''

'' I should think so. I said, Well, if you won't sing, you shan't sleep, anyway; and if you fellows had let me alone I would have made him shin out of Galilee quicker than any turtle ever did yet. But it isn't any matter now — let it go. The skin is all off the back of my neck.''

About ten in the morning we halted at Joseph's Pit. This is a ruined Khan of the Middle Ages, in one of whose side courts is a great walled and arched pit with water in it, and this pit, one tradition says, is the one Joseph's brethren cast him into. A more authentic tradition, aided by the geography of the country, places the pit in Dothan, some two days journey from here. However, since there are many who believe in this present pit as the true one, it has its interest.

It is hard to make a choice of the most beautiful passage in a book which is so gemmed with beautiful passages as the Bible; but it is certain that not many things within its lids may take rank above the exquisite story of Joseph. Who taught those ancient writers their simplicity of language, their felicity of expression, their pathos, and, above all, their faculty of sinking themselves entirely out of sight of the reader and making the narrative stand out alone and seem to tell itself? Shakespeare is always present when one reads his book; Macaulay is present when we follow the march of his stately sentences; but the Old Testament writers are hidden from view.

If the pit I have been speaking of is the right one, a scene transpired there, long ages ago, which is familiar to us all in pictures. The sons of Jacob had been pasturing their flocks near there. Their father grew uneasy at their long absence, and sent Joseph, his favorite, to see if anything had gone wrong with them. He traveled six or seven days' journey; he was only seventeen years old, and, boy like, he toiled through that long stretch of the vilest, rockiest, dustiest country in Asia, arrayed in the pride of his heart, his beautiful claw-hammer coat of many colors. Joseph was the favorite, and that was one crime in the eyes of his brethren; he had dreamed dreams, and interpreted them to foreshadow his elevation far above all his family in the far future, and that was another; he was dressed well and had doubtless displayed the harmless vanity of youth in keeping the fact prominently before his brothers. These were crimes his elders fretted over among themselves and proposed to punish when the opportunity should offer. When they saw him coming up from the Sea of Galilee, they recognized him and were glad. They said, " Lo, here is this dreamer — let us kill him.'' But Reuben pleaded for his life, and they spared it. But they seized the boy, and stripped the hated coat from his back and pushed him into the pit. *They* intended to let him die there, but Reuben intended to liberate him secretly. However, while Reuben was away for a little while, the brethren sold Joseph to some Ishmaelitish merchants who were journeying toward Egypt. Such is the history of the pit. And the self-same pit is there in that place, even to this day;

and there it will remain until the next detachment of image-breakers and tomb-desecrators arrives from the *Quaker City* excursion, and they will infallibly dig it up and carry it away with them. For behold in them is no reverence for the solemn monuments of the past, and whithersoever they go they destroy and spare not.

Joseph became rich, distinguished, powerful — as the Bible expresses it, "lord over all the land of Egypt." Joseph was the real king, the strength, the brain of the monarchy, though Pharaoh held the title. Joseph is one of the truly great men of the Old Testament. And he was the noblest and the manliest, save Esau. Why shall we not say a good word for the princely Bedouin? The only crime that can be brought against him is that he was unfortunate. Why must everybody praise Joseph's great-hearted generosity to his cruel brethren, without stint of fervent language, and fling only a reluctant bone of praise to Esau for his still sublimer generosity to the brother who had wronged him? Jacob took advantage of Esau's consuming hunger to rob him of his birthright and the great honor and consideration that belonged to the position; by treachery and falsehood he robbed him of his father's blessing; he made of him a stranger in his home, and a wanderer. Yet after twenty years had passed away and Jacob met Esau and fell at his feet quaking with fear and begging piteously to be spared the punishment he knew he deserved, what did that magnificent savage do? He fell upon his neck and embraced him! When Jacob — who was incapable of comprehending nobility of character — still doubting, still fearing, insisted upon "finding grace with my lord" by the bribe of a present of cattle, what did the gorgeous son of the desert say?

"Nay, I have enough, my brother; keep that thou hast unto thyself!"

Esau found Jacob rich, beloved by wives and children, and traveling in state, with servants, herds of cattle and trains of camels — but he himself was still the uncourted outcast this brother had made him. After thirteen years of romantic mystery, the brethren who had wronged Joseph, came, strangers in a strange land, hungry and humble, to buy "a little food"; and being summoned to a palace, charged with crime, they beheld in its owner their wronged brother; they were trembling beggars — he, the lord of a mighty empire! What Joseph that ever lived would have thrown away such a chance to "show off"? Who stands first — outcast Esau forgiving Jacob in prosperity, or Joseph on a king's throne forgiving the ragged tremblers whose happy rascality placed him there?

Just before we came to Joseph's Pit, we had "raised" a hill, and there, a few miles before us, with not a tree or a shrub to interrupt the view, lay a vision which millions of worshipers in the far lands of the earth would give half their possessions to see — the sacred Sea of Galilee!

Therefore we tarried only a short time at the pit. We rested the horses and ourselves, and felt for a few minutes the blessed shade of the ancient buildings. We were out of water, but the two or three scowling Arabs, with their long guns, who were idling about the place, said they had none and that there was none in the vicinity. They knew there was a little brackish water in the pit, but they venerated a place made sacred by their ancestor's imprisonment too much to be willing to see Christian dogs drink from it. But Ferguson tied rags and handkerchiefs together till he made a rope long enough to lower a vessel to the bottom, and we drank and then rode on; and in a short time we dismounted on those shores which the feet of the Saviour have made holy ground.

At noon we took a swim in the Sea of Galilee — a blessed privilege in this roasting climate — and then lunched under a neglected old fig tree at the fountain they call Ain-et-Tin, a hundred yards from ruined Capernaum. Every rivulet that gurgles out of the rocks and sands of this part of the world is dubbed with the title of "fountain," and people familiar with the Hudson, the Great Lakes, and the Mississippi fall into transports of admiration over them, and exhaust their powers of composition in writing their praises. If all the poetry and nonsense that have been discharged upon the fountains and the bland scenery of this region were collected in a book, it would make a most valuable volume to burn.

During luncheon, the pilgrim enthusiasts of our
party, who had been so light-hearted and happy
ever since they touched holy ground that they did
little but mutter incoherent rhapsodies, could scarcely
eat, so anxious were they to "take shipping" and
sail in very person upon the waters that had borne
the vessels of the Apostles. Their anxiety grew and
their excitement augmented with every fleeting moment, until my fears were aroused and I began to
have misgivings that in their present condition they
might break recklessly loose from all considerations
of prudence and buy a whole fleet of ships to sail in
instead of hiring a single one for an hour, as quiet
folk are wont to do. I trembled to think of the
ruined purses this day's performances might result
in. I could not help reflecting bodingly upon the
intemperate zeal with which middle-aged men are
apt to surfeit themselves upon a seductive folly
which they have tasted for the first time. And yet
I did not feel that I had a right to be surprised at
the state of things which was giving me so much con-
cern. These men had been taught from infancy to
revere, almost to worship, the holy places whereon
their happy eyes were resting now. For many and
many a year this very picture had visited their
thoughts by day and floated through their dreams by
night. To stand before it in the flesh — to see it as
they saw it now — to sail upon the hallowed sea,
and kiss the holy soil that compassed it about; these
were aspirations they had cherished while a genera-

tion dragged its lagging seasons by and left its
furrows in their faces and its frosts upon their hair.
To look upon this picture, and sail upon this sea,
they had forsaken home and its idols and journeyed
thousands and thousands of miles, in weariness and
tribulation. What wonder that the sordid lights of
work-day prudence should pale before the glory of
a hope like theirs in the full splendor of its fruition?
Let them squander millions! I said — who speaks
of money at a time like this?

In this frame of mind I followed, as fast as I
could, the eager footsteps of the pilgrims, and stood
upon the shore of the lake, and swelled, with hat
and voice, the frantic hail they sent after the
" ship " that was speeding by. It was a success.
The toilers of the sea ran in and beached their bark.
Joy sat upon every countenance.

" How much? — ask him how much, Ferguson! —
how much to take us all — eight of us, and you — to
Bethsaida, yonder, and to the mouth of Jordan, and
to the place where the swine ran down into the
sea — quick! — and we want to coast around everywhere — everywhere! — all day long! — *I* could sail
a year in these waters! — and tell him we'll stop at
Magdala and finish at Tiberias! — ask him how
much! — anything — anything whatever! — tell him
we don't care what the expense is!" [I said to
myself, I knew how it would be.]

Ferguson — (interpreting) —" He says two napoleons — eight dollars."

One or two countenances fell. Then a pause.

"Too much! — we'll give him one!"

I never shall know how it was — I shudder yet when I think how the place is given to miracles — but in a single instant of time, as it seemed to me, that ship was twenty paces from the shore, and speeding away like a frightened thing! Eight crest-fallen creatures stood upon the shore, and oh, to think of it! this — this — after all that overmastering ecstasy! Oh, shameful, shameful ending, after such unseemly boasting! It was too much like "Ho! let me at him!" followed by a prudent "Two of you hold him — one can hold me!"

Instantly there was wailing and gnashing of teeth in the camp. The two napoleons were offered — more if necessary — and pilgrims and dragoman shouted themselves hoarse with pleadings to the retreating boatmen to come back. But they sailed serenely away and paid no further heed to pilgrims who had dreamed all their lives of some day skimming over the sacred waters of Galilee and listening to its hallowed story in the whisperings of its waves, and had journeyed countless leagues to do it, and — and then concluded that the fare was too high. Impertinent Mohammedan Arabs, to think such things of gentlemen of another faith.

Well, there was nothing to do but just submit and forego the privilege of voyaging on Gennesaret, after coming half around the globe to taste that pleasure. There was a time, when the Saviour taught here, that boats were plenty among the fishermen of the coasts — but boats and fishermen both are gone now; and old Josephus had a fleet of men-of-war in these waters eighteen centuries ago — a hundred and thirty bold canoes — but they, also, have passed away and left no sign. They battle here no more by sea, and the commercial marine of Galilee numbers only two small ships, just of a pattern with the little skiffs the disciples knew. One was lost to us for good — the other was miles away and far out of hail. So we mounted the horses and rode grimly on toward Magdala, cantering along in the edge of the water for want of the means of passing over it.

How the pilgrims abused each other! Each said it was the other's fault, and each in turn denied it. No word was spoken by the sinners — even the mildest sarcasm might have been dangerous at such a time. Sinners that have been kept down and had examples held up to them, and suffered frequent lectures, and been so put upon in a moral way and in the matter of going slow and being serious and bottling up slang, and so crowded in regard to the matter of being proper and always and forever behaving, that their lives have become a burden to them, would not lag behind pilgrims at such a time as this, and wink furtively, and be joyful, and commit other such crimes — because it would not occur to them to do it. Otherwise they would. But they did do it, though — and it did them a world of good to hear the pilgrims abuse each other, too. We

took an unworthy satisfaction in seeing them fall
out, now and then, because it showed that they were
only poor human people like us, after all.

So we all rode down to Magdala, while the gnashing of teeth waxed and waned by turns, and harsh
words troubled the holy calm of Galilee.

Lest any man think I mean to be ill-natured when
I talk about our pilgrims as I have been talking, I
wish to say in all sincerity that I do not. I would
not listen to lectures from men I did not like and
could not respect; and none of these can say I ever
took their lectures unkindly, or was restive under
the infliction, or failed to try to profit by what they
said to me. They are better men than I am; I can
say that honestly; they are good friends of mine,
too — and besides, if they did not wish to be stirred
up occasionally in print, why in the mischief did
they travel with me? They knew me. They knew
my liberal way — that I like to give and take —
when it is for me to give and other people to take.
When one of them threatened to leave me in
Damascus when I had the cholera, he had no real
idea of doing it — I know his passionate nature and
the good impulses that underlie it. And did I not
overhear Church, another pilgrim, say he did not
care who went or who stayed, *he* would stand by me
till I walked out of Damascus on my own feet or was
carried out in a coffin, if it was a year? And do I
not include Church every time I abuse the pilgrims
— and would I be likely to speak ill-naturedly of

him? I wish to stir them up and make them healthy; that is all.

We had left Capernaum behind us. It was only a shapeless ruin. It bore no semblance to a town, and had nothing about it to suggest that it had ever been a town. But all desolate and unpeopled as it was, it was illustrious ground. From it sprang that tree of Christianity whose broad arms overshadow so many distant lands to-day. After Christ was tempted of the devil in the desert, he came here and began his teachings; and during the three or four years he lived afterward, this place was his home almost altogether. He began to heal the sick, and his fame soon spread so widely that sufferers came from Syria and beyond Jordan, and even from Jerusalem, several days journey away, to be cured of their diseases. Here he healed the centurion's servant and Peter's mother-in-law, and multitudes of the lame and the blind and persons possessed of devils; and here, also, he raised Jairus' daughter from the dead. He went into a ship with his disciples, and when they roused him from sleep in the midst of a storm, he quieted the winds and lulled the troubled sea to rest with his voice. He passed over to the other side, a few miles away, and relieved two men of devils, which passed into some swine. After his return he called Matthew from the receipt of customs, performed some cures, and created scandal by eating with publicans and sinners. Then he went healing and teaching through Galilee, and even

17**

journeyed to Tyre and Sidon. He chose the twelve disciples, and sent them abroad to preach the new gospel. He worked miracles in Bethsaida and Chorazin — villages two or three miles from Capernaum. It was near one of them that the miraculous draft of fishes is supposed to have been taken, and it was in the desert places near the other that he fed the thousands by the miracles of the loaves and fishes. He cursed them both, and Capernaum also, for not repenting, after all the great works he had done in their midst, and prophesied against them. They are all in ruins now — which is gratifying to the pilgrims, for, as usual, they fit the eternal words of gods to the evanescent things of this earth; Christ, it is more probable, referred to the *people*, not their shabby villages of wigwams; he said it would be sad for them at "the Day of Judgment"— and what business have mud-hovels at the Day of Judgment? it would not affect the prophecy in the least — it would neither prove it nor disprove it — if these towns were splendid cities now instead of the almost vanished ruins they are. Christ visited Magdala, which is near by Capernaum, and he also visited Cesarea Philippi. He went up to his old home at Nazareth, and saw his brothers Joses, and Judas, and James, and Simon — those persons who, being own brothers to Jesus Christ, one would expect to hear mentioned sometimes, yet who ever saw their names in a newspaper or heard them from a pulpit? Who ever inquires what manner of youths they were; and whether they slept with Jesus, played with him and romped about him; quarreled with him concerning toys and trifles; struck him in anger, not suspecting what he was? Who ever wonders what they thought when they saw him come back to Nazareth a celebrity, and looked long at his unfamiliar face to make sure, and then said, "It *is* Jesus?" Who wonders what passed in their minds when they saw this brother (who was *only* a brother to them, however much he might be to others a mysterious stranger who was a god and had stood face to face with God above the clouds) doing strange miracles with crowds of astonished people for witnesses? Who wonders if the brothers of Jesus asked him to come home with them, and said his mother and his sisters were grieved at his long absence, and would be wild with delight to see his face again? Who ever gives a thought to the sisters of Jesus at all? — yet he had sisters; and memories of them must have stolen into his mind often when he was ill-treated among strangers; when he was homeless and said he had not where to lay his head; when all deserted him, even Peter, and he stood alone among his enemies.

Christ did few miracles in Nazareth, and stayed but a little while. The people said, "*This* the Son of God! Why, his father is nothing but a carpenter. We know the family. We see them every day. Are not his brothers named so and so, and his sisters so and so, and is not his mother the person

17 **

they call Mary? This is absurd." He did not curse his home, but he shook its dust from his feet and went away.

Capernaum lies close to the edge of the little sea, in a small plain some five miles long and a mile or two wide, which is mildly adorned with oleanders which look all the better contrasted with the bald hills and the howling deserts which surround them, but they are not as deliriously beautiful as the books paint them. If one be calm and resolute he can look upon their comeliness and live.

One of the most astonishing things that have yet fallen under our observation is the exceedingly small portion of the earth from which sprang the now flourishing plant of Christianity. The longest journey our Saviour ever performed was from here to Jerusalem — about one hundred to one hundred and twenty miles. The next longest was from here to Sidon — say about sixty or seventy miles. Instead of being wide apart — as American appreciation of distances would naturally suggest — the places made most particularly celebrated by the presence of Christ are nearly all right here in full view, and within cannon-shot of Capernaum. Leaving out two or three short journeys of the Saviour, he spent his life, preached his gospel, and performed his miracles within a compass no larger than an ordinary county in the United States. It is as much as I can do to comprehend this stupefying fact. How it wears a man out to have to read up a hundred pages of history every two or three miles — for verily the celebrated localities of Palestine occur that close together. How wearily, how bewilderingly they swarm about your path!

In due time we reached the ancient village of Magdala.

CHAPTER XXI.

MAGDALA is not a beautiful place. It is thoroughly Syrian, and that is to say that it is thoroughly ugly, and cramped, squalid, uncomfortable, and filthy — just the style of cities that have adorned the country since Adam's time, as all writers have labored hard to prove, and have succeeded. The streets of Magdala are anywhere from three to six feet wide, and reeking with uncleanliness. The houses are from five to seven feet high, and all built upon one arbitrary plan — the ungraceful form of a drygoods box. The sides are daubed with a smooth white plaster, and tastefully frescoed aloft and alow with disks of camel-dung placed there to dry. This gives the edifice the romantic appearance of having been riddled with cannon-balls, and imparts to it a very warlike aspect. When the artist has arranged his materials with an eye to just proportion — the small and the large flakes in alternate rows, and separated by carefully-considered intervals — I know of nothing more cheerful to look upon than a spirited Syrian fresco. The flat, plastered roof is garnished by picturesque stacks of

fresco materials, which, having become thoroughly
dried and cured, are placed there where it will be
convenient. It is used for fuel. There is no timber
of any consequence in Palestine — none at all to
waste upon fires — and neither are there any mines
of coal. If my description has been intelligible,
you will perceive, now, that a square, flat-roofed
hovel, neatly frescoed, with its wall-tops gallantly
bastioned and turreted with dried camel-refuse, gives
to a landscape a feature that is exceedingly festive
and picturesque, especially if one is careful to remember to stick in a cat wherever, about the
premises, there is room for a cat to sit. There are
no windows to a Syrian hut, and no chimneys.
When I used to read that they let a bedridden man
down through the roof of a house in Capernaum to
get him into the presence of the Saviour, I generally
had a three-story brick in my mind, and marveled
that they did not break his neck with the strange
experiment. I perceive now, however, that they
might have taken him by the heels and thrown him
clear over the house without discommoding him
very much. Palestine is not changed any since
those days, in manners, customs, architecture, or
people.

As we rode into Magdala not a soul was visible.
But the ring of the horses' hoofs roused the stupid
population, and they all came trooping out — old
men and old women, boys and girls, the blind, the
crazy, and the crippled, all in ragged, soiled, and

scanty raiment, and all abject beggars by nature, instinct, and education.   How the vermin-tortured vagabonds did swarm!   How they showed their scars
and sores, and piteously pointed to their maimed and
crooked limbs, and begged with their pleading eyes
for charity!   We had invoked a spirit we could not
lay.   They hung to the horses' tails, clung to their
manes and. the stirrups, closed in on every side in
scorn of dangerous hoofs — and out of their infidel
throats, with one accord, burst an agonizing and
most infernal chorus: " Howajji, bucksheesh!
howajji, bucksheesh! howajji, bucksheesh! bucksheesh! bucksheesh! "   I never was in a storm like
that before.

As we paid the bucksheesh out to sore-eyed
children and brown, buxom girls with repulsively
tattooed lips and chins, we filed through the town
and by many an exquisite fresco, till we came to a
bramble-infested inclosure and a Roman looking ruin
which had been the veritable dwelling of St. Mary
Magdalene, the friend and follower of Jesus.   The
guide believed it, and so did I.   I could not well do
otherwise, with the house right there before my eyes
as plain as day.   The pilgrims took down portions
of the front wall for specimens, as is their honored
custom, and then we departed.

We are camped in this place, now, just within the
city walls of Tiberias.   We went into the town before nightfall and looked at its people — we cared
nothing about its houses.   Its people are best ex-

amined at a distance. They are particularly uncomely Jews, Arabs, and negroes. Squalor and
poverty are the pride of Tiberias. The young
women wear their dower strung upon a strong wire
that curves downward from the top of the head to
the jaw — Turkish silver coins which they have raked
together or inherited. Most of these maidens were
not wealthy, but some few had been very kindly
dealt with by fortune. I saw heiresses there worth,
in their own right — worth, well, I suppose I might
venture to say, as much as nine dollars and a half.
But such cases are rare. When you come across one
of these, she naturally puts on airs. She will not
ask for bucksheesh. She will not even permit of
undue familiarity. She assumes a crushing dignity
and goes on serenely practicing with her fine-tooth
comb and quoting poetry just the same as if you
were not present at all. Some people cannot stand
prosperity.

They say that the long-nosed, lanky, dyspeptic-
looking body-snatchers, with the indescribable hats
on, and a long curl dangling down in front of each
ear, are the old, familiar, self-righteous Pharisees we
read of in the Scriptures. Verily, they look it.
Judging merely by their general style, and without
other evidence, one might easily suspect that self-
righteousness was their specialty.

From various authorities I have culled information
concerning Tiberias. It was built by Herod Antipas,
the murderer of John the Baptist, and named after

the Emperor Tiberius. It is believed that it stands upon the site of what must have been, ages ago, a city of considerable architectural pretensions, judging by the fine porphyry pillars that are scattered through Tiberias and down the lake shore southward. These were fluted once, and yet, although the stone is about as hard as iron, the flutings are almost worn away. These pillars are small, and doubtless the edifices they adorned were distinguished more for elegance than grandeur. This modern town — Tiberias — is only mentioned in the New Testament; never in the Old.

The Sanhedrim met here last, and for three hundred years Tiberias was the metropolis of the Jews in Palestine. It is one of the four holy cities of the Israelites, and is to them what Mecca is to the Mohammedan and Jerusalem to the Christian. It has been the abiding place of many learned and famous Jewish rabbins. They lie buried here, and near them lie also twenty-five thousand of their faith who traveled far to be near them while they lived and lie with them when they died. The great Rabbi Ben Israel spent three years here in the early part of the third century. He is dead, now.

The celebrated Sea of Galilee is not so large a sea as Lake Tahoe* by a good deal — it is just about

---

* I measure all lakes by Tahoe, partly because I am far more familiar with it than with any other, and partly because I have such a high admiration for it and such a world of pleasant recollections of it, that it is very nearly impossible for me to speak of lakes and not mention it.

two-thirds as large. And when we come to speak of beauty, this sea is no more to be compared to Tahoe than a meridian of longitude is to a rainbow. The dim waters of this pool cannot suggest the limpid brilliancy of Tahoe; these low, shaven, yellow hillocks of rocks and sand, so devoid of perspective, cannot suggest the grand peaks that compass Tahoe like a wall, and whose ribbed and chasmed fronts are clad with stately pines that seem to grow small and smaller as they climb, till one might fancy them reduced to weeds and shrubs far upward, where they join the everlasting snows. Silence and solitude brood over Tahoe; and silence and solitude brood also over this lake of Gennesaret. But the solitude of the one is as cheerful and fascinating as the solitude of the other is dismal and repellent.

In the early morning one watches the silent battle of dawn and darkness upon the waters of Tahoe with a placid interest; but when the shadows sulk away and one by one the hidden beauties of the shore unfold themselves in the full splendor of noon; when the still surface is belted like a rainbow with broad bars of blue and green and white, half the distance from circumference to center; when, in the lazy summer afternoon, he lies in a boat, far out to where the dead blue of the deep water begins, and smokes the pipe of peace and idly winks at the distant crags and patches of snow from under his cap-brim; when the boat drifts shoreward to the white water, and he lolls over the gunwale and gazes by the hour down through the crystal depths and notes the colors of the pebbles and reviews the finny armies gliding in procession a hundred feet below; when at night he sees moon and stars, mountain ridges feathered with pines, jutting white capes, bold promontories, grand sweeps of rugged scenery topped with bald, glimmering peaks, all magnificently pictured in the polished mirror of the lake, in richest, softest detail, the tranquil interest that was born with the morning deepens and deepens, by sure degrees, till it culminates at last in resistless fascination!

It is solitude, for birds and squirrels on the shore and fishes in the water are all the creatures that are near to make it otherwise, but it is not the sort of solitude to make one dreary. Come to Galilee for that. If these unpeopled deserts, these rusty mounds of barrenness, that never, never, never do shake the glare from their harsh outlines, and fade and faint into vague perspective; that melancholy ruin of Capernaum; this stupid village of Tiberias, slumbering under its six funereal plumes of palms; yonder desolate declivity where the swine of the miracle ran down into the sea, and doubtless thought it was better to swallow a devil or two and get drowned into the bargain than have to live longer in such a place; this cloudless, blistering sky; this solemn, sailless, tintless lake, reposing within its rim of yellow hills and low, steep banks, and looking just as expressionless and unpoetical (when we leave its sublime history out of the question), as any metropolitan reservoir in Christendom — if these things are not food for rock me to sleep, mother, none exist, I think.

But I should not offer the evidence for the prosecution and leave the defense unheard. Wm. C. Grimes deposes as follows:

" We had taken ship to go over to the other side. The sea was not more than six miles wide. Of the beauty of the scene, however, I can not say enough, nor can I imagine where those travelers carried their eyes who have described the scenery of the lake as tame or uninteresting. The first great characteristic of it is the deep basin in which it lies. This is from three to four hundred feet deep on all sides except at the lower end, and the sharp slope of the banks, which are all of the richest green, is broken and diversified by the wâdys and water-courses which work their way down through the sides of the basin, forming dark chasms or light sunny valleys. Near Tiberias these banks are rocky, and ancient sepulchres open in them, with their doors toward the water. They selected grand spots, as did the Egyptians of old, for burial places, as if they designed that when the voice of God should reach the sleepers they should walk forth and open their eyes on scenes of glorious beauty. On the east, the wild and desolate mountains contrast finely with the deep blue lake; and toward the north, sublime and majestic, Hermon looks down on the sea, lifting his white crown to heaven with the pride of a hill that has seen the departing footsteps of a hundred generations. On the northeast shore of the sea was a single tree, and this is the only tree of any size visible from the water of the lake, except a few lonely palms in the city of Tiberias, and by its solitary position attracts more attention than would a forest. The whole appearance of the scene is precisely what we would expect and desire the scenery of Gennesaret to be, grand beauty, but quiet calm. The very mountains are calm."

It is an ingeniously written description, and well calculated to deceive. But if the paint and the ribbons and the flowers be stripped from it, a skeleton will be found beneath.

So stripped, there remains a lake six miles wide and neutral in color; with steep green banks, unrelieved by shrubbery; at one end bare, unsightly rocks, with (almost invisible) holes in them of no consequence to the picture; eastward, "wild and desolate mountains" (low, desolate hills, he should have said); in the north, a mountain called Hermon, with snow on it; peculiarity of the picture, "calmness"; its prominent feature, one tree.

No ingenuity could make such a picture beautiful — to one's actual vision.

I claim the right to correct misstatements, and have so corrected the color of the water in the above recapitulation. The waters of Gennesaret are of an exceedingly mild blue, even from a high elevation and a distance of five miles. Close at hand (the witness was sailing on the lake), it is hardly proper to call them blue at all, much less "deep" blue. I wish to state, also, not as a correction, but as a matter of opinion, that Mount Hermon is not a striking or picturesque mountain, by any means, being too near the height of its immediate neighbors to be so. That is all. I do not object to the witness dragging a mountain forty-five miles to help the scenery under consideration, because it is entirely proper to do it, and, besides, the picture needs it.

"C. W. E." (of "Life in the Holy Land"), deposes as follows:

"A beautiful sea lies unbosomed among the Galilean hills, in the midst of that land once possessed by Zebulon and Naphtali, Asher and

Dan. The azure of the sky penetrates the depths of the lake, and the waters are sweet and cool. On the west, stretch broad fertile plains; on the north the rocky shores rise step by step until in the far distance tower the snowy heights of Hermon; on the east through a misty veil are seen the high plains of Perea, which stretch away in rugged mountains leading the mind by varied paths toward Jerusalem the Holy. Flowers bloom in this terrestrial paradise, once beautiful and verdant with waving trees; singing birds enchant the ear; the turtle-dove soothes with its soft note; the crested lark sends up its song toward heaven, and the grave and stately stork inspires the mind with thought, and leads it on to meditation and repose. Life here was once idyllic, charming; here were once no rich, no poor, no high, no low. It was a world of ease, simplicity, and beauty; now it is a scene of desolation and misery."

This is not an ingenious picture. It is the worst I ever saw. It describes in elaborate detail what it terms a " terrestrial paradise," and closes with the startling information that this paradise is " a scene of *desolation and misery.*"

I have given two fair, average specimens of the character of the testimony offered by the majority of the writers who visit this region. One says, " Of the beauty of the scene I cannot say enough," and then proceeds to cover up with a woof of glittering sentences a thing which, when stripped for inspection, proves to be only an unobtrusive basin of water, some mountainous desolation, and one tree. The other, after a conscientious effort to build a terrestrial paradise out of the same materials, with the addition of a " grave and stately stork," spoils it all by blundering upon the ghastly truth at the last.

Nearly every book concerning Galilee and its lake describes the scenery as beautiful. No — not always so straightforward as that. Sometimes the *impres-*

sion intentionally conveyed is that it is beautiful, at the same time that the author is careful not to *say* that it is, in plain Saxon.   But a careful analysis of these descriptions will show that the materials of which they are formed are not individually beautiful and cannot be wrought into combinations that are beautiful.   The veneration and the affection which some of these men felt for the scenes they were speaking of heated their fancies and biased their judgment; but the pleasant falsities they wrote were full of honest sincerity, at any rate.   Others wrote as they did, because they feared it would be unpopular to write otherwise.   Others were hypocrites and deliberately meant to deceive.   Any of them would say in a moment, if asked, that it was *always* right and always *best* to tell the truth.   They would say that, at any rate, if they did not perceive the drift of the question.

But why should not the truth be spoken of this region?   Is the truth harmful?   Has it ever needed to hide its face?   God made the Sea of Galilee and its surroundings as they are.   Is it the province of Mr. Grimes to improve upon the work?

I am sure, from the tenor of books I have read, that many who have visited this land in years gone by, were Presbyterians, and came seeking evidences in support of their particular creed; they found a Presbyterian Palestine, and they had already made up their minds to find no other, though possibly they did not know it, being blinded by their zeal.

Others were Baptists, seeking Baptist evidences and
a Baptist Palestine.   Others were Catholics, Metho-
dists, Episcopalians, seeking evidences indorsing their
several creeds, and a Catholic, a Methodist, an
Episcopalian Palestine.   Honest as these men's in-
tentions may have been, they were full of partialities
and prejudices, they entered the country with their
verdicts already prepared, and they could no more
write dispassionately and impartially about it than
they could about their own wives and children.
Our pilgrims have brought *their* verdicts with them.
They have shown it in their conversation ever since
we left Beirout.   I can almost tell, in set phrase,
what they will say when they see Tabor, Nazareth,
Jericho, and Jerusalem — *because I have the books
they will "smouch" their ideas from.*   These authors
write pictures and frame rhapsodies, and lesser men
follow and see with the author's eyes instead of their
own, and speak with his tongue.   What the pilgrims
said at Cesarea Philippi surprised me with its wisdom.
I found it afterwards in Robinson.   What they said
when Gennesaret burst upon their vision charmed
me with its grace.   I find it in Mr. Thompson's
"Land and the Book."   They have spoken often, in
happily-worded language which never varied, of how
they mean to lay their weary heads upon a stone at
Bethel, as Jacob did, and close their dim eyes, and
dream, perchance, of angels descending out of
heaven on a ladder.   It was very pretty.   But I
have recognized the weary head and the dim eyes,
18**

finally. They borrowed the idea — and the words
— and the construction — and the punctuation —
from Grimes. The pilgrims will tell of Palestine,
when they get home, not as it appeared to *them*, but
as it appeared to Thompson and Robinson and
Grimes — with the tints varied to suit each pilgrim's
creed.

Pilgrims, sinners, and Arabs are all abed, now, and
the camp is still. Labor in loneliness is irksome.
Since I made my last few notes, I have been sitting
outside the tent for half an hour. Night is the time
to see Galilee. Gennesaret under these lustrous stars
has nothing repulsive about it. Gennesaret with the
glittering reflections of the constellations flecking its
surface, almost makes me regret that I ever saw the
rude glare of the day upon it. Its history and its
associations are its chiefest charm, in any eyes, and
the spells they weave are feeble in the searching light
of the sun. *Then*, we scarcely feel the fetters. Our
thoughts wander constantly to the practical concerns
of life, and refuse to dwell upon things that seem
vague and unreal. But when the day is done, even
the most unimpressible must yield to the dreamy influences of this tranquil starlight. The old traditions
of the place steal upon his memory and haunt his
reveries, and then his fancy clothes all sights and
sounds with the supernatural. In the lapping of the
waves upon the beach, he hears the dip of ghostly
oars; in the secret noises of the night he hears spirit
voices; in the soft sweep of the breeze, the rush of

invisible wings. Phantom ships are on the sea, the dead of twenty centuries come forth from the tombs, and in the dirges of the night wind the songs of old forgotten ages find utterance again.

In the starlight, Galilee has no boundaries but the broad compass of the heavens, and is a theater meet for great events; meet for the birth of a religion able to save a world; and meet for the stately Figure appointed to stand upon its stage and proclaim its high decrees. But in the sunlight, one says: Is it for the deeds which were done and the words which were spoken in this little acre of rocks and sand eighteen centuries gone, that the bells are ringing to-day in the remote islands of the sea and far and wide over continents that clasp the circumference of the huge globe?

One can comprehend it only when night has hidden all incongruities and created a theater proper for so grand a drama.

CHAPTER XXII.

WE took another swim in the Sea of Galilee at twilight yesterday, and another at sunrise this morning. We have not sailed, but three swims are equal to a sail, are they not? There were plenty of fish visible in the water, but we have no outside aids in this pilgrimage but "Tent Life in the Holy Land," "The Land and the Book," and other literature of like description — no fishing tackle. There were no fish to be had in the village of Tiberias. True, we saw two or three vagabonds mending their nets, but never trying to catch anything with them.

We did not go to the ancient warm baths two miles below Tiberias. I had no desire in the world to go there. This seemed a little strange, and prompted me to try to discover what the cause of this unreasonable indifference was. It turned out to be simply because Pliny mentions them. I have conceived a sort of unwarrantable unfriendliness toward Pliny and St. Paul, because it seems as if I can never ferret out a place that I can have to myself. It always and eternally transpires that St. Paul has been to that place, and Pliny has "mentioned" it.

In the early morning we mounted and started. And then a weird apparition marched forth at the head of the procession — a pirate, I thought, if ever a pirate dwelt upon land. It was a tall Arab, as swarthy as an Indian, young — say thirty years of age. On his head he had closely bound a gorgeous yellow and red striped silk scarf, whose ends, lavishly fringed with tassels, hung down between his shoulders and dallied with the wind. From his neck to his knees, in ample folds, a robe swept down that was a very star-spangled banner of curved and sinuous bars of black and white. Out of his back, somewhere, apparently, the long stem of a chibouk projected, and reached far above his right shoulder. Athwart his back, diagonally, and extending high above his left shoulder, was an Arab gun of Saladin's time, that was splendid with silver plating from stock clear up to the end of its measureless stretch of barrel. About his waist was bound many and many a yard of elaborately figured but sadly tarnished stuff that came from sumptuous Persia, and among the baggy folds in front the sunbeams glinted from a formidable battery of old brass-mounted horse pistols and the gilded hilts of bloodthirsty knives. There were holsters for more pistols appended to the wonderful stack of long-haired goat-skins and Persian carpets, which the man had been taught to regard in the light of a saddle; and down among the pen-

R **

dulous rank of vast tassels that swung from that sad·
dle, and clanging against the iron shovel of a stirrup
that propped the warrior's knees up toward his chin,
was a crooked, silver-clad scimetar of such awful
dimensions and such implacable expression that no
man might hope to look upon it and not shudder.
The fringed and bedizened prince whose privilege it
is to ride the pony and lead the elephant into a
country village is poor and naked compared to this
chaos of paraphernalia, and the happy vanity of the
one is the very poverty of satisfaction compared to
the majestic serenity, the overwhelming complacency
of the other.

" *Who* is this? *What* is this? " That was the
trembling inquiry all down the line.

" Our guard! From Galilee to the birthplace of
the Saviour, the country is infested with fierce
Bedouins, whose sole happiness it is, in this life, to
cut and stab and mangle and murder unoffending
Christians. Allah be with us! "

" Then hire a regiment! Would you send us out
among these desperate hordes, with no salvation in
our utmost need but this old turret? "

The dragoman laughed—not at the facetiousness of
the simile, for verily, that guide or that courier or
that dragoman never yet lived upon earth who had
in him the faintest appreciation of a joke, even
though that joke were so broad and so ponderous
that if it fell on him it would flatten him out like a
postage-stamp — the dragoman laughed, and then,

emboldened by some thought that was in his brain, no doubt, proceeded to extremities and winked.

In straits like these, when a man laughs, it is encouraging; when he winks, it is positively reassuring. He finally intimated that one guard would be sufficient to protect us, but that that one was an absolute necessity. It was because of the moral weight his awful panoply would have with the Bedouins. Then I said we didn't want any guard at all. If one fantastic vagabond could protect eight armed Christians and a pack of Arab servants from all harm, surely that detachment could protect themselves. He shook his head doubtfully. Then I said, just think of how it looks — think of how it would read, to self-reliant Americans, that we went sneaking through this deserted wilderness under the protection of this masquerading Arab, who would break his neck getting out of the country if a man that *was* a man ever started after him. It was a mean, low, degrading position. Why were we ever told to bring navy revolvers with us if we had to be protected at last by this infamous star-spangled scum of the desert? These appeals were vain — the dragoman only smiled and shook his head.

I rode to the front and struck up an acquaintance with King Solomon-in-all-his-glory, and got him to show me his lingering eternity of a gun. It had a rusty flint lock; it was ringed and barred and plated with silver from end to end, but it was as desperately out of the perpendicular as are the billiard cues of

'49 that one finds yet in service in the ancient mining camps of California. The muzzle was eaten by the rust of centuries into a ragged filigree-work, like the end of a burnt-out stovepipe. I shut one eye and peered within — it was flaked with iron rust like an old steamboat boiler. I borrowed the ponderous pistols and snapped them. They were rusty inside, too — had not been loaded for a generation. I went back, full of encouragement, and reported to the guide, and asked him to discharge this dismantled fortress. It came out, then. This fellow was a retainer of the Sheik of Tiberias. He was a source of Government revenue. He was to the Empire of Tiberias what the customs are to America. The Sheik imposed guards upon travelers and charged them for it. It is a lucrative source of emolument, and sometimes brings into the national treasury as much as thirty-five or forty dollars a year.

I knew the warrior's secret now; I knew the hollow vanity of his rusty trumpery, and despised his asinine complacency. I told on him, and with reckless daring the cavalcade rode straight ahead into the perilous solitudes of the desert, and scorned his frantic warnings of the mutilation and death that hovered about them on every side.

Arrived at an elevation of twelve hundred feet above the lake (I ought to mention that the lake lies six hundred feet below the level of the Mediterranean — no traveler ever neglects to flourish that fragment of news in his letters), as bald and unthrilling a panorama as any land can afford, perhaps, was spread out before us. Yet it was so crowded with historical interest, that if all the pages that have been written about it were spread upon its surface, they would flag it from horizon to horizon like a pavement. Among the localities comprised in this view, were Mount Hermon; the hills that border Cesarea Philippi, Dan, the Sources of the Jordan and the Waters of Merom; Tiberias; the Sea of Galilee; Joseph's Pit; Capernaum; Bethsaida; the supposed scenes of the Sermon on the Mount, the feeding of the multitudes and the miraculous draught of fishes; the declivity down which the swine ran to the sea; the entrance and the exit of the Jordan; Safed, "the city set upon a hill," one of the four holy cities of the Jews, and the place where they believe the real Messiah will appear when he comes to redeem the world; part of the battlefield of Hattin, where the knightly Crusaders fought their last fight, and in a blaze of glory passed from the stage and ended their splendid career forever; Mount Tabor, the traditional scene of the Lord's Transfiguration. And down toward the southeast lay a landscape that suggested to my mind a quotation (imperfectly remembered, no doubt):

"The Ephraimites, not being called upon to share in the rich spoils of the Ammonitish war, assembled a mighty host to fight against Jeptha, Judge of Israel; who being apprised of their approach, gathered together the men of Israel and gave them battle and put them to flight. To make his victory the more secure, he stationed guards at the different fords and passages of the Jordan, with instructions to let none pass who could not say Shibboleth. The Ephraimites, being of a different tribe, could not frame to pronounce the word aright, but called it Sibboleth, which proved them enemies and cost them their lives; wherefore forty and two thousand fell at the different fords and passages of the Jordan that day."

We jogged along peacefully over the great caravan route from Damascus to Jerusalem and Egypt, past Lubia and other Syrian hamlets, perched, in the unvarying style, upon the summit of steep mounds and hills, and fenced round about with giant cactuses (the sign of worthless land), with prickly pears upon them like hams, and came at last to the battlefield of Hattin.

It is a grand, irregular plateau, and looks as if it might have been created for a battlefield. Here the peerless Saladin met the Christian host some seven hundred years ago, and broke their power in Palestine for all time to come. There had long been a truce between the opposing forces, but according to the Guide-Book, Raynauld of Chatillon, Lord of Kerak, broke it by plundering a Damascus caravan, and refusing to give up either the merchants or their goods when Saladin demanded them. This conduct of an insolent petty chieftain stung the Sultan to the quick, and he swore that he would slaughter Raynauld with his own hand, no matter how, or when, or where he found him. Both armies prepared for war. Under the weak King of Jerusalem was the very flower of the Christian chivalry. He foolishly compelled them to undergo a long, exhausting march, in the scorching sun, and then, without water or other refreshment, ordered them to encamp in this open plain. The splendidly mounted masses of Moslem soldiers swept round the north end of Gennesaret, burning and destroying as they came, and pitched their camp in front of the opposing lines. At dawn the terrific fight began. Surrounded on all sides by the Sultan's swarming battalions, the Christian Knights fought on without a hope for their lives. They fought with desperate valor, but to no purpose; the odds of heat and numbers and consuming thirst were too great against them. Toward the middle of the day the bravest of their band cut their way through the Moslem ranks and gained the summit of a little hill, and there, hour after hour, they closed around the banner of the Cross, and beat back the charging squadrons of the enemy.

But the doom of the Christian power was sealed. Sunset found Saladin Lord of Palestine, the Christian chivalry strewn in heaps upon the field, and the King of Jerusalem, the Grand Master of the Templars, and Raynauld of Chatillon, captives in the Sultan's tent. Saladin treated two of the prisoners with princely courtesy, and ordered refreshments to be set before them. When the King handed an iced Sherbet to Chatillon, the Sultan said, "It is thou that givest it to him, not I." He remembered his oath, and slaughtered the hapless Knight of Chatillon with his own hand.

It was hard to realize that this silent plain had

once resounded with martial music and trembled to the tramp of armed men. It was hard to people this solitude with rushing columns of cavalry, and stir its torpid pulses with the shouts of victors, the shrieks of the wounded, and the flash of banner and steel above the surging billows of war. A desolation is here that not even imagination can grace with the pomp of life and action.

We reached Tabor safely, and considerably in advance of that old iron-clad swindle of a guard. We never saw a human being on the whole route, much less lawless hordes of Bedouins. Tabor stands solitary and alone, a giant sentinel above the Plain of Esdraelon. It rises some fourteen hundred feet above the surrounding level, a green, wooded cone, symmetrical and full of grace — a prominent landmark, and one that is exceedingly pleasant to eyes surfeited with the repulsive monotony of desert Syria. We climbed the steep path to its summit, through breezy glades of thorn and oak. The view presented from its highest peak was almost beautiful. Below, was the broad, level plain of Esdraelon, checkered with fields like a chessboard, and full as smooth and level, seemingly; dotted about its borders with white, compact villages, and faintly penciled, far and near, with the curving lines of roads and trails. When it is robed in the fresh verdure of spring, it must form a charming picture, even by itself. Skirting its southern border rises "Little Hermon," over whose summit a glimpse of

Gilboa is caught.   Nain, famous for the raising of
the widow's son, and Endor, as famous for the performances of her witch, are in view.   To the eastward lies the Valley of the Jordan and beyond it the
mountains of Gilead.   Westward is Mount Carmel.
Hermon in the north — the table-lands of Bashan —
Safed, the holy city, gleaming white upon a tall spur
of the mountains of Lebanon — a steel-blue corner
of the Sea of Galilee — saddle-peaked Hattin, traditional " Mount of Beatitudes " and mute witness of
the last brave fight of the Crusading host for Holy
Cross — these fill up the picture.

To glance at the salient features of this landscape
through the picturesque framework of a ragged and
ruined stone window-arch of the time of Christ, thus
hiding from sight all that is unattractive, is to secure
to yourself a pleasure worth climbing the mountain
to enjoy.   One must stand on his head to get the
best effect in a fine sunset, and set a landscape in a
bold, strong framework that is very close at hand,
to bring out all its beauty.   One learns this latter
truth never more to forget it, in that mimic land
of enchantment, the wonderful garden of my lord
the Count Pallavicini, near Genoa.   You go wandering for hours among hills and wooded glens, art-
fully contrived to leave the impression that Nature
shaped them and not man; following winding paths
and coming suddenly upon leaping cascades and
rustic bridges; finding sylvan lakes where you expected them not; loitering through battered mediæ-

val castles in miniature that seem hoary with age and
yet were built a dozen years ago; meditating over
ancient crumbling tombs, whose marble columns
were marred and broken purposely by the modern
artist that made them; stumbling unawares upon
toy palaces, wrought of rare and costly materials,
and again upon a peasant's hut, whose dilapidated
furniture would never suggest that it was made so to
order; sweeping round and round in the midst of a
forest on an enchanted wooden horse that is moved
by some invisible agency; traversing Roman roads
and passing under majestic triumphal arches; resting in quaint bowers where unseen spirits discharge
jets of water on you from every possible direction,
and where even the flowers you touch assail you
with a shower; boating on a subterranean lake
among caverns and arches royally draped with
clustering stalactites, and passing out into open day
upon another lake, which is bordered with sloping
banks of grass and gay with patrician barges that
swim at anchor in the shadow of a miniature marble
temple that rises out of the clear water and glasses
its white statues, its rich capitals and fluted columns
in the tranquil depths. So, from marvel to marvel
you have drifted on, thinking all the time that the
one last seen must be the chiefest. And, verily,
the chiefest wonder *is* reserved until the last, but
you do not see it until you step ashore, and passing
through a wilderness of rare flowers, collected from
every corner of the earth, you stand at the door of

one more mimic temple. Right in this place the
artist taxed his genius to the utmost, and fairly
opened the gates of fairy land. You look through
an unpretending pane of glass, stained yellow; the
first thing you see is a mass of quivering foliage, ten
short steps before you, in the midst of which is a
ragged opening like a gateway — a thing that is
common enough in nature, and not apt to excite
suspicions of a deep human design — and above the
bottom of the gateway, project, in the most careless
way, a few broad tropic leaves and brilliant flowers.
All of a sudden, through this bright, bold gateway,
you catch a glimpse of the faintest, softest, richest
picture that ever graced the dream of a dying Saint,
since John saw the New Jerusalem glimmering above
the clouds of Heaven. A broad sweep of sea,
flecked with careening sails; a sharp, jutting cape,
and a lofty lighthouse on it; a sloping lawn behind
it; beyond, a portion of the old "city of palaces,"
with its parks and hills and stately mansions; beyond
these, a prodigious mountain, with its strong outlines sharply cut against ocean and sky; and, over
all, vagrant shreds and flakes of cloud, floating in a
sea of gold. The ocean is gold, the city is gold,
the meadow, the mountain, the sky — everything is
golden — rich, and mellow, and dreamy as a vision
of Paradise. No artist could put upon canvas its
entrancing beauty, and yet, without the yellow
glass, and the carefully contrived accident of a
framework that cast it into enchanted distance and

shut out from it all unattractive features, it was not a picture to fall into ecstasies over. Such is life, and the trail of the serpent is over us all.

There is nothing for it now but to come back to old Tabor, though the subject is tiresome enough, and I cannot stick to it for wandering off to scenes that are pleasanter to remember. I think I will skip, anyhow. There is nothing about Tabor (except we concede that it was the scene of the Transfiguration), but some gray old ruins, stacked up there in all ages of the world from the days of stout Gideon and parties that flourished thirty centuries ago to the fresh yesterday of Crusading times. It has its Greek Convent, and the coffee there is good, but never a splinter of the true cross or bone of a hallowed saint to arrest the idle thoughts of worldlings and turn them into graver channels. A Catholic church is nothing to me that has no relics.

The plain of Esdraelon—"the battlefield of the nations"—only sets one to dreaming of Joshua, and Benhadad, and Saul, and Gideon; Tamerlane, Tancred, Cœur de Lion, and Saladin; the warrior Kings of Persia, Egypt's heroes, and Napoleon—for they all fought here. If the magic of the moonlight could summon from the graves of forgotten centuries and many lands the countless myriads that have battled on this wide, far-reaching floor, and array them in the thousand strange costumes of their hundred nationalities, and send the vast host sweeping down the plain, splendid with plumes and ban-

ners and glittering lances, I could stay here an age
to see the phantom pageant.   But the magic of the
moonlight is a vanity and a fraud; and whoso
putteth his trust in it shall suffer sorrow and disappointment.

Down at the foot of Tabor, and just at the edge
of the storied Plain of Esdraelon, is the insignificant
village of Deburieh, where Deborah, prophetess of
Israel, lived.   It is just like Magdala.

19**

CHAPTER XXIII.

WE descended from Mount Tabor, crossed a deep ravine, and followed a hilly, rocky road to Nazareth — distant two hours. All distances in the East are measured by hours, not miles. A good horse will walk three miles an hour over nearly any kind of a road; therefore, an hour here always stands for three miles. This method of computation is bothersome and annoying; and until one gets thoroughly accustomed to it, it carries no intelligence to his mind until he has stopped and translated the pagan hours into Christian miles, just as people do with the spoken words of a foreign language they are acquainted with, but not familiarly enough to catch the meaning in a moment. Distances traveled by human feet are also estimated by hours and minutes, though I do not know what the base of the calculation is. In Constantinople you ask, " How far is it to the Consulate?" and they answer, " About ten minutes." " How far is it to the Lloyds' Agency?" " Quarter of an hour." " How far is it to the lower bridge?" " Four minutes." I cannot be positive about it, but I think that there, when a man orders a pair of pantaloons,

he says he wants them a quarter of a minute in the
legs and nine seconds around the waist.

Two hours from Tabor to Nazareth — and as it was
an uncommonly narrow, crooked trail, we necessarily met all the camel trains and jackass caravans
between Jericho and Jacksonville in that particular
place and nowhere else. The donkeys do not matter
so much, because they are so small that you can
jump your horse over them if he is an animal of
spirit, but a camel is not jumpable. A camel is as
tall as any ordinary dwelling-house in Syria — which
is to say a camel is from one to two, and sometimes
nearly three feet taller than a good-sized man. In
this part of the country his load is oftenest in the
shape of colossal sacks — one on each side. He
and his cargo take up as much room as a carriage.
Think of meeting this style of obstruction in a
narrow trail. The camel would not turn out for a
king. He stalks serenely along, bringing his cushioned stilts forward with the long, regular swing of
a pendulum, and whatever is in the way must get
out of the way peaceably, or be wiped out forcibly
by the bulky sacks. It was a tiresome ride to us,
and perfectly exhausting to the horses. We were
compelled to jump over upward of eighteen hundred
donkeys, and only one person in the party was un-
seated less than sixty times by the camels. This
seems like a powerful statement, but the poet has
said, " Things are not what they seem." I cannot
think of anything now more certain to make one

19**

shudder, than to have a soft-footed camel sneak up behind him and touch him on the ear with its cold, flabby under lip. A camel did this for one of the boys, who was drooping over his saddle in a brown study. He glanced up and saw the majestic apparition hovering above him, and made frantic efforts to get out of the way, but the camel reached out and bit him on the shoulder before he accomplished it. This was the only pleasant incident of the journey.

At Nazareth we camped in an olive grove near the Virgin Mary's fountain, and that wonderful Arab "guard" came to collect some bucksheesh for his "services" in following us from Tiberias and warding off invisible dangers with the terrors of his armament. The dragoman had paid his master, but that counted as nothing — if you hire a man to sneeze for you here, and another man chooses to help him, you have got to pay both. They do nothing whatever without pay. How it must have surprised these people to hear the way of salvation offered to them " *without money and without price.*" If the manners, the people, or the customs of this country have changed since the Saviour's time, the figures and metaphors of the Bible are not the evidences to prove it by.

We entered the great Latin Convent which is built over the traditional dwelling-place of the Holy Family. We went down a flight of fifteen steps below the ground level, and stood in a small chapel tricked out with tapestry hangings, silver lamps, and oil paintings. A spot marked by a cross, in the marble floor, under the altar, was exhibited as the place made forever holy by the feet of the Virgin when she stood up to receive the message of the angel. So simple, so unpretending a locality, to be the scene of so mighty an event! The very scene of the Annunciation — an event which has been commemorated by splendid shrines and august temples all over the civilized world, and one which the princes of art have made it their loftiest ambition to picture worthily on their canvas; a spot whose history is familiar to the very children of every house, and city, and obscure hamlet of the furthest lands of Christendom; a spot which myriads of men would toil across the breadth of a world to see, would consider it a priceless privilege to look upon. It was easy to think these thoughts. But it was not easy to bring myself up to the magnitude of the situation. I could sit off several thousand miles and imagine the angel appearing, with shadowy wings and lustrous countenance, and note the glory that streamed downward upon the Virgin's head while the message from the Throne of God fell upon her ears — any one can do that, beyond the ocean, but few can do it here. I saw the little recess from which the angel stepped, but could not fill its void. The angels that I know are creatures of unstable fancy — they will not fit in niches of substantial stone. Imagination labors best in distant fields. I doubt if any man can stand in the Grotto of the

S**

Annunciation and people with the phantom images of his mind its too tangible walls of stone.

They showed us a broken granite pillar, depending from the roof, which they said was hacked in two by the Moslem conquerors of Nazareth, in the vain hope of pulling down the sanctuary. But the pillar remained miraculously suspended in the air, and, unsupported itself, supported then and still supports the roof. By dividing this statement up among eight, it was found not difficult to believe it.

These gifted Latin monks never do anything by halves. If they were to show you the Brazen Serpent that was elevated in the wilderness, you could depend upon it that they had on hand the pole it was elevated on also, and even the hole it stood in. They have got the " Grotto " of the Annunciation here; and just as convenient to it as one's throat is to his mouth, they have also the Virgin's Kitchen, and even her sitting-room, where she and Joseph watched the infant Saviour play with Hebrew toys eighteen hundred years ago. All under one roof, and all clean, spacious, comfortable " grottoes." It seems curious that personages intimately connected with the Holy Family always lived in grottoes — in Nazareth, in Bethlehem, in imperial Ephesus — and yet nobody else in their day and generation thought of doing anything of the kind. If they ever did, their grottoes are all gone, and I suppose we ought to wonder at the peculiar marvel of the preservation of these I speak of. When the

Virgin fled from Herod's wrath, she hid in a grotto in Bethlehem, and the same is there to this day. The slaughter of the innocents in Bethlehem was done in a grotto; the Saviour was born in a grotto — both are shown to pilgrims yet. It is exceedingly strange that these tremendous events all happened in grottoes — and exceedingly fortunate, likewise, because the strongest houses must crumble to ruin in time, but a grotto in the living rock will last forever. It is an imposture — this grotto stuff — but it is one that all men ought to thank the Catholics for. Wherever they ferret out a lost locality made holy by some Scriptural event, they straightway build a massive — almost imperishable — church there, and preserve the memory of that locality for the gratification of future generations. If it had been left to Protestants to do this most worthy work, we would not even know where Jerusalem is to-day, and the man who could go and put his finger on Nazareth would be too wise for this world. The world owes the Catholics its good will even for the happy rascality of hewing out these bogus grottoes in the rock; for it is infinitely more satisfactory to look at a grotto, where people have faithfully believed for centuries that the Virgin once lived, than to have to imagine a dwelling-place for her somewhere, anywhere, nowhere, loose and at large all over this town of Nazareth. There is too large a scope of country. The imagination cannot work. There is no one particular spot to chain your eye, rivet your interest, and make you think. The memory of the Pilgrims cannot perish while Plymouth Rock remains to us. The old monks are wise. They know how to drive a stake through a pleasant tradition that will hold it to its place forever.

We visited the places where Jesus worked for fifteen years as a carpenter, and where he attempted to teach in the synagogue and was driven out by a mob. Catholic chapels stand upon these sites and protect the little fragments of the ancient walls which remain. Our pilgrims broke off specimens. We visited, also, a new chapel, in the midst of the town, which is built around a bowlder some twelve feet long by four feet thick; the priests discovered, a few years ago, that the disciples had sat upon this rock to rest once, when they had walked up from Capernaum. They hastened to preserve the relic. Relics are very good property. Travelers are expected to pay for seeing them, and they do it cheerfully. We like the idea. One's conscience can never be the worse for the knowledge that he has paid his way like a man. Our pilgrims would have liked very well to get out their lampblack and stencil-plates and paint their names on that rock, together with the names of the villages they hail from in America, but the priests permit nothing of that kind. To speak the strict truth, however, our party seldom offend in that way, though we have men in the ship who never lose an opportunity to do it. Our pilgrims' chief sin is their lust for

"specimens." I suppose that by this time they
know the dimensions of that rock to an inch, and
its weight to a ton; and I do not hesitate to charge
that they will go back there to-night and try to
carry it off.

This "Fountain of the Virgin" is the one which
tradition says Mary used to get water from, twenty
times a day, when she was a girl, and bear it away
in a jar upon her head. The water streams through
faucets in the face of a wall of ancient masonry
which stands removed from the houses of the village.
The young girls of Nazareth still collect about it by
the dozen and keep up a riotous laughter and sky-
larking. The Nazarene girls are homely. Some of
them have large, lustrous eyes, but none of them
have pretty faces. These girls wear a single garment, usually, and it is loose, shapeless, of unde-
cided color; it is generally out of repair, too.
They wear, from crown to jaw, curious strings of
old coins, after the manner of the belles of Tiberias,
and brass jewelry upon their wrists and in their ears.
They wear no shoes and stockings. They are the
most human girls we have found in the country yet,
and the best natured. But there is no question that
these picturesque maidens sadly lack comeliness.

A pilgrim — the "Enthusiast"— said: "See that
tall, graceful girl! look at the Madonna-like beauty
of her countenance!"

Another pilgrim came along presently and said:
"Observe that tall, graceful girl; what queenly

Madonna-like gracefulness of beauty is in her
countenance.''

I said: '' She is not tall, she is short; she is not
beautiful, she is homely; she is graceful enough, I
grant, but she is rather boisterous.''

The third and last pilgrim moved by, before long,
and he said: '' Ah, what a tall, graceful girl! what
Madonna-like gracefulness of queenly beauty !''

The verdicts were all in. It was time, now, to
look up the authorities for all these opinions. I
found this paragraph, which follows. Written by
whom? Wm. C. Grimes:

"After we were in the saddle, we rode down to the spring to have
a last look at the women of Nazareth, who were, as a class, much the
prettiest that we had seen in the East.   As we approached the crowd a
tall girl of nineteen advanced toward Miriam and offered her a cup of
water.   Her movement was graceful and queenly.   We exclaimed on
the spot at the Madonna-like beauty of her countenance.   Whitely was
suddenly thirsty, and begged for water, and drank it slowly, with his
eyes over the top of the cup, fixed on her large black eyes, which gazed
on him quite as curiously as he on her.   Then Moreright wanted water.
She gave it to him and he managed to spill it so as to ask for another
cup, and by the time she came to me she saw through the operation;
her eyes were full of fun as she looked at me.   I laughed outright, and
she joined me in as gay a shout as ever country maiden in old Orange
county.   I wished for a picture of her.   A Madonna, whose face was a
portrait of that beautiful Nazareth girl, would be a ' thing of beauty ' and
' a joy forever.' ''

That is the kind of gruel which has been served
out from Palestine for ages. Commend me to
Fenimore Cooper to find beauty in the Indians,
and to Grimes to find it in the Arabs. Arab men
are often fine looking, but Arab women are not.

We can all believe that the Virgin Mary was beautiful; it is not natural to think otherwise; but does it follow that it is our duty to find beauty in these present women of Nazareth?

I love to quote from Grimes, because he is so dramatic. And because he is so romantic. And because he seems to care but little whether he tells the truth or not, so he scares the reader or excites his envy or his admiration.

He went through this peaceful land with one hand forever on his revolver, and the other on his pocket-handkerchief. Always, when he was not on the point of crying over a holy place, he was on the point of killing an Arab. More surprising things happened to him in Palestine than ever happened to any traveler here or elsewhere since Munchausen died.

At Beit Jin, where nobody had interfered with him, he crept out of his tent at dead of night and shot at what he took to be an Arab lying on a rock, some distance away, planning evil. The ball killed a wolf. Just before he fired, he makes a dramatic picture of himself — as usual, to scare the reader:

"Was it imagination, or did I see a moving object on the surface of the rock? If it were a man, why did he not now drop me? He had a beautiful shot as I stood out in my black boornoose against the white tent. I had the sensation of an entering bullet in my throat, breast, brain."

Reckless creature!

Riding toward Gennesaret, they saw two Bedouins, and "we looked to our pistols and loosened them quietly in our shawls," etc.   Always cool.

In Samaria, he charged up a hill, in the face of a volley of stones; he fired into the crowd of men who threw them.   He says:

"*I never lost an opportunity* of impressing the Arabs with the perfection of American and English weapons, and the danger of attacking any one of the armed Franks.   I think the lesson of that ball not lost."

At Beitin he gave his whole band of Arab muleteers a piece of his mind, and then —

"I contented myself with a solemn assurance that if there occurred another instance of disobedience to orders, I would thrash the responsible party as he never dreamed of being thrashed, and if I could not find who was responsible, I would whip them all, from first to last, whether there was a governor at hand to do it or I had to do it myself."

Perfectly fearless, this man.

He rode down the perpendicular path in the rocks, from the Castle of Banias to the oak grove, at a flying gallop, his horse striding "thirty feet" at every bound.   I stand prepared to bring thirty reliable witnesses to prove that Putnam's famous feat at Horseneck was insignificant compared to this.

Behold him — always theatrical — looking at Jerusalem — this time, by an oversight, with his hand off his pistol for once.

"I stood in the road, my hand on my horse's neck, and with my dim eyes sought to trace the outlines of the holy places which I had long before fixed in my mind, but the fast-flowing tears forbade my succeeding.   There were our Mohammedan servants, a Latin monk, two

Armenians, and a Jew in our cortège, and all alike gazed with overflow-
ing eyes.''

If Latin monks and Arabs cried, I know to a
moral certainty that the horses cried also, and so
the picture is complete.

But when necessity demanded he could be firm as
adamant.   In the Lebanon Valley an Arab youth —
a Christian; he is particular to explain that Mohammedans do not steal — robbed him of a paltry ten
dollars' worth of powder and shot.   He convicted
him before a sheik and looked on while he was
punished by the terrible bastinado.   Hear him:

> "He (Mousa) was on his back in a twinkling, howling, shouting,
> screaming, but he was carried out to the piazza before the door, where
> we could see the operation, and laid face down.   One man sat on his
> back and one on his legs, the latter holding up his feet, while a third
> laid on the bare soles a rhinoceros-hide koorbash * that whizzed through
> the air at every stroke.   Poor Moreright was in agony, and Nama and
> Nama the Second (mother and sister of Mousa) were on their faces
> begging and wailing, now embracing my knees and now Whitely's, while
> the brother, outside, made the air ring with cries louder than Mousa's.
> Even Yusef came and asked me on his knees to relent, and last of all,
> Betuni — the rascal had lost a feed-bag in their house and had been
> loudest in his denunciations that morning — besought the Howajji to
> have mercy on the fellow."

But not he!   The punishment was '' suspended,''
at the *fifteenth blow*, to hear the confession.   Then
Grimes and his party rode away, and left the entire

---

* "A koorbash is Arabic for cowhide, the cow being a rhinoceros.
It is the most cruel whip known to fame.   Heavy as lead and flexible
as India-rubber, usually about forty inches long and tapering gradually
from an inch in diameter to a point, it administers a blow which *leaves
its mark for time*." — *Scow Life in Egypt*, bv the same author.

Christian family to be fined and as severely punished as the *Mohammedan sheik* should deem proper.

"As I mounted, Yusef once more begged me to interfere and have mercy on them, but I looked around at the dark faces of the crowd, and I couldn't find one drop of pity in my heart for them."

He closes his picture with a rollicking burst of humor which contrasts finely with the grief of the mother and her children.

One more paragraph:

"Then once more I bowed my head. It is no shame to have wept in Palestine. I wept when I saw Jerusalem, I wept when I lay in the starlight at Bethlehem, I wept on the blessed shores of Galilee. My hand was no less firm on the rein, my finger did not tremble on the trigger of my pistol when I rode with it in my right hand along the shore of the blue sea" (weeping.) "My eye was not dimmed by those tears nor my heart in aught weakened. Let him who would sneer at my emotion close this volume here, for he will find little to his taste in my journeyings through Holy Land."

He never bored but he struck water.

I am aware that this is a pretty voluminous notice of Mr. Grimes' book. However, it is proper and legitimate to speak of it, for "Nomadic Life in Palestine" is a representative book — the representative of a *class* of Palestine books — and a criticism upon it will serve for a criticism upon them all. And since I am treating it in the comprehensive capacity of a representative book, I have taken the liberty of giving to both book and author fictitious names. Perhaps it is in better taste, anyhow, to do this.

CHAPTER XXIV.

NAZARETH is wonderfully interesting because the town has an air about it of being precisely as Jesus left it, and one finds himself saying, all the time, "The boy Jesus has stood in this doorway — has played in that street — has touched these stones with his hands — has rambled over these chalky hills." Whoever shall write the Boyhood of Jesus ingeniously, will make a book which will possess a vivid interest for young and old alike. I judge so from the greater interest we found in Nazareth than any of our speculations upon Capernaum and the Sea of Galilee gave rise to. It was not possible, standing by the Sea of Galilee, to frame more than a vague, far-away idea of the majestic Personage who walked upon the crested waves as if they had been solid earth, and who touched the dead and they rose up and spoke. I read among my notes, now, with a new interest, some sentences from an edition of 1621 of the Apocryphal New Testament. [Extract.]

"Christ, kissed by a bride made dumb by sorcerers, cures her. A leprous girl cured by the water in which the infant Christ was washed, and becomes the servant of Joseph and Mary. The leprous son of a Prince cured in like manner.

"A young man who had been bewitched and turned into a mule, miraculously cured by the infant Saviour being put on his back, and is married to the girl who had been cured of leprosy. Whereupon the bystanders praise God.

"Chapter 16. Christ miraculously widens or contracts gates, milk-pails, sieves, or boxes not properly made by Joseph, he not being skillful at his carpenter's trade. The King of Jerusalem gives Joseph an order for a throne. Joseph works on it for two years and makes it two spans too short. The King being angry with him, Jesus comforts him — commands him to pull one side of the throne while he pulls the other, and brings it to its proper dimensions.

"Chapter 19. Jesus, charged with throwing a boy from the roof of a house, miraculously causes the dead boy to speak and acquit him; fetches water for his mother, breaks the pitcher and miraculously gathers the water in his mantle and brings it home.

"Sent to a schoolmaster, refuses to tell his letters, and the school-master going to whip him, his hand withers."

Further on in this quaint volume of rejected gospels is an epistle of St. Clement to the Corinthians, which was used in the churches and considered genuine fourteen or fifteen hundred years ago. In it this account of the fabled phœnix occurs:

" 1. Let us consider that wonderful type of the resurrection, which is seen in the Eastern countries, that is to say, in Arabia.

" 2. There is a certain bird called a phœnix. Of this there is never but one at a time, and that lives five hundred years. And when the time of its dissolution draws near, that it must die, it makes itself a nest of frankincense, and myrrh, and other spices, into which, when its time is fulfilled, it enters and dies.

" 3. But its flesh, putrefying, breeds a certain worm, which being nourished by the juice of the dead bird, brings forth feathers; and when it is grown to a perfect state, it takes up the nest in which the bones of its parent lie, and carries it from Arabia into Egypt, to a city called Heliopolis:

" 4. And flying in open day in the sight of all men, lays it upon the altar of the sun, and so returns from whence it came.

" 5. The priests then search into the records of the time, and find that it returned precisely at the end of five hundred years."

Business is business, and there is nothing like punctuality, especially in a phœnix.

The few chapters relating to the infancy of the Saviour contain many things which seem frivolous and not worth preserving. A large part of the remaining portions of the book read like good Scripture, however. There is one verse that ought not to have been rejected, because it so evidently prophetically refers to the general run of Congresses of the United States:

" 199. They carry themselves high, and as prudent men; and though they are fools, yet would seem to be teachers."

I have set these extracts down, as I found them. Everywhere, among the cathedrals of France and Italy, one finds traditions of personages that do not figure in the Bible, and of miracles that are not mentioned in its pages. But they are all in this Apocryphal New Testament, and though they have been ruled out of our modern Bible, it is claimed that they were accepted gospel twelve or fifteen centuries ago, and ranked as high in credit as any. One needs to read this book before he visits those venerable cathedrals, with their treasures of tabooed and forgotten tradition.

They imposed another pirate upon us at Nazareth — another invincible Arab guard. We took our

20**

last look at the city, clinging like a whitewashed wasp's nest to the hillside, and at eight o'clock in the morning, departed. We dismounted and drove the horses down a bridle-path which I think was fully as crooked as a corkscrew; which I know to be as steep as the downward sweep of a rainbow, and which I believe to be the worst piece of road in the geography, except one in the Sandwich Islands, which I remember painfully, and possibly one or two mountain trails in the Sierra Nevadas. Often, in this narrow path, the horse had to poise himself nicely on a rude stone step and then drop his fore-feet over the edge and down something more than half his own height. This brought his nose near the ground, while his tail pointed up toward the sky somewhere, and gave him the appearance of pre-paring to stand on his head. A horse cannot look dignified in this position. We accomplished the long descent at last, and trotted across the great Plain of Esdraelon.

Some of us will be shot before we finish this pilgrimage. The pilgrims read "Nomadic Life" and keep themselves in a constant state of Quixotic heroism. They have their hands on their pistols all the time, and every now and then, when you least expect it, they snatch them out and take aim at Bedouins who are not visible, and draw their knives and make savage passes at other Bedouins who do not exist. I am in deadly peril always, for these spasms are sudden and irregular, and, of course, I cannot tell when to be getting out of the way. If I am accidentally murdered, some time, during one of these romantic frenzies of the pilgrims, Mr. Grimes must be rigidly held to answer as an accessory before the fact. If the pilgrims would take deliberate aim and shoot at a man, it would be all right and proper — because that man would not be in any danger; but these random assaults are what I object to. I do not wish to see any more places like Esdraelon, where the ground is level and people can gallop. It puts melodramatic nonsense into the pilgrims' heads. All at once, when one is jogging along stupidly in the sun, and thinking about something ever so far away, here they come, at a stormy gallop, spurring and whooping at those ridgy old sore-backed plugs till their heels fly higher than their heads, and, as they whiz by, out comes a little potato gun of a revolver, there is a startling little pop, and a small pellet goes singing through the air. Now that I have begun this pilgrimage, I intend to go through with it, though, sooth to say, nothing but the most desperate valor has kept me to my purpose up to the present time. I do not mind Bedouins,— I am not afraid of them; because neither Bedouins nor ordinary Arabs have shown any disposition to harm us, but I *do* feel afraid of my own comrades.

Arriving at the furthest verge of the Plain, we rode a little way up a hill and found ourselves at Endor, famous for its witch. Her descendants are there yet. They were the wildest horde of half-

20**

naked savages we have found thus far. They swarmed out of mud beehives; out of hovels of the drygoods box pattern; out of gaping caves under shelving rocks; out of crevices in the earth. In five minutes the dead solitude and silence of the place were no more, and a begging, screeching, shouting mob were struggling about the horses' feet and blocking the way. "Bucksheesh! bucksheesh! bucksheesh! howajji, bucksheesh!" It was Magdala over again, only here the glare from the infidel eyes was fierce and full of hate. The population numbers two hundred and fifty, and more than half the citizens live in caves in the rock. Dirt, degradation, and savagery are Endor's specialty. We say no more about Magdala and Deburieh now. Endor heads the list. It is worse than any Indian *campoodie*. The hill is barren, rocky, and forbidding. No sprig of grass is visible, and only one tree. This is a fig tree, which maintains a precarious footing among the rocks at the mouth of the dismal cavern once occupied by the veritable Witch of Endor. In this cavern, tradition says, Saul, the King, sat at midnight, and stared and trembled, while the earth shook, the thunders crashed among the hills, and out of the midst of fire and smoke the spirit of the dead prophet rose up and confronted him. Saul had crept to this place in the darkness, while his army slept, to learn what fate awaited him in the morrow's battle. He went away a sad man, to meet disgrace and death.

A spring trickles out of the rock in the gloomy recesses of the cavern, and we were thirsty. The citizens of Endor objected to our going in there. They do not mind dirt; they do not mind rags; they do not mind vermin; they do not mind barbarous ignorance and savagery; they do not mind a reasonable degree of starvation, but they *do* like to be pure and holy before their god, whoever he may be, and therefore they shudder and grow almost pale at the idea of Christian lips polluting a spring whose waters must descend into their sanctified gullets. We had no wanton desire to wound even *their* feelings or trample upon their prejudices, but we were out of water, thus early in the day, and were burning up with thirst. It was at this time and under these circumstances that I framed an aphorism which has already become celebrated. I said: "Necessity knows no law." We went in and drank.

We got away from the noisy wretches, finally, dropping them in squads and couples as we filed over the hills — the aged first, the infants next, the young girls further on; the strong men ran beside us a mile, and only left when they had secured the last possible piastre in the way of bucksheesh.

In an hour, we reached Nain, where Christ raised the widow's son to life. Nain is Magdala on a small scale. It has no population of any consequence. Within a hundred yards of it is the original graveyard, for aught I know; the tomb-

T**

stones lie flat on the ground, which is Jewish fashion in Syria. I believe the Moslems do not allow them to have upright tombstones. A Moslem grave is usually roughly plastered over and whitewashed, and has at one end an upright projection which is shaped into exceedingly rude attempts at ornamentation. In the cities, there is often no appearance of a grave at all; a tall, slender marble tombstone, elaborately lettered, gilded and painted, marks the burial place, and this is surmounted by a turban, so carved and shaped as to signify the dead man's rank in life.

They showed a fragment of ancient wall which they said was one side of the gate out of which the widow's dead son was being brought so many centuries ago when Jesus met the procession:

"Now when he came nigh to the gate of the city, behold there was a dead man carried out, the only son of his mother, and she was a widow; and much people of the city was with her.

"And when the Lord saw her, he had compassion on her, and said, Weep not.

"And he came and touched the bier: and they that bare him stood still. And he said, Young man, I say unto thee, arise.

"And he that was dead sat up, and began to speak. And he delivered him to his mother.

"And there came a fear on all. And they glorified God, saying, That a great prophet is risen up among us; and That God hath visited his people."

A little mosque stands upon the spot which tradition says was occupied by the widow's dwelling. Two or three aged Arabs sat about its door. We entered, and the pilgrims broke specimens from the foundation walls, though they had to touch, and

even step, upon the "praying carpets" to do it.
It was almost the same as breaking pieces from the
hearts of those old Arabs. To step rudely upon
the sacred praying mats, with booted feet — a thing
not done by any Arab — was to inflict pain upon
men who had not offended us in any way. Suppose
a party of armed foreigners were to enter a village
church in America and break ornaments from the
altar railings for curiosities, and climb up and walk
upon the Bible and the pulpit cushions? However,
the cases are different. One is the profanation of a
temple of our faith — the other only the profanation
of a pagan one.

We descended to the Plain again, and halted a
moment at a well — of Abraham's time, no doubt.
It was in a desert place. It was walled three feet
above ground with squared and heavy blocks of
stone, after the manner of Bible pictures. Around
it some camels stood, and others knelt. There was a
group of sober little donkeys with naked, dusky
children clambering about them, or sitting astride
their rumps, or pulling their tails. Tawny, black-
eyed, barefooted maids, arrayed in rags and adorned
with brazen armlets and pinchbeck earrings, were
poising water-jars upon their heads, or drawing water
from the well. A flock of sheep stood by, waiting
for the shepherds to fill the hollowed stones with
water, so that they might drink — stones which, like
those that walled the well, were worn smooth and
deeply creased by the chafing chins of a hundred

generations of thirsty animals. Picturesque Arabs sat upon the ground, in groups, and solemnly smoked their long-stemmed chibouks. Other Arabs were filling black hog-skins with water — skins which, well filled, and distended with water till the short legs projected painfully out of the proper line, looked like the corpses of hogs bloated by drowning. Here was a grand Oriental picture which I had worshiped a thousand times in soft, rich steel engravings! But in the engraving there was no desolation; no dirt; no rags; no fleas; no ugly features; no sore eyes; no feasting flies; no besotted ignorance in the countenances; no raw places on the donkeys' backs; no disagreeable jabbering in unknown tongues; no stench of camels; no suggestion that a couple of tons of powder placed under the party and touched off would heighten the effect and give to the scene a genuine interest and a charm which it would always be pleasant to recall, even though a man lived a thousand years.

Oriental scenes look best in steel engravings. I cannot be imposed upon any more by that picture of the Queen of Sheba visiting Solomon. I shall say to myself, You look fine, madam, but your feet are not clean, and you smell like a camel.

Presently, a wild Arab in charge of a camel train recognized an old friend in Ferguson, and they ran and fell upon each other's necks and kissed each other's grimy, bearded faces upon both cheeks. It explained instantly a something which had always

seemed to me only a far-fetched Oriental figure of
speech. I refer to the circumstance of Christ's
rebuking a Pharisee, or some such character, and
reminding him that from him he had received no
"kiss of welcome." It did not seem reasonable to
me that men should kiss each other, but I am aware,
now, that they did. There was reason in it, too.
The custom was natural and proper; because people
must kiss, and a man would not be likely to kiss one
of the women of this country of his own free will
and accord. One must travel, to learn. Every day,
now, old Scriptural phrases that never possessed any
significance for me before take to themselves a
meaning.

We journeyed around the base of the mountain —
"Little Hermon," — past the old Crusaders' castle
of El Fuleh, and arrived at Shunem. This was
another Magdala, to a fraction, frescoes and all.
Here, tradition says, the prophet Samuel was born,
and here the Shunamite woman built a little house
upon the city wall for the accommodation of the prophet Elisha. Elisha asked her what she expected
in return. It was a perfectly natural question, for
these people are and were in the habit of proffering
favors and services and then expecting and begging
for pay. Elisha knew them well. He could not
comprehend that anybody should build for him that
humble little chamber for the mere sake of old
friendship, and with no selfish motive whatever. It
used to seem a very impolite, not to say a rude

question, for Elisha to ask the woman, but it does
not seem so to me now. The woman said she expected nothing. Then, for her goodness and her
unselfishness, he rejoiced her heart with the news
that she should bear a son. It was a high reward — but she would not have thanked him for a
daughter — daughters have always been unpopular
here. The son was born, grew, waxed strong, died.
Elisha restored him to life in Shunem.

We found here a grove of lemon trees — cool,
shady, hung with fruit. One is apt to overestimate
beauty when it is rare, but to me this grove seemed
very beautiful. It *was* beautiful. I do not overestimate it. I must always remember Shunem gratefully, as a place which gave to us this leafy shelter
after our long, hot ride. We lunched, rested,
chatted, smoked our pipes an hour, and then
mounted and moved on.

As we trotted across the Plain of Jezreel, we met
half a dozen Digger Indians (Bedouins) with very
long spears in their hands, cavorting around on old
crowbait horses, and spearing imaginary enemies;
whooping, and fluttering their rags in the wind, and
carrying on in every respect like a pack of hopeless
lunatics. At last, here were the " wild, free sons
of the desert, speeding over the plain like the wind,
on their beautiful Arabian mares " we had read so
much about and longed so much to see! Here were
the " picturesque costumes " ! This was the " gallant spectacle " ! Tatterdemalion vagrants — cheap

braggadocio — "Arabian mares" spined and necked
like the ichthyosaurus in the museum, and humped
and cornered like a dromedary! To glance at the
genuine son of the desert is to take the romance out
of him forever — to behold his steed is to long in
charity to strip his harness off and let him fall to
pieces.

Presently we came to a ruinous old town on a hill,
the same being the ancient Jezreel.

Ahab, King of Samaria (this was a very vast kingdom, for those days, and was very nearly half as
large as Rhode Island) dwelt in the city of Jezreel,
which was his capital. Near him lived a man by the
name of Naboth, who had a vineyard. The King
asked him for it, and when he would not give it,
offered to buy it. But Naboth refused to sell it.
In those days it was considered a sort of crime
to part with one's inheritance at any price — and
even if a man did part with it, it reverted to himself
or his heirs again at the next jubilee year. So this
spoiled child of a King went and lay down on the
bed with his face to the wall, and grieved sorely.
The Queen, a notorious character in those days, and
whose name is a byword and a reproach even in
these, came in and asked him wherefore he sorrowed,
and he told her. Jezebel said she could secure the
vineyard; and she went forth and forged letters to
the nobles and wise men, in the King's name, and
ordered them to proclaim a fast and set Naboth on
high before the people, and suborn two witnesses to

swear that he had blasphemed. They did it, and the people stoned the accused by the city wall, and he died. Then Jezebel came and told the King, and said, Behold, Naboth is no more — rise up and seize the vineyard. So Ahab seized the vineyard, and went into it to possess it. But the Prophet Elijah came to him there and read his fate to him, and the fate of Jezebel; and said that in the place where dogs licked the blood of Naboth, dogs should also lick his blood — and he said, likewise, the dogs should eat Jezebel by the wall of Jezreel. In the course of time, the King was killed in battle, and when his chariot wheels were washed in the pool of Samaria, the dogs licked the blood. In after years, Jehu, who was King of Israel, marched down against Jezreel, by order of one of the Prophets, and administered one of those convincing rebukes so common among the people of those days: he killed many kings and their subjects, and as he came along he saw Jezebel, painted and finely dressed, looking out of a window, and ordered that she be thrown down to him. A servant did it, and Jehu's horse trampled her under foot. Then Jehu went in and sat down to dinner; and presently he said, Go and bury this cursed woman, for she is a King's daughter. The spirit of charity came upon him too late, however, for the prophecy had already been fulfilled — the dogs had eaten her, and they "found no more of her than the skull, and the feet, and the palms of her hands."

Ahab, the late King, had left a helpless family behind him, and Jehu killed seventy of the orphan sons.
Then he killed all the relatives, and teachers, and
servants and friends of the family, and rested from
his labors, until he was come near to Samaria, where
he met forty-two persons and asked them who they
were; they said they were brothers of the King of
Judah. He killed them. When he got to Samaria,
he said he would show his zeal for the Lord; so he
gathered all the priests and people together that
worshiped Baal, pretending that he was going to
adopt that worship and offer up a great sacrifice;
and when they were all shut up where they could
not defend themselves, he caused every person of
them to be killed. Then Jehu, the good missionary,
rested from his labors once more.

We went back to the valley, and rode to the Fountain of Ain Jelüd. They call it the Fountain of
Jezreel, usually. It is a pond about one hundred
feet square and four feet deep, with a stream of
water trickling into it from under an overhanging
ledge of rocks. It is in the midst of a great solitude.
Here Gideon pitched his camp in the old times;
behind Shunem lay the " Midianites, the Amalekites,
and the Children of the East," who were " as grass-
hoppers for multitude; both they and their camels
were without number, as the sand by the seaside for
multitude." Which means that there were one hundred and thirty-five thousand men, and that they had
transportation service accordingly.

Gideon, with only three hundred men, surprised them in the night, and stood by and looked on while they butchered each other until a hundred and twenty thousand lay dead on the field.

We camped at Jenin before night, and got up and started again at one o'clock in the morning. Somewhere towards daylight we passed the locality where the best authenticated tradition locates the pit into which Joseph's brethren threw him, and about noon, after passing over a succession of mountain tops, clad with groves of fig and olive trees, with the Mediterranean in sight some forty miles away, and going by many ancient Biblical cities whose inhabitants glowered savagely upon our Christian procession, and were seemingly inclined to practice on it with stones, we came to the singularly terraced and unlovely hills that betrayed that we were out of Galilee and into Samaria at last.

We climbed a high hill to visit the city of Samaria, where the woman may have hailed from who conversed with Christ at Jacob's Well, and from whence, no doubt, came also the celebrated Good Samaritan. Herod the Great is said to have made a magnificent city of this place, and a great number of coarse limestone columns, twenty feet high and two feet through, that are almost guiltless of architectural grace of shape and ornament, are pointed out by many authors as evidence of the fact. They would not have been considered handsome in ancient Greece, however.

The inhabitants of this camp are particularly vicious, and stoned two parties of our pilgrims a day or two ago who brought about the difficulty by showing their revolvers when they did not intend to use them — a thing which is deemed bad judgment in the Far West, and ought certainly to be so considered anywhere. In the new Territories, when a man puts his hand on a weapon, he knows that he must use it; he must use it instantly or expect to be shot down where he stands. Those pilgrims had been reading Grimes.

There was nothing for us to do in Samaria but buy handfuls of old Roman coins at a franc a dozen, and look at a dilapidated church of the Crusaders and a vault in it which once contained the body of John the Baptist. This relic was long ago carried away to Genoa.

Samaria stood a disastrous siege, once, in the days of Elisha, at the hands of the King of Syria. Provisions reached such a figure that " an ass's head was sold for eighty pieces of silver and the fourth part of a cab of dove's dung for five pieces of silver."

An incident recorded of that heavy time will give one a very good idea of the distress that prevailed within these crumbling walls. As the King was walking upon the battlements one day, " a woman cried out, saying, Help, my lord, O King! And the King said, What aileth thee? and she answered, This woman said unto me, Give thy son, that we may eat him to-day, and we will eat my son to-morrow. So we boiled my son, and did eat him; and I said unto her on the next day, Give thy son that we may eat him; and she hath hid her son."

The prophet Elisha declared that within four and twenty hours the prices of food should go down to nothing, almost, and it was so. The Syrian army broke camp and fled, for some cause or other, the famine was relieved from without, and many a shoddy speculator in dove's dung and ass's meat was ruined.

We were glad to leave this hot and dusty old village and hurry on. At two o'clock we stopped to lunch and rest at ancient Shechem, between the historic Mounts of Gerizim and Ebal where in the old times the books of the law, the curses and the blessings, were read from the heights to the Jewish multitudes below.

CHAPTER XXV.

THE narrow cañon in which Nablous, or Shechem, is situated, is under high cultivation, and the soil is exceedingly black and fertile. It is well watered, and its affluent vegetation gains effect by contrast with the barren hills that tower on either side. One of these hills is the ancient Mount of Blessings and the other the Mount of Curses; and wise men who seek for fulfillments of prophecy think they find here a wonder of this kind — to wit, that the Mount of Blessings is strangely fertile and its mate as strangely unproductive. We could not see that there was really much difference between them in this respect, however.

Shechem is distinguished as one of the residences of the patriarch Jacob, and as the seat of those tribes that cut themselves loose from their brethren of Israel and propagated doctrines not in conformity with those of the original Jewish creed. For thousands of years this clan have dwelt in Shechem under strict *tabu*, and having little commerce or fellowship with their fellow-men of any religion or nationality. For generations they have not numbered more than

one or two hundred, but they still adhere to their
ancient faith and maintain their ancient rites and
ceremonies. Talk of family and old descent! Princes
and nobles pride themselves upon lineages they can
trace back some hundreds of years. What is this trifle
to this handful of old first families of Shechem, who
can name their fathers straight back without a flaw for
thousands — straight back to a period so remote that
men reared in a country where the days of two hundred years ago are called "ancient" times grow
dazed and bewildered when they try to comprehend
it! Here is respectability for you — here is
"family" — here is high descent worth talking
about. This sad, proud remnant of a once mighty
community still hold themselves aloof from all the
world; they still live as their fathers lived, labor as
their fathers labored, think as they did, feel as they
did, worship in the same place, in sight of the same
landmarks, and in the same quaint, patriarchal way
their ancestors did more than thirty centuries ago.
I found myself gazing at any straggling scion of
this strange race with a riveted fascination, just as
one would stare at a living mastodon, or a megather-
ium that had moved in the gray dawn of creation and
seen the wonders of that mysterious world that was
before the flood.

Carefully preserved among the sacred archives of
this curious community is a MS. copy of the ancient
Jewish law, which is said to be the oldest document
on earth. It is written on vellum, and is some four

or five thousand years old. Nothing but bucksheesh can purchase a sight. Its fame is somewhat dimmed in these latter days, because of the doubts so many authors of Palestine travels have felt themselves privileged to cast upon it. Speaking of this MS. reminds me that I procured from the high priest of this ancient Samaritan community, at great expense, a secret document of still higher antiquity and far more extraordinary interest, which I propose to publish as soon as I have finished translating it.

Joshua gave his dying injunction to the children of Israel at Shechem, and buried a valuable treasure secretly under an oak tree there about the same time. The superstitious Samaritans have always been afraid to hunt for it. They believe it is guarded by fierce spirits invisible to men.

About a mile and a half from Shechem we halted at the base of Mount Ebal, before a little square area, inclosed by a high stone wall, neatly whitewashed. Across one end of this enclosure is a tomb built after the manner of the Moslems. It is the tomb of Joseph. No truth is better authenticated than this.

When Joseph was dying he prophesied that exodus of the Israelites from Egypt which occurred four hundred years afterwards. At the same time he exacted of his people an oath that when they journeyed to the land of Canaan, they would bear his bones with them and bury them in the ancient inheritance of his fathers. The oath was kept.

"And the bones of Joseph, which the children of Israel brought up
21 **

out of Egypt, buried they in Shechem, in a parcel of ground which Jacob bought of the sons of Hamor the father of Shechem, for a hundred pieces of silver.''

Few tombs on earth command the veneration of so many races and men of divers creeds as this of Joseph. "Samaritan and Jew, Moslem and Christian alike, revere it, and honor it with their visits. The tomb of Joseph, the dutiful son, the affectionate, forgiving brother, the virtuous man, the wise Prince and ruler. Egypt felt his influence — the world knows his history.''

In this same "parcel of ground'' which Jacob bought of the sons of Hamor for a hundred pieces of silver, is Jacob's celebrated well. It is cut in the solid rock, and is nine feet square and ninety feet deep. The name of this unpretending hole in the ground, which one might pass by and take no notice of, is as familiar as household words to even the children and the peasants of many a far-off country.

It is more famous than the Parthenon; it is older than the Pyramids.

It was by this well that Jesus sat and talked with a woman of that strange, antiquated Samaritan community I have been speaking of, and told her of the mysterious water of life. As descendants of old English nobles still cherish in the traditions of their houses how that this king or that king tarried a day with some favored ancestor three hundred years ago, no doubt the descendants of the woman of Samaria, living there in Shechem, still refer with pardonable vanity to this conversation of their ancestor, held some little time gone by, with the Messiah of the Christians. It is not likely that they undervalue a distinction such as this. Samaritan nature is human nature, and human nature remembers contact with the illustrious, always.

For an offense done to the family honor, the sons of Jacob exterminated all Shechem once.

We left Jacob's Well and traveled till eight in the evening, but rather slowly, for we had been in the saddle nineteen hours, and the horses were cruelly tired. We got so far ahead of the tents that we had to camp in an Arab village, and sleep on the ground. We could have slept in the largest of the houses; but there were some little drawbacks; it was populous with vermin, it had a dirt floor, it was in no respect cleanly, and there was a family of goats in the only bedroom, and two donkeys in the parlor. Outside there were no inconveniences, except that the dusky, ragged, earnest-eyed villagers of both sexes and all ages grouped themselves on their haunches all around us, and discussed us and criticised us with noisy tongues till midnight. We did not mind the noise, being tired, but, doubtless, the reader is aware that it is almost an impossible thing to go to sleep when you know that people are looking at you. We went to bed at ten, and got up again at two and started once more. Thus are people persecuted by dragomen, whose sole ambition in life is to get ahead of each other.

About daylight we passed Shiloh, where the Ark

of the Covenant rested three hundred years, and at whose gates good old Eli fell down and " brake his neck " when the messenger, riding hard from the battle, told him of the defeat of his people, the death of his sons, and, more than all, the capture of Israel's pride, her hope, her refuge, the ancient Ark her forefathers brought with them out of Egypt. It is little wonder that under circumstances like these he fell down and brake his neck. But Shiloh had no charms for us. We were so cold that there was no comfort but in motion, and so drowsy we could hardly sit upon the horses.

After a while we came to a shapeless mass of ruins, which still bears the name of Beth-el. It was here that Jacob lay down and had that superb vision of angels flitting up and down a ladder that reached from the clouds to earth, and caught glimpses of their blessed home through the open gates of Heaven.

The pilgrims took what was left of the hallowed ruin, and we pressed on toward the goal of our crusade, renowned Jerusalem.

The further we went the hotter the sun got, and the more rocky and bare, repulsive and dreary the landscape became. There could not have been more fragments of stone strewn broadcast over this part of the world, if every ten square feet of the land had been occupied by a separate and distinct stone-cutter's establishment for an age. There was hardly a tree or a shrub anywhere. Even the olive and the cactus, those fast friends of a worthless soil, had almost deserted the country. No landscape exists that is more tiresome to the eye than that which bounds the approaches to Jerusalem. The only difference between the roads and the surrounding country, perhaps, is that there are rather more rocks in the roads than in the surrounding country.

We passed Ramah and Beroth, and on the right saw the tomb of the prophet Samuel, perched high upon a commanding eminence. Still no Jerusalem came in sight. We hurried on impatiently. We halted a moment at the ancient Fountain of Beira, but its stones, worn deeply by the chins of thirsty animals that are dead and gone centuries ago, had no interest for us — we longed to see Jerusalem. We spurred up hill after hill, and usually began to stretch our necks minutes before we got to the top — but disappointment always followed — more stupid hills beyond — more unsightly landscape — no Holy City.

At last, away in the middle of the day, ancient bits of wall and crumbling arches began to line the way — we toiled up one more hill, and every pilgrim and every sinner swung his hat on high! Jerusalem!

Perched on its eternal hills, white and domed and solid, massed together and hooped with high gray walls, the venerable city gleamed in the sun. So small! Why, it was no larger than an American village of four thousand inhabitants, and no larger than an ordinary Syrian city of thirty thousand. Jerusalem numbers only fourteen thousand people.

We dismounted and looked, without speaking a dozen sentences, across the wide intervening valley for an hour or more; and noted those prominent features of the city that pictures make familiar to all men from their school days till their death. We could recognize the Tower of Hippicus, the Mosque of Omar, the Damascus Gate, the Mount of Olives, the Valley of Jehoshaphat, the Tower of David, and the Garden of Gethsemane — and dating from these landmarks could tell very nearly the localities of many others we were not able to distinguish.

I record it here as a notable but not discreditable fact that not even our pilgrims wept. I think there was no individual in the party whose brain was not teeming with thoughts and images and memories invoked by the grand history of the venerable city that lay before us, but still among them all was no "voice of them that wept."

There was no call for tears. Tears would have been out of place. The thoughts Jerusalem suggests are full of poetry, sublimity, and more than all, dignity. Such thoughts do not find their appropriate expression in the emotions of the nursery.

Just after noon we entered these narrow, crooked streets, by the ancient and the famed Damascus Gate, and now for several hours I have been trying to comprehend that I am actually in the illustrious old city where Solomon dwelt, where Abraham held converse with the Deity, and where walls still stand that witnessed the spectacle of the Crucifixion.

CHAPTER XXVI.

A FAST walker could go outside the walls of Jerusalem and walk entirely around the city in an hour. I do not know how else to make one understand how small it is. The appearance of the city is peculiar. It is as knobby with countless little domes as a prison door is with bolt-heads. Every house has from one to half a dozen of these white plastered domes of stone, broad and low, sitting in the center of, or in a cluster upon, the flat roof. Wherefore, when one looks down from an eminence, upon the compact mass of houses (so closely crowded together, in fact, that there is no appearance of streets at all, and so the city looks solid) he sees the knobbiest town in the world, except Constantinople. It looks as if it might be roofed, from center to circumference, with inverted saucers. The monotony of the view is interrupted only by the great Mosque of Omar, the Tower of Hippicus, and one or two other buildings that rise into commanding prominence.

The houses are generally two stories high, built strongly of masonry, whitewashed or plastered outside, and have a cage of wooden lattice-work projecting in front of every window. To reproduce a Jerusalem street, it would only be necessary to up-end a chicken-coop and hang it before each window in an alley of American houses.

The streets are roughly and badly paved with stone, and are tolerably crooked — enough so to make each street appear to close together constantly and come to an end about a hundred yards ahead of a pilgrim as long as he chooses to walk in it. Projecting from the top of the lower story of many of the houses is a very narrow porch-roof or shed, without supports from below; and I have several times seen cats jump across the street from one shed to the other when they were out calling. The cats could have jumped double the distance without extraordinary exertion. I mention these things to give an idea of how narrow the streets are. Since a cat can jump across them without the least inconvenience, it is hardly necessary to state that such streets are too narrow for carriages. These vehicles cannot navigate the Holy City.

The population of Jerusalem is composed of Moslems, Jews, Greeks, Latins, Armenians, Syrians, Copts, Abyssinians, Greek Catholics, and a handful of Protestants. One hundred of the latter sect are all that dwell now in this birthplace of Christianity. The nice shades of nationality comprised in the above list, and the languages spoken by them, are altogether too numerous to mention. It seems to

me that all the races and colors and tongues of the
earth must be represented among the fourteen thousand souls that dwell in Jerusalem.   Rags, wretched-
ness, poverty, and dirt, those signs and symbols that
indicate the presence of Moslem rule more surely
than the crescent-flag itself, abound.   Lepers, cripples, the blind, and the idiotic, assail you on every
hand, and they know but one word of but one
language apparently — the eternal "bucksheesh."
To see the numbers of maimed, malformed, and diseased humanity that throng the holy places and
obstruct the gates, one might suppose that the
ancient days had come again, and that the angel of
the Lord was expected to descend at any moment to
stir the waters of Bethesda.   Jerusalem is mournful,
and dreary, and lifeless.   I would not desire to live
here.

One naturally goes first to the Holy Sepulchre.
It is right in the city, near the western gate; it and
the place of the Crucifixion, and, in fact, every other
place intimately connected with that tremendous
event, are ingeniously massed together and covered
by one roof — the dome of the Church of the Holy
Sepulchre.

Entering the building, through the midst of the
usual assemblage of beggars, one sees on his left a
few Turkish guards — for Christians of different
sects will not only quarrel, but fight, also, in this
sacred place, if allowed to do it.   Before you is a
marble slab, which covers the Stone of Unction,

whereon the Saviour's body was laid to prepare it
for burial. It was found necessary to conceal the
real stone in this way in order to save it from destruction. Pilgrims were too much given to chipping off pieces of it to carry home. Near by is a
circular railing which marks the spot where the
Virgin stood when the Lord's body was anointed.

Entering the great Rotunda, we stand before the
most sacred locality in Christendom — the grave of
Jesus. It is in the center of the church, and immediately under the great dome. It is inclosed in a
sort of little temple of yellow and white stone, of
fanciful design. Within the little temple is a portion of the very stone which was rolled away from
the door of the Sepulchre, and on which the angel
was sitting when Mary came thither "at early
dawn." Stooping low, we enter the vault — the
Sepulchre itself. It is only about six feet by seven,
and the stone couch on which the dead Saviour lay
extends from end to end of the apartment and occu-
pies half its width. It is covered with a marble slab
which has been much worn by the lips of pilgrims.
This slab serves as an altar now. Over it hang
some fifty gold and silver lamps, which are kept
always burning, and the place is otherwise scandal-
ized by trumpery gewgaws and tawdry ornamentation.

All sects of Christians (except Protestants) have
chapels under the roof of the Church of the Holy
Sepulchre, and each must keep to itself and not

venture upon another's ground. It has been proven conclusively that they cannot worship together around the grave of the Saviour of the World in peace. The chapel of the Syrians is not handsome; that of the Copts is the humblest of them all. It is nothing but a dismal cavern, roughly hewn in the living rock of the Hill of Calvary. In one side of it two ancient tombs are hewn, which are claimed to be those in which Nicodemus and Joseph of Arimathea were buried.

As we moved among the great piers and pillars of another part of the church, we came upon a party of black-robed, animal-looking Italian monks, with candles in their hands, who were chanting something in Latin, and going through some kind of religious performance around a disk of white marble let into the floor. It was there that the risen Saviour appeared to Mary Magdalen in the likeness of a gardener. Near by was a similar stone, shaped like a star — here the Magdalen herself stood, at the same time. Monks were performing in this place also. They perform everywhere — all over the vast building, and at all hours. Their candles are always flitting about in the gloom, and making the dim old church more dismal than there is any necessity that it should be, even though it is a tomb.

We were shown the place where our Lord appeared to His mother after the Resurrection. Here, also, a marble slab marks the place where St. Helena, the mother of the Emperor Constantine,

found the crosses about three hundred years after
the Crucifixion. According to the legend, this great
discovery elicited extravagant demonstrations of joy.
But they were of short duration. The question
intruded itself: "Which bore the blessed Saviour,
and which the thieves?" To be in doubt, in so
mighty a matter as this — to be uncertain which one
to adore — was a grievous misfortune. It turned
the public joy to sorrow. But when lived there a
holy priest who could not set so simple a trouble as
this at rest? One of these soon hit upon a plan
that would be a certain test. A noble lady lay very
ill in Jerusalem. The wise priests ordered that the
three crosses be taken to her bedside one at a time.
It was done. When her eyes fell upon the first one,
she uttered a scream that was heard beyond the
Damascus Gate, and even upon the Mount of Olives,
it was said, and then fell back in a deadly swoon.
They recovered her and brought the second cross.
Instantly she went into fearful convulsions, and it
was with the greatest difficulty that six strong men
could hold her. They were afraid, now, to bring in
the third cross. They began to fear that possibly
they had fallen upon the wrong crosses, and that the
true cross was not with this number at all. However, as the woman seemed likely to die with the
convulsions that were tearing her, they concluded
that the third could do no more than put her out of
her misery with a happy dispatch. So they brought
it, and behold, a miracle! The woman sprang from

her bed, smiling and joyful, and perfectly restored to health. When we listen to evidence like this, we cannot but believe. We would be ashamed to doubt, and properly, too. Even the very part of Jerusalem where this all occurred is there yet. So there is really no room for doubt.

The priest tried to show us, through a small screen, a fragment of the genuine Pillar of Flagellation, to which Christ was bound when they scourged him. But we could not see it, because it was dark inside the screen. However, a baton is kept here, which the pilgrim thrusts through a hole in the screen, and then he no longer doubts that the true Pillar of Flagellation is in there. He cannot have any excuse to doubt it, for he can feel it with the stick. He can feel it as distinctly as he could feel anything.

Not far from here was a niche where they used to preserve a piece of the True Cross, but it is gone now. This piece of the cross was discovered in the sixteenth century. The Latin priests say it was stolen away, long ago, by priests of another sect. That seems like a hard statement to make, but we know very well that it *was* stolen, because we have seen it ourselves in several of the cathedrals of Italy and France.

But the relic that touched us most was the plain old sword of that stout Crusader, Godfrey of Bouillon — King Godfrey of Jerusalem. No blade in Christendom wields such enchantment as this — no blade of all that rust in the ancestral halls of Europe is able to invoke such visions of romance in the brain of him who looks upon it — none that can prate of such chivalric deeds or tell such brave tales of the warrior days of old. It stirs within a man every memory of the Holy Wars that has been sleeping in his brain for years, and peoples his thoughts with mail-clad images, with marching armies, with battles and with sieges. It speaks to him of Baldwin, and Tancred, the princely Saladin, and great Richard of the Lion Heart. It was with just such blades as these that these splendid heroes of romance used to segregate a man, so to speak, and leave the half of him to fall one way and the other half the other. This very sword has cloven hundreds of Saracen Knights from crown to chin in those old times when Godfrey wielded it. It was enchanted, then, by a genius that was under the command of King Solomon. When danger approached its master's tent it always struck the shield and clanged out a fierce alarm upon the startled ear of night. In times of doubt, or in fog or darkness, if it were drawn from its sheath it would point instantly toward the foe, and thus reveal the way — and it would also attempt to start after them of its own accord. A Christian could not be so disguised that it would not know him and refuse to hurt him — nor a Moslem so disguised that it would not leap from its scabbard and take his life. These statements are all well authenticated in many legends that are among the most trustworthy legends the good old Catholic monks preserve. I can never forget old Godfrey's sword now. I tried it on a Moslem, and clove him in twain like a doughnut. The spirit of Grimes was upon me, and if I had had a graveyard I would have destroyed all the infidels in Jerusalem. I wiped the blood off the old sword and handed it back to the priest — I did not want the fresh gore to obliterate those sacred spots that crimsoned its brightness one day six hundred years ago and thus gave Godfrey warning that before the sun went down his journey of life would end.

Still moving through the gloom of the Church of the Holy Sepulchre we came to a small chapel, hewn out of the rock — a place which has been known as "The Prison of Our Lord" for many centuries. Tradition says that here the Saviour was confined just previously to the crucifixion. Under an altar by the door was a pair of stone stocks for human legs. These things are called the "Bonds of Christ," and the use they were once put to has given them the name they now bear.

The Greek Chapel is the most roomy, the richest and the showiest chapel in the Church of the Holy Sepulchre. Its altar, like that of all the Greek churches, is a lofty screen that extends clear across the chapel, and is gorgeous with gilding and pictures. The numerous lamps that hang before it are of gold and silver, and cost great sums.

But the feature of the place is a short column that
22**

rises from the middle of the marble pavement of the chapel, and marks the exact *center of the earth*. The most reliable traditions tell us that this was known to be the earth's center, ages ago, and that when Christ was upon earth he set all doubts upon the subject at rest forever, by stating with his own lips that the tradition was correct. Remember He said that that particular column stood upon the center of the world. If the center of the world changes, the column changes its position accordingly. This column has moved three different times, of its own accord. This is because, in great convulsions of nature, at three different times, masses of the earth — whole ranges of mountains, probably — have flown off into space, thus lessening the diameter of the earth, and changing the exact locality of its center by a point or two. This is a very curious and interesting circumstance, and is a withering rebuke to those philosophers who would make us believe that it is not possible for any portion of the earth to fly off into space.

To satisfy himself that this spot was really the center of the earth, a skeptic once paid well for the privilege of ascending to the dome of the church to see if the sun gave him a shadow at noon. He came down perfectly convinced. The day was very cloudy and the sun threw no shadows at all; but the man was satisfied that if the sun had come out and made shadows it could not have made any for him. Proofs like these are not to be set aside by

THE TOMB OF ADAM

the idle tongues of cavilers. To such as are not bigoted, and are willing to be convinced, they carry a conviction that nothing can ever shake.

If even greater proofs than those I have mentioned are wanted, to satisfy the headstrong and the foolish that this is the genuine center of the earth, they are here. The greatest of them lies in the fact that from under this very column was taken the *dust from which Adam was made*. This can surely be regarded in the light of a settler. It is not likely that the original first man would have been made from an inferior quality of earth when it was entirely convenient to get first quality from the world's center. This will strike any reflecting mind forcibly. That Adam was formed of dirt procured in this very spot is amply proven by the fact that in six thousand years no man has ever been able to prove that the dirt was *not* procured here whereof he was made.

It is a singular circumstance that right under the roof of this same great church, and not far away from that illustrious column, Adam himself, the father of the human race, lies buried. There is no question that he is actually buried in the grave which is pointed out as his — there can be none — because it has never yet been proven that that grave is not the grave in which he is buried.

The tomb of Adam! How touching it was, here in a land of strangers, far away from home, and friends, and all who cared for me, thus to discover the grave of a blood relation. True, a distant one,

22**

but still a relation. The unerring instinct of nature thrilled its recognition. The fountain of my filial affection was stirred to its profoundest depths, and I gave way to tumultuous emotion. I leaned upon a pillar and burst into tears. I deem it no shame to have wept over the grave of my poor dead relative. Let him who would sneer at my emotion close this volume here, for he will find little to his taste in my journeyings through Holy Land. Noble old man — he did not live to see me — he did not live to see his child. And I — I — alas, I did not live to see *him*. Weighed down by sorrow and disappointment, he died before I was born — six thousand brief summers before I was born. But let us try to bear it with fortitude. Let us trust that he is better off where he is. Let us take comfort in the thought that his loss is our eternal gain.

The next place the guide took us to in the holy church was an altar dedicated to the Roman soldier who was of the military guard that attended at the Crucifixion to keep order, and who — when the vail of the Temple was rent in the awful darkness that followed; when the rock of Golgotha was split asunder by an earthquake; when the artillery of heaven thundered, and in the baleful glare of the lightnings the shrouded dead flitted about the streets of Jerusalem — shook with fear and said, "Surely this was the Son of God!" Where this altar stands now, that Roman soldier stood then, in full view of the crucified Saviour — in full sight and hearing of

all the marvels that were transpiring far and wide
about the circumference of the Hill of Calvary.
And in this self-same spot the priests of the Temple
beheaded him for those blasphemous words he had
spoken.

In this altar they used to keep one of the most
curious relics that human eyes ever looked upon —
a thing that had power to fascinate the beholder in
some mysterious way and keep him gazing for hours
together.   It was nothing less than the copper plate
Pilate put upon the Saviour's cross, and upon which
he wrote, "THIS IS THE KING OF THE JEWS."   I
think St. Helena, the mother of Constantine, found
this wonderful memento when she was here in the
third century.   She traveled all over Palestine, and
was always fortunate.   Whenever the good old enthusiast found a thing mentioned in her Bible, Old
or New, she would go and search for that thing, and
never stop until she found it.   If it was Adam, she
would find Adam; if it was the Ark, she would find
the Ark; if it was Goliah, or Joshua, she would
find *them*.   She found the inscription here that I
was speaking of, I think.   She found it in this very
spot, close to where the martyred Roman soldier
stood.   That copper plate is in one of the churches
in Rome now.   Any one can see it there.   The
inscription is very distinct.

We passed along a few steps and saw the altar built
over the very spot where the good Catholic priests
say the soldiers divided the raiment of the Saviour.

V **

Then we went down into a cavern which cavilers say was once a cistern. It is a chapel now, however — the Chapel of St. Helena. It is fifty-one feet long by forty-three wide. In it is a marble chair which Helena used to sit in while she superintended her workmen when they were digging and delving for the True Cross. In this place is an altar dedicated to St. Dimas, the penitent thief. A new bronze statue is here — a statue of St. Helena. It reminded us of poor Maximilian, so lately shot. He presented it to this chapel when he was about to leave for his throne in Mexico.

From the cistern we descended twelve steps into a large roughly-shaped grotto, carved wholly out of the living rock. Helena blasted it out when she was searching for the true cross. She had a laborious piece of work here, but it was richly rewarded. Out of this place she got the crown of thorns, the nails of the cross, the true cross itself, and the cross of the penitent thief. When she thought she had found everything and was about to stop, she was told in a dream to continue a day longer. It was very fortunate. She did so, and found the cross of the other thief.

The walls and roof of this grotto still weep bitter tears in memory of the event that transpired on Calvary, and devout pilgrims groan and sob when these sad tears fall upon them from the dripping rock. The monks call this apartment the " Chapel of the Invention of the Cross "— a name which is unfortunate, because it leads the ignorant to imagine that a tacit acknowledgment is thus made that the tradition that Helena found the true cross here is a fiction — an invention. It is a happiness to know, however, that intelligent people do not doubt the story in any of its particulars.

Priests of any of the chapels and denominations in the Church of the Holy Sepulchre can visit this sacred grotto to weep and pray and worship the gentle Redeemer. Two different congregations are not allowed to enter at the same time, however, because they always fight.

Still marching through the venerable Church of the Holy Sepulchre, among chanting priests in coarse long robes and sandals; pilgrims of all colors and many nationalities, in all sorts of strange costumes; under dusky arches and by dingy piers and columns; through a somber cathedral gloom, freighted with smoke and incense, and faintly starred with scores of candles that appeared suddenly and as suddenly disappeared, or drifted mysteriously hither and thither about the distant aisles like ghostly jack-o'-lanterns — we came at last to a small chapel which is called the "Chapel of the Mocking." Under the altar was a fragment of a marble column; this was the seat Christ sat on when he was reviled, and mockingly made King, crowned with a crown of thorns and sceptered with a reed. It was here that they blindfolded him and struck him, and said in derision, "Prophesy who it is that smote thee.'' The tradition that this is the identical spot of the mocking is a very ancient one. The guide said that Saewulf was the first to mention it. I do not know Saewulf, but still, I cannot well refuse to receive his evidence — none of us can.

They showed us where the great Godfrey and his brother Baldwin, the first Christian Kings of Jerusalem, once lay buried by that sacred sepulchre they had fought so long and so valiantly to wrest from the hands of the infidel. But the niches that had contained the ashes of these renowned crusaders were empty. Even the coverings of their tombs were gone — destroyed by devout members of the Greek church, because Godfrey and Baldwin were Latin princes, and had been reared in a Christian faith whose creed differed in some unimportant respects from theirs.

We passed on, and halted before the tomb of Melchisedek! You will remember Melchisedek, no doubt; he was the King who came out and levied a tribute on Abraham the time that he pursued Lot's captors to Dan, and took all their property from them. That was about four thousand years ago, and Melchisedek died shortly afterward. However, his tomb is in a good state of preservation.

When one enters the Church of the Holy Sepulchre, the Sepulchre itself is the first thing he desires to see, and really is almost the first thing he does see. The next thing he has a strong yearning to see is the spot where the Saviour was crucified. But

this they exhibit last.   It is the crowning glory of
the place.   One is grave and thoughtful when he
stands in the little Tomb of the Saviour — he could
not well be otherwise in such a place — but he has
not the slightest possible belief that ever the Lord
lay there, and so the interest he feels in the spot is
very, very greatly marred by that reflection.   He
looks at the place where Mary stood, in another
part of the church, and where John stood, and Mary
Magdalen; where the mob derided the Lord; where
the angel sat; where the crown of thorns was found,
and the true cross; where the risen Saviour appeared — he looks at all these places with interest,
but with the same conviction he felt in the case of the
Sepulchre, that there is nothing genuine about them,
and that they are imaginary holy places created by
the monks.   But the place of the Crucifixion affects
him differently.   He fully believes that he is looking
upon the very spot where the Saviour gave up his
life.   He remembers that Christ was very celebrated,
long before he came to Jerusalem; he knows that
his fame was so great that crowds followed him all
the time; he is aware that his entry into the city
produced a stirring sensation, and that his reception
was a kind of ovation; he cannot overlook the fact
that when he was crucified there were very many in
Jerusalem who believed that he was the true Son of
God.   To publicly execute such a personage was
sufficient in itself to make the locality of the execution a memorable place for ages; added to this, the

storm, the darkness, the earthquake, the rending of the vail of the Temple, and the untimely waking of the dead, were events calculated to fix the execution and the scene of it in the memory of even the most thoughtless witness. Fathers would tell their sons about the strange affair, and point out the spot; the sons would transmit the story to their children, and thus a period of three hundred years would easily be spanned*— at which time Helena came and built a church upon Calvary to commemorate the death and burial of the Lord and preserve the sacred place in the memories of men; since that time there has always been a church there. It is not possible that there can be any mistake about the locality of the Crucifixion. Not half a dozen persons knew where they buried the Saviour, perhaps, and a burial is not a startling event, anyhow; therefore, we can be pardoned for unbelief in the Sepulchre, but not in the place of the Crucifixion. Five hundred years hence there will be no vestige of Bunker Hill Monument left, but America will still know where the battle was fought and where Warren fell. The crucifixion of Christ was too notable an event in Jerusalem, and the Hill of Calvary made too cele-brated by it, to be forgotten in the short space of three hundred years. I climbed the stairway in the church which brings one to the top of the small in-closed pinnacle of rock, and looked upon the place

---

* The thought is Mr. Prime's, not mine, and is full of good sense. I borrowed it from his "Tent Life."— M. T.

where the true cross once stood, with a far more absorbing interest than I had ever felt in anything earthly before. I could not believe that the three holes in the top of the rock were the actual ones the crosses stood in, but I felt satisfied that those crosses had stood so near the place now occupied by them, that the few feet of possible difference were a matter of no consequence.

When one stands where the Saviour was crucified, he finds it all he can do to keep it strictly before his mind that Christ was not crucified in a Catholic church. He must remind himself every now and then that the great event transpired in the open air, and not in a gloomy, candle-lighted cell in a little corner of a vast church, up stairs — a small cell all bejeweled and bespangled with flashy ornamentation, in execrable taste.

Under a marble altar like a table, is a circular hole in the marble floor, corresponding with the one just under it in which the true cross stood. The first thing every one does is to kneel down and take a candle and examine this hole. He does this strange prospecting with an amount of gravity that can never be estimated or appreciated by a man who has not seen the operation. Then he holds his candle before a richly engraved picture of the Saviour, done on a massy slab of gold, and wonderfully rayed and starred with diamonds, which hangs above the hole within the altar, and his solemnity changes to lively admiration. He rises and faces the

finely wrought figures of the Saviour and the male-
factors uplifted upon their crosses behind the altar,
and bright with a metallic luster of many colors.
He turns next to the figures close to them of the
Virgin and Mary Magdalen; next to the rift in the
living rock made by the earthquake at the time of
the crucifixion, and an extension of which he had
seen before in the wall of one of the grottoes below;
he looks next at the show-case with a figure of the
Virgin in it, and is amazed at the princely fortune in
precious gems and jewelry that hangs so thickly
about the form as to hide it like a garment almost.
All about the apartment the gaudy trappings of the
Greek church offend the eye and keep the mind on
the rack to remember that this is the Place of the
Crucifixion — Golgotha — the Mount of Calvary.
And the last thing he looks at is that which was also
the first — the place where the true cross stood.
That will chain him to the spot and compel him to
look once more, and once again, after he has satisfied all curiosity and lost all interest concerning the
other matters pertaining to the locality.

And so I close my chapter on the Church of the
Holy Sepulchre — the most sacred locality on earth
to millions and millions of men, and women, and
children, the noble and the humble, bond and free.
In its history from the first, and in its tremendous
associations, it is the most illustrious edifice in
Christendom. With all its clap-trap side-shows and
unseemly impostures of every kind, it is still grand,

reverend, venerable — for a god died there; for fifteen hundred years its shrines have been wet with the tears of pilgrims from the earth's remotest confines; for more than two hundred, the most gallant knights that ever wielded sword wasted their lives away in a struggle to seize it and hold it sacred from infidel pollution. Even in our own day a war, that cost millions of treasure and rivers of blood, was fought because two rival nations claimed the sole right to put a new dome upon it. History is full of this old Church of the Holy Sepulchre — full of blood that was shed because of the respect and the veneration in which men held the last resting-place of the meek and lowly, the mild and gentle Prince of Peace!

CHAPTER XXVII.

WE were standing in a narrow street, by the Tower of Antonio. "On these stones that are crumbling away," the guide said, "the Saviour sat and rested before taking up the cross. This is the beginning of the Sorrowful Way, or the Way of Grief." The party took note of the sacred spot, and moved on. We passed under the "Ecce Homo Arch," and saw the very window from which Pilate's wife warned her husband to have nothing to do with the persecution of the Just Man. This window is in an excellent state of preservation, considering its great age. They showed us where Jesus rested the second time, and where the mob refused to give him up, and said, "Let his blood be upon our heads, and upon our children's children forever." The French Catholics are building a church on this spot, and with their usual veneration for historical relics, are incorporating into the new such scraps of ancient walls as they have found there. Further on, we saw the spot where the fainting Saviour fell under the weight of his cross. A great granite column of some ancient temple lay there at the time, and the heavy cross struck it such a blow that it broke in two in the middle. Such was the guide's story when he halted us before the broken column.

We crossed a street, and came presently to the former residence of St. Veronica. When the Saviour passed there, she came out, full of womanly compassion, and spoke pitying words to him, undaunted by the hootings and the threatenings of the mob, and wiped the perspiration from his face with her handkerchief. We had heard so much of St. Veronica, and seen her picture by so many masters, that it was like meeting an old friend unexpectedly to come upon her ancient home in Jerusalem. The strangest thing about the incident that has made her name so famous, is, that when she wiped the perspiration away, the print of the Saviour's face remained upon the handkerchief, a perfect portrait, and so remains unto this day. We knew this, because we saw this handkerchief in a cathedral in Paris, in another in Spain, and in two others in Italy. In the Milan cathedral it costs five francs to see it, and at St. Peter's, at Rome, it is almost impossible to see it at any price. No tradition is so amply verified as this of St. Veronica and her handkerchief.

At the next corner we saw a deep indentation in the hard stone masonry of the corner of a house, but might have gone heedlessly by it but that the guide said it was made by the elbow of the Saviour, who stumbled here and fell. Presently we came to just such another indentation in a stone wall. The guide said the Saviour fell here, also, and made this depression with his elbow.

There were other places where the Lord fell, and others where he rested; but one of the most curious landmarks of ancient history we found on this morning walk through the crooked lanes that lead toward Calvary, was a certain stone built into a house — a stone that was so seamed and scarred that it bore a sort of grotesque resemblance to the human face. The projections that answered for cheeks were worn smooth by the passionate kisses of generations of pilgrims from distant lands. We asked "Why?" The guide said it was because this was one of "the very stones of Jerusalem" that Christ mentioned when he was reproved for permitting the people to cry "Hosannah!" when he made his memorable entry into the city upon an ass. One of the pilgrims said, "But there is no evidence that the stones *did* cry out — Christ said that if the people stopped from shouting Hosannah, the very stones *would* do it." The guide was perfectly serene. He said, calmly, "This is one of the stones that *would* have cried out." It was of little use to try to shake this fellow's simple faith — it was easy to see that.

And so we came at last to another wonder, of deep and abiding interest — the veritable house where the unhappy wretch once lived who has been celebrated in song and story for more than eighteen hundred years as the Wandering Jew. On the

memorable day of the Crucifixion he stood in this
old doorway with his arms akimbo, looking out upon
the struggling mob that was approaching, and when
the weary Saviour would have sat down and rested
him a moment, pushed him rudely away and said,
" Move on!" The Lord said, " Move on, thou,
likewise," and the command has never been revoked
from that day to this. All men know how that the
miscreant upon whose head that just curse fell has
roamed up and down the wide world, for ages and
ages, seeking rest and never finding it — courting
death but always in vain — longing to stop, in city,
in wilderness, in desert solitudes, yet hearing always
that relentless warning to march — march on! They
say — do these hoary traditions — that when Titus
sacked Jerusalem and slaughtered eleven hundred
thousand Jews in her streets and byways, the Wandering Jew was seen always in the thickest of the
fight, and that when battle-axes gleamed in the air,
he bowed his head beneath them; when swords
flashed their deadly lightnings, he sprang in their
way; he bared his breast to whizzing javelins, to
hissing arrows, to any and to every weapon that
promised death and forgetfulness, and rest. But it
was useless — he walked forth out of the carnage
without a wound. And it is said that five hundred
years afterward he followed Mahomet when he carried destruction to the cities of Arabia, and then
turned against him, hoping in this way to win the
death of a traitor. His calculations were wrong

23**

again.   No quarter was given to any living creature but one, and that was the only one of all the host that did not want it.   He sought death five hundred years later, in the wars of the Crusades, and offered himself to famine and pestilence at Ascalon.   He escaped again — he could not die.   These repeated annoyances could have at last but one effect — they shook his confidence.   Since then the Wandering Jew has carried on a kind of desultory toying with the most promising of the aids and implements of destruction, but with small hope, as a general thing. He has speculated some in cholera and railroads, and has taken almost a lively interest in infernal machines and patent medicines.   He is old, now, and grave, as becomes an age like his; he indulges in no light amusements save that he goes sometimes to executions, and is fond of funerals.

There is one thing he cannot avoid; go where he will about the world, he must never fail to report in Jerusalem every fiftieth year.   Only a year or two ago he was here for the thirty-seventh time since Jesus was crucified on Calvary.   They say that many old people, who are here now, saw him then, and had seen him before.   He looks always the same — old, and withered, and hollow-eyed, and listless, save that there is about him something which seems to suggest that he is looking for some one, expecting some one — the friends of his youth, perhaps.   But the most of them are dead, now.   He always pokes about the old streets looking lonesome, making his

mark on a wall here and there, and eying the oldest
buildings with a sort of friendly half interest; and
he sheds a few tears at the threshold of his ancient
dwelling, and bitter, bitter tears they are. Then he
collects his rent and leaves again. He has been seen
standing near the Church of the Holy Sepulchre on
many a starlight night, for he has cherished an idea
for many centuries that if he could only enter there,
he could rest. But when he approaches, the doors
slam to with a crash, the earth trembles, and all the
lights in Jerusalem burn a ghastly blue! He does
this every fifty years, just the same. It is hopeless,
but then it is hard to break habits one has been
eighteen hundred years accustomed to. The old
tourist is far away on his wanderings, now. How
he must smile to see a pack of blockheads like us,
galloping about the world, and looking wise, and
imagining we are finding out a good deal about it!
He must have a consuming contempt for the ignorant,
complacent asses that go skurrying about the world
in these railroading days and call it traveling.

When the guide pointed out where the Wandering
Jew had left his familiar mark upon a wall, I was
filled with astonishment. It read:

"S. T. — 1860 — X."

All I have revealed about the Wandering Jew can
be amply proven by reference to our guide.

The mighty Mosque of Omar, and the paved court
around it, occupy *a fourth part* of Jerusalem. They
are upon Mount Moriah, where King Solomon's

23**

Temple stood. This Mosque is the holiest place the Mohammedan knows, outside of Mecca. Up to within a year or two past, no Christian could gain admission to it or its court for love or money. But the prohibition has been removed, and we entered freely for bucksheesh.

I need not speak of the wonderful beauty and the exquisite grace and symmetry that have made this Mosque so celebrated — because I did not see them. One cannot see such things at an instant glance — one frequently only finds out how really beautiful a really beautiful woman is after considerable acquaintance with her; and the rule applies to Niagara Falls, to majestic mountains, and to mosques — especially to mosques.

The great feature of the Mosque of Omar is the prodigious rock in the center of its rotunda. It was upon this rock that Abraham came so near offering up his son Isaac — this, at least, is authentic — it is very much more to be relied on than most of the traditions, at any rate. On this rock, also, the angel stood and threatened Jerusalem, and David persuaded him to spare the city. Mahomet was well acquainted with this stone. From it he ascended to heaven. The stone tried to follow him, and if the angel Gabriel had not happened by the merest good luck to be there to seize it, it would have done it. Very few people have a grip like Gabriel — the prints of his monstrous fingers, two inches deep, are to be seen in that rock to-day.

This rock, large as it is, is suspended in the air. It does not touch anything at all. The guide said so. This is very wonderful. In the place on it where Mahomet stood, he left his footprints in the solid stone. I should judge that he wore about eighteens. But what I was going to say, when I spoke of the rock being suspended, was, that in the floor of the cavern under it they showed us a slab which they said covered a hole which was a thing of extraordinary interest to all Mohammedans, because that hole leads down to perdition, and every soul that is transferred from thence to Heaven must pass up through this orifice. Mahomet stands there and lifts them out by the hair. All Mohammedans shave their heads, but they are careful to leave a lock of hair for the Prophet to take hold of. Our guide observed that a good Mohammedan would consider himself doomed to stay with the damned forever if he were to lose his scalp-lock and die before it grew again. The most of them that I have seen ought to stay with the damned, anyhow, without reference to how they were barbered.

For several ages no woman has been allowed to enter the cavern where that important hole is. The reason is that one of the sex was once caught there blabbing everything she knew about what was going on above ground, to the rapscallions in the infernal regions down below. She carried her gossiping to such an extreme that nothing could be kept private — nothing could be done or said on earth but every-

W**

body in perdition knew all about it before the sun went down. It was about time to suppress this woman's telegraph, and it was promptly done. Her breath subsided about the same time.

The inside of the great mosque is very showy with variegated marble walls and with windows and inscriptions of elaborate mosaic. The Turks have their sacred relics, like the Catholics. The guide showed us the veritable armor worn by the great son-in-law and successor of Mahomet, and also the buckler of Mahomet's uncle. The great iron railing which surrounds the rock was ornamented in one place with a thousand rags tied to its open work. These are to remind Mahomet not to forget the worshipers who placed them there. It is considered the next best thing to tying threads around his finger by way of reminders.

Just outside the mosque is a miniature temple, which marks the spot where David and Goliah used to sit and judge the people.*

Everywhere about the Mosque of Omar are portions of pillars, curiously wrought altars, and fragments of elegantly carved marble — precious remains of Solomon's Temple. These have been dug from all depths in the soil and rubbish of Mount Moriah, and the Moslems have always shown a disposition to preserve them with the utmost care. At that por-

---

* A pilgrim informs me that it was not David and Goliah, but David and Saul. I stick to my own statement — the guide told me, and he ought to know.

tion of the ancient wall of Solomon's Temple which
is called the Jew's Place of Wailing, and where the
Hebrews assemble every Friday to kiss the venerated
stones and weep over the fallen greatness of Zion,
anyone can see a part of the unquestioned and un-
disputed Temple of Solomon, the same consisting of
three or four stones lying one upon the other, each
of which is about twice as long as a seven-octave
piano, and about as thick as such a piano is high.
But, as I have remarked before, it is only a year or
two ago that the ancient edict prohibiting Christian
rubbish like ourselves to *enter* the Mosque of Omar
and see the costly marbles that once adorned the
inner Temple was annulled. The designs wrought
upon these fragments are all quaint and peculiar, and
so the charm of novelty is added to the deep interest
they naturally inspire. One meets with these venerable scraps at every turn, especially in the neighboring Mosque el Aksa, into whose inner walls a very
large number of them are carefully built for preservation. These pieces of stone, stained and dusty
with age, dimly hint at a grandeur we have all been
taught to regard as the princeliest ever seen on earth;
and they call up pictures of a pageant that is familiar
to all imaginations — camels laden with spices and
treasure — beautiful slaves, presents for Solomon's
harem — a long cavalcade of richly caparisoned
beasts and warriors — and Sheba's Queen in the van
of this vision of "Oriental magnificence." These
elegant fragments bear a richer interest than the

solemn vastness of the stones the Jews kiss in the Place of Wailing can ever have for the heedless sinner.

Down in the hollow ground, underneath the olives and the orange trees that flourish in the court of the great Mosque, is a wilderness of pillars — remains of the ancient Temple; they supported it. There are ponderous archways down there, also, over which the destroying " plough " of prophecy passed harmless. It is pleasant to know we are disappointed, in that we never dreamed we might see portions of the actual Temple of Solomon, and yet experience no shadow of suspicion that they were a monkish humbug and a fraud.

We are surfeited with sights. Nothing has any fascination for us, now, but the Church of the Holy Sepulchre. We have been there every day, and have not grown tired of it; but we are weary of everything else. The sights are too many. They swarm about you at every step; no single foot of ground in all Jerusalem or within its neighborhood seems to be without a stirring and important history of its own. It is a very relief to steal a walk of a hundred yards without a guide along to talk unceasingly about every stone you step upon and drag you back ages and ages to the day when it achieved celebrity.

It seems hardly real when I find myself leaning for a moment on a ruined wall and looking *listlessly* down into the historic pool of Bethesda. I did not think such things *could* be so crowded together as to diminish their interest. But, in serious truth, we have been drifting about, for several days, using our eyes and our ears from a sense of duty than any higher and worthier reason. And too often we have been glad when it was time to go home and be distressed no more about illustrious localities.

Our pilgrims compress too much into one day. One can gorge sights to repletion as well as sweetmeats. Since we breakfasted, this morning, we have seen enough to have furnished us food for a year's reflection if we could have seen the various objects in comfort and looked upon them deliberately. We visited the pool of Hezekiah, where David saw Uriah's wife coming from the bath and fell in love with her.

We went out of the city by the Jaffa gate, and of course were told many things about its Tower of Hippicus.

We rode across the Valley of Hinnom, between two of the Pools of Gihon, and by an aqueduct built by Solomon, which still conveys water to the city. We ascended the Hill of Evil Counsel, where Judas received his thirty pieces of silver, and we also lingered a moment under the tree a venerable tradition says he hanged himself on.

We descended to the cañon again, and then the guide began to give name and history to every bank and boulder we came to: " This was the Field of Blood; these cuttings in the rocks were shrines and temples of Moloch; here they sacrificed children; yonder is the Zion Gate; the Tyropean Valley; the Hill of Ophel; here is the junction of the Valley of Jehoshaphat — on your right is the Well of Job." We turned up Jehoshaphat. The recital went on.

"This is the Mount of Olives; this is the Hill of Offense; the nest of huts is the Village of Siloam; here, yonder, everywhere, is the King's Garden; under this great tree Zacharias, the high priest, was murdered; yonder is Mount Moriah and the Temple wall; the tomb of Absalom; the tomb of St. James; the tomb of Zacharias; beyond, are the Garden of Gethsemane and the tomb of the Virgin Mary; here is the Pool of Siloam, and —"

We said we would dismount, and quench our thirst, and rest. We were burning up with the heat. We were failing under the accumulated fatigue of days and days of ceaseless marching. All were willing.

The Pool is a deep, walled ditch, through which a clear stream of water runs, that comes from under Jerusalem somewhere, and passing through the Fountain of the Virgin, or being supplied from it, reaches this place by way of a tunnel of heavy masonry. The famous pool looked exactly as it looked in Solomon's time, no doubt, and the same dusky, Oriental women, came down in their old Oriental way and carried off jars of the water on their heads, just as they did three thousand years ago, and just as they will do fifty thousand years hence if any of them are still left on earth.

We went away from there and stopped at the Fountain of the Virgin. But the water was not good, and there was no comfort or peace anywhere, on account of the regiment of boys and girls and beggars that persecuted us all the time for bucksheesh. The guide wanted us to give them some money, and we did it; but when he went on to say that they were starving to death we could not but feel that we had done a great sin in throwing obstacles in the way of such a desirable consummation, and so we tried to collect it back, but it could not be done.

We entered the Garden of Gethsemane, and we visited the Tomb of the Virgin, both of which we had seen before. It is not meet that I should speak of them now. A more fitting time will come.

I cannot speak now of the Mount of Olives or its view of Jerusalem, the Dead Sea, and the mountains of Moab; nor of the Damascus Gate or the tree that was planted by King Godfrey of Jerusalem. One ought to feel pleasantly when he talks of these things. I cannot say anything about the stone column that projects over Jehoshaphat from the Temple wall like a cannon, except that the Moslems believe Mahomet will sit astride of it when he comes to judge the world. It is a pity he could not judge it from some roost of his own in Mecca, without trespassing on *our* holy ground. Close by is the Golden Gate, in the Temple wall — a gate that was an elegant piece of sculpture in the time of the Temple, and is even so yet. From it, in ancient times, the

Jewish High Priest turned loose the scapegoat and let him flee to the wilderness and bear away his twelvemonth load of the sins of the people. If they were to turn one loose now, he would not get as far as the Garden of Gethsemane, till these miserable vagabonds here would gobble him up,* sins and all. *They* wouldn't care. Mutton-chops and sin is good enough living for them. The Moslems watch the Golden Gate with a jealous eye, and an anxious one, for they have an honored tradition that when it falls, Islamism will fall, and with it the Ottoman Empire. It did not grieve me any to notice that the old gate was getting a little shaky.

We are at home again. We are exhausted. The sun has roasted us, almost.

We have full comfort in one reflection, however. Our experiences in Europe have taught us that in time this fatigue will be forgotten; the heat will be forgotten; the thirst, the tiresome volubility of the guide, the persecutions of the beggars — and then, all that will be left will be pleasant memories of Jerusalem, memories we shall call up with always increasing interest as the years go by, memories which some day will become all beautiful when the last annoyance that incumbers them shall have faded out of our minds never again to return. Schoolboy days are no happier than the days of after life, but we look back upon them regretfully because we have for-

---

* Favorite pilgrim expression.

gotten our punishments at school, and how we grieved when our marbles were lost and our kites destroyed — because we have forgotten all the sorrows and privations of that canonized epoch and remember only its orchard robberies, its wooden sword pageants, and its fishing holidays. We are satisfied. We can wait. Our reward will come. To us, Jerusalem and to-day's experiences will be an enchanted memory a year hence — a memory which money could not buy from us.

CHAPTER XXVIII.

WE cast up the account. It footed up pretty fairly. There was nothing more at Jerusalem to be seen, except the traditional houses of Dives and Lazarus of the parable, the Tombs of the Kings, and those of the Judges; the spot where they stoned one of the disciples to death, and beheaded another; the room and the table made celebrated by the Last Supper; the fig-tree that Jesus withered; a number of historical places about Gethsemane and the Mount of Olives, and fifteen or twenty others in different portions of the city itself.

We were approaching the end. Human nature asserted itself, now. Overwork and consequent exhaustion began to have their natural effect. They began to master the energies and dull the ardor of the party. Perfectly secure now against failing to accomplish any detail of the pilgrimage, they felt like drawing in advance upon the holiday soon to be placed to their credit. They grew a little lazy. They were late to breakfast and sat long at dinner. Thirty or forty pilgrims had arrived from the ship, by the short routes, and much swapping of gossip had to be indulged in. And in hot afternoons, they showed a strong disposition to lie on the cool divans in the hotel and smoke and talk about pleasant experiences of a month or so gone by — for even thus early do episodes of travel which were sometimes annoying, sometimes exasperating, and full as often of no consequence at all when they transpired, begin to rise above the dead level of monotonous reminiscences and become shapely landmarks in one's memory. The fog-whistle, smothered among a million of trifling sounds, is not noticed a block away, in the city, but the sailor hears it far at sea, whither none of those thousands of trifling sounds can reach. When one is in Rome, all the domes are alike; but when he has gone away twelve miles, the city fades utterly from sight and leaves St. Peter's swelling above the level plain like an anchored balloon. When one is traveling in Europe, the daily incidents seem all alike; but when he has placed them all two months and two thousand miles behind him, those that were worthy of being remembered are prominent, and those that were really insignificant have vanished. This disposition to smoke and idle and talk was not well. It was plain that it must not be allowed to gain ground. A diversion must be tried, or demoralization would ensue. The Jordan, Jericho, and the Dead Sea were suggested. The remainder of Jerusalem must be left unvisited, for a little while. The journey was approved at once. New life stirred in every pulse. In the saddle —

abroad on the plains — sleeping in beds bounded only by the horizon: fancy was at work with these things in a moment. It was painful to note how readily these town-bred men had taken to the free life of the camp and the desert. The nomadic instinct is a human instinct; it was born with Adam and transmitted through the patriarchs, and after thirty centuries of steady effort, civilization has not educated it entirely out of us yet. It has a charm which, once tasted, a man will yearn to taste again. The nomadic instinct cannot be educated out of an Indian at all.

The Jordan journey being approved, our dragoman was notified.

At nine in the morning the caravan was before the hotel door and we were at breakfast. There was a commotion about the place. Rumors of war and bloodshed were flying everywhere. The lawless Bedouins in the Valley of the Jordan and the deserts down by the Dead Sea were up in arms, and were going to destroy all comers. They had had a battle with a troop of Turkish cavalry and defeated them; several men killed. They had shut up the inhabitants of a village and a Turkish garrison in an old fort near Jericho, and were besieging them. They had marched upon a camp of our excursionists by the Jordan, and the pilgrims only saved their lives by stealing away and flying to Jerusalem under whip and spur in the darkness of the night. Another of our parties had been fired on from an ambush and then attacked in the open day. Shots were fired on both sides. Fortunately, there was no bloodshed. We spoke with the very pilgrim who had fired one of the shots, and learned from his own lips how, in this imminent deadly peril, only the cool courage of the pilgrims, their strength of numbers and imposing display of war material, had saved them from utter destruction. It was reported that the Consul had requested that no more of our pilgrims should go to the Jordan while this state of things lasted; and further, that he was unwilling that any more should go, at least without an unusually strong military guard. Here was trouble. But with the horses at the door and everybody aware of what they were there for, what would *you* have done? Acknowledged that you were afraid, and backed shamefully out? Hardly. It would not be human nature, where there were so many women. You would have done as we did: said you were not afraid of a million Bedouins — and made your will and proposed quietly to yourself to take up an unostentatious position in the rear of the procession.

I think we must all have determined upon the same line of tactics, for it did seem as if we never would get to Jericho. I had a notoriously slow horse, but somehow I could not keep him in the rear, to save my neck. He was forever turning up in the lead. In such cases I trembled a little, and got down to fix my saddle. But it was not of any use. The others all got down to fix their saddles, too. I never

24**

saw such a time with saddles. It was the first time any of them had got out of order in three weeks, and now they had all broken down at once. I tried walking, for exercise — I had not had enough in Jerusalem searching for holy places. But it was a failure. The whole mob were suffering for exercise, and it was not fifteen minutes till they were all on foot and I had the lead again. It was very discouraging.

This was all after we got beyond Bethany. We stopped at the village of Bethany, an hour out from Jerusalem. They showed us the tomb of Lazarus. I had rather live in it than in any house in the town. And they showed us also a large "Fountain of Lazarus," and in the center of the village the ancient dwelling of Lazarus. Lazarus appears to have been a man of property. The legends of the Sunday-schools do him great injustice; they give one the impression that he was poor. It is because they get him confused with that Lazarus who had no merit but his virtue, and virtue never has been as respectable as money. The house of Lazarus is a three-story edifice, of stone masonry, but the accumulated rubbish of ages has buried all of it but the upper story. We took candles and descended to the dismal cell-like chambers where Jesus sat at meat with Martha and Mary, and conversed with them about their brother. We could not but look upon these old dingy apartments with a more than common interest.

We had had a glimpse, from a mountain top, of
the Dead Sea, lying like a blue shield in the plain of
the Jordan, and now we were marching down a close,
flaming, rugged, desolate defile, where no living
creature could enjoy life, except, perhaps, a sal-
amander. It was such a dreary, repulsive, horrible
solitude! It was the " wilderness " where John
preached, with camel's hair about his loins — raiment enough — but he never could have got his
locusts and wild honey here. We were moping
along down through this dreadful place, every man
in the rear. Our guards — two gorgeous young
Arab sheiks, with cargoes of swords, guns, pistols,
and daggers on board — were loafing ahead.

" Bedouins! "

Every man shrunk up and disappeared in his
clothes like a mud-turtle. My first impulse was to
dash forward and destroy the Bedouins. My second
was to dash to the rear to see if there were any coming in that direction. I acted on the latter impulse.
So did all the others. If any Bedouins had approached us, then, from that point of the compass,
they would have paid dearly for their rashness. We
all remarked that, afterwards. There would have
been scenes of riot and bloodshed there that no pen
could describe. I know that, because each man told
what he would have done, individually; and such a
medley of strange and unheard-of inventions of
cruelty you could not conceive of. One man said
he had calmly made up his mind to perish where he

24**

stood, if need be, but never yield an inch; he was going to wait, with deadly patience, till he could count the stripes upon the first Bedouin's jacket, and then count them and let him have it. Another was going to sit still till the first lance reached within an inch of his breast, and then dodge it and seize it. I forbear to tell what he was going to do to that Bedouin that owned it. It makes my blood run cold to think of it. Another was going to scalp such Bedouins as fell to his share, and take his bald-headed sons of the desert home with him alive for trophies. But the wild-eyed pilgrim rhapsodist was silent. His orbs gleamed with a deadly light, but his lips moved not. Anxiety grew, and he was questioned. If he had got a Bedouin, what would he have done with him — shot him? He smiled a smile of grim contempt and shook his head. Would he have stabbed him? Another shake. Would he have quartered him — flayed him? More shakes. Oh! horror, what *would* he have done?

" Eat him ! "

Such was the awful sentence that thundered from his lips. What was grammar to a desperado like that? I was glad in my heart that I had been spared these scenes of malignant carnage. No Bedouins attacked our terrible rear. And none attacked the front. The newcomers were only a re-enforcement of cadaverous Arabs, in shirts and bare legs, sent far ahead of us to brandish rusty guns, and shout and brag, and carry on like lunatics, and thus scare away all bands of marauding Bedouins that might lurk about our path. What a shame it is that armed white Christians must travel under guard of vermin like this as a protection against the prowling vagabonds of the desert — those sanguinary outlaws who are always going to do something desperate, but never do it. I may as well mention here that on our whole trip we saw no Bedouins, and had no more use for an Arab guard than we could have had for patent-leather boots and white kid gloves. The Bedouins that attacked the other parties of pilgrims so fiercely were provided for the occasion by the Arab guards of those parties, and shipped from Jerusalem for temporary service as Bedouins. They met together in full view of the pilgrims, after the battle, and took lunch, divided the bucksheesh extorted in the season of danger, and then accompanied the cavalcade home to the city! The nuisance of an Arab guard is one which is created by the Sheiks and the Bedouins together, for mutual profit, it is said, and no doubt there is a good deal of truth in it.

We visited the fountain the prophet Elisha sweetened (it is sweet yet); where he remained some time and was fed by the ravens.

Ancient Jericho is not very picturesque as a ruin. When Joshua marched around it seven times, some three thousand years ago, and blew it down with his trumpet, he did the work so well and so completely that he hardly left enough of the city to cast a shadow. The curse pronounced against the rebuild-

X**

ing of it has never been removed.   One king, holding the curse in light estimation, made the attempt,
but was stricken sorely for his presumption.   Its
site will always remain unoccupied; and yet it is
one of the very best locations for a town we have
seen in all Palestine.

At two in the morning they routed us out of bed
— another piece of unwarranted cruelty, another
stupid effort of our dragoman to get ahead of a
rival.   It was not two hours to the Jordan.   However, we were dressed and under way before any one
thought of looking to see what time it was, and so
we drowsed on through the chill night air and
dreamed of camp fires, warm beds, and other comfortable things.

There was no conversation.   People do not talk
when they are cold, and wretched, and sleepy.   We
nodded in the saddle, at times, and woke up with a
start to find that the procession had disappeared in
the gloom.   Then there was energy and attention to
business until its dusky outlines came in sight again.
Occasionally the order was passed in a low voice
down the line: "Close up — close up!   Bedouins
lurk here, everywhere!"   What an exquisite shudder it sent shivering along one's spine!

We reached the famous river before four o'clock,
and the night was so black that we could have ridden
into it without seeing it.   Some of us were in an
unhappy frame of mind.   We waited and waited for'
daylight, but it did not come.   Finally we went

away in the dark and slept an hour on the ground, in the bushes, and caught cold. It was a costly nap, on that account, but otherwise it was a paying investment because it brought unconsciousness of the dreary minutes and put us in a somewhat fitter mood for a first glimpse of the sacred river.

With the first suspicion of dawn, every pilgrim took off his clothes and waded into the dark torrent, singing:

> "On Jordan's stormy banks I stand,
> And cast a wistful eye
> To Canaan's fair and happy land,
> Where my possessions lie."

But they did not sing long. The water was so fearfully cold that they were obliged to stop singing and scamper out again. Then they stood on the bank shivering, and so chagrined and so grieved, that they merited honest compassion. Because another dream, another cherished hope, had failed. They had promised themselves all along that they would cross the Jordan where the Israelites crossed it when they entered Canaan from their long pilgrimage in the desert. They would cross where the twelve stones were placed in memory of that great event. While they did it they would picture to themselves that vast army of pilgrims marching through the cloven waters, bearing the hallowed ark of the covenant and shouting hosannahs, and singing songs of thanksgiving and praise. Each had promised himself that he would be the first to cross. They were at the goal of their hopes at last, but the current was too swift, the water was too cold!

It was then that Jack did them a service. With that engaging recklessness of consequences which is natural to youth, and so proper and so seemly, as well, he went and led the way across the Jordan, and all was happiness again. Every individual waded over, then, and stood upon the further bank. The water was not quite breast deep, anywhere. If it had been more, we could hardly have accomplished the feat, for the strong current would have swept us down the stream, and we would have been exhausted and drowned before reaching a place where we could make a landing. The main object compassed, the drooping, miserable party sat down to wait for the sun again, for all wanted to see the water as well as feel it. But it was too cold a pastime. Some cans were filled from the holy river, some canes cut from its banks, and then we mounted and rode reluctantly away to keep from freezing to death. So we saw the Jordan very dimly. The thickets of bushes that bordered its banks threw their shadows across its shallow, turbulent waters ("stormy," the hymn makes them, which is rather a complimentary stretch of fancy), and we could not judge of the width of the stream by the eye. We knew by our wading experience, however, that many streets in America are double as wide as the Jordan.

Daylight came, soon after we got under way, and in the course of an hour or two we reached the Dead Sea. Nothing grows in the flat, burning desert around it but weeds and the Dead Sea apple the poets say is beautiful to the eye, but crumbles to ashes and dust when you break it. Such as we found were not handsome, but they were bitter to the taste. They yielded no dust. It was because they were not ripe, perhaps.

The desert and the barren hills gleam painfully in the sun, around the Dead Sea, and there is no pleasant thing or living creature upon it or about its borders to cheer the eye. It is a scorching, arid, repulsive solitude. A silence broods over the scene that is depressing to the spirits. It makes one think of funerals and death.

The Dead Sea is small. Its waters are very clear, and it has a pebbly bottom and is shallow for some distance out from the shores. It yields quantities of asphaltum; fragments of it lie all about its banks; this stuff gives the place something of an unpleasant smell.

All our reading had taught us to expect that the first plunge into the Dead Sea would be attended with distressing results — our bodies would feel as if they were suddenly pierced by millions of red-hot needles; the dreadful smarting would continue for hours; we might even look to be blistered from head to foot, and suffer miserably for many days. We were disappointed. Our eight sprang in at the same time that another party of pilgrims did, and nobody screamed once. None of them ever did complain of anything more than a slight pricking sensation in places where their skin was abraded, and then only for a short time. My face smarted for a couple of hours, but it was partly because I got it badly sunburned while I was bathing, and stayed in so long that it became plastered over with salt.

No, the water did not blister us; it did not cover us with a slimy ooze and confer upon us an atrocious fragrance; it was not very slimy; and I could not discover that we smelt really any worse than we have always smelt since we have been in Palestine. It was only a different kind of smell, but not conspicuous on that account, because we have a great deal of variety in that respect. We didn't smell, there on the Jordan, the same as we do in Jerusalem; and we don't smell in Jerusalem just as we did in Nazareth, or Tiberias, or Cesarea Philippi, or any of those other ruinous ancient towns in Galilee. No, we change all the time, and generally for the worse. We do our own washing.

It was a funny bath. We could not sink. One could stretch himself at full length on his back, with his arms on his breast, and all of his body above a line drawn from the corner of his jaw past the middle of his side, the middle of his leg and through his ankle bone, would remain out of water. He could lift his head clear out if he chose. No position can be retained long; you lose your balance and whirl over, first on your back and then on your face, and so on. You can lie comfortably, on your back, with your head out, and your legs out from your knees down, by steadying yourself with your hands. You can sit, with your knees drawn up to your chin and your arms clasped around them, but you are bound to turn over presently, because you are topheavy in that position. You can stand up straight in water that is over your head, and from the middle of your breast upward you will not be wet. But you cannot remain so. The water will soon float your feet to the surface. You cannot swim on your back and make any progress of any consequence, because your feet stick away above the surface, and there is nothing to propel yourself with but your heels. If you swim on your face, you kick up the water like a stern-wheel boat. You make no headway. A horse is so topheavy that he can neither swim nor stand up in the Dead Sea. He turns over on his side at once. Some of us bathed for more than an hour, and then came out coated with salt till we shone like icicles. We scrubbed it off with a coarse towel and rode off with a splendid brand-new smell, though it was one which was not any more disagreeable than those we have been for several weeks enjoying. It was the variegated villainy and novelty of it that charmed us. Salt crystals glitter in the sun about the shores of the lake. In places they coat the ground like a brilliant crust of ice.

When I was a boy I somehow got the impression that the river Jordan was four thousand miles long and thirty-five miles wide. It is only ninety miles long, and so crooked that a man does not know

which side of it he is on half the time. In going
ninety miles it does not get over more than fifty
miles of ground. It is not any wider than Broadway in New York. There is the Sea of Galilee and
this Dead Sea — neither of them twenty miles long
or thirteen wide. And yet when I was in Sunday-
school I thought they were sixty thousand miles in
diameter.

Travel and experience mar the grandest pictures
and rob us of the most cherished traditions of our
boyhood. Well, let them go. I have already seen
the Empire of King Solomon diminish to the size of
the State of Pennsylvania; I suppose I can bear the
reduction of the seas and the river.

We looked everywhere, as we passed along, but
never saw grain or crystal of Lot's wife. It was a
great disappointment. For many and many a year
we had known her sad story, and taken that interest
in her which misfortune always inspires. But she
was gone. Her picturesque form no longer looms
above the desert of the Dead Sea to remind the
tourist of the doom that fell upon the lost cities.

I cannot describe the hideous afternoon's ride
from the Dead Sea to Mars Saba. It oppresses me
yet, to think of it. The sun so pelted us that the
tears ran down our cheeks once or twice. The
ghastly, treeless, grassless, breathless cañons smothered us as if we had been in an oven. The sun had
positive *weight* to it, I think. Not a man could sit
erect under it. All drooped low in the saddles.

John preached in this " Wilderness" !   It must have
been exhausting work.   What a very heaven the
massy towers and ramparts of vast Mars Saba looked
to us when we caught a first glimpse of them !

We stayed at this great convent all night, guests
of the hospitable priests.   Mars Saba, perched upon
a crag, a human nest stuck high up against a perpendicular mountain wall, is a world of grand
masonry that rises, terrace upon terrace, away above
your head, like the terraced and retreating colonnades
one sees in fanciful pictures of Belshazzar's Feast
and the palaces of the ancient Pharaohs.   No other
human dwelling is near.   It was founded many ages
ago by a holy recluse who lived at first in a cave in
the rock — a cave which is inclosed in the convent
walls now, and was reverently shown to us by the
priests.   This recluse, by his rigorous torturing of
his flesh, his diet of bread and water, his utter with-
drawal from all society and from the vanities of the
world, and his constant prayer and saintly contem-
plation of a skull, inspired an emulation that brought
about him many disciples.   The precipice on the
opposite side of the cañon is well perforated with
the small holes they dug in the rock to live in.   The
present occupants of Mars Saba, about seventy in
number, are all hermits.   They wear a coarse robe,
an ugly, brimless stovepipe of a hat, and go without shoes.   They eat nothing whatever but bread
and salt; they drink nothing but water.   As long as
they live they can never go outside the walls, or

set in the floor bears a Latin inscription to that
effect.   It is polished with the kisses of many generations of worshiping pilgrims.   The grotto was
tricked out in the usual tasteless style observable in
all the holy places of Palestine.   As in the Church
of the Holy Sepulchre, envy and uncharitableness
were apparent here.   The priests and the members
of the Greek and Latin churches cannot come by
the same corridor to kneel in the sacred birthplace
of the Redeemer, but are compelled to approach
and retire by different avenues, lest they quarrel
and fight on this holiest ground on earth.

I have no "meditations," suggested by this spot
where the very first "Merry Christmas!" was uttered in all the world, and from whence the friend
of my childhood, Santa Claus, departed on his first
journey to gladden and continue to gladden roaring
firesides on wintry mornings in many a distant land
forever and forever.   I touch, with reverent finger,
the actual spot where the infant Jesus lay, but I
think — nothing.

You *cannot* think in this place any more than you
can in any other in Palestine that would be likely to
inspire reflection.   Beggars, cripples, and monks
compass you about, and make you think only of
bucksheesh when you would rather think of something more in keeping with the character of the spot.

I was glad to get away, and glad when we had
walked through the grottoes where Eusebius wrote,
and Jerome fasted, and Joseph prepared for the

flight into Egypt, and the dozen other distinguished grottoes, and knew we were done. The Church of the Nativity is almost as well packed with exceeding holy places as the Church of the Holy Sepulchre itself. They even have in it a grotto wherein twenty thousand children were slaughtered by Herod when he was seeking the life of the infant Saviour.

We went to the Milk Grotto, of course — a cavern where Mary hid herself for a while before the flight into Egypt. Its walls were black before she entered, but in suckling the Child, a drop of her milk fell upon the floor and instantly changed the darkness of the walls to its own snowy hue. We took many little fragments of stone from here, because it is well known in all the East that a barren woman hath need only to touch her lips to one of these and her failing will depart from her. We took many specimens, to the end that we might confer happiness upon certain households that we wot of.

We got away from Bethlehem and its troops of beggars and relic-peddlers in the afternoon, and after spending some little time at Rachel's tomb, hurried to Jerusalem as fast as possible. I never was *so* glad to get home again before. I never have enjoyed rest as I have enjoyed it during these last few hours. The journey to the Dead Sea, the Jordan, and Bethlehem was short, but it was an exhausting one. Such roasting heat, such oppressive solitude, and such dismal desolation cannot surely exist elsewhere on earth. And *such* fatigue !

25**

CHAPTER XXIX.

WE visited all the holy places about Jerusalem which we had left unvisited when we journeyed to the Jordan, and then, about three o'clock one afternoon, we fell into procession and marched out at the stately Damascus gate, and the walls of Jerusalem shut us out forever. We paused on the summit of a distant hill and took a final look and made a final farewell to the venerable city which had been such a good home to us.

For about four hours we traveled down hill constantly. We followed a narrow bridle-path which traversed the beds of the mountain gorges, and when we could we got out of the way of the long trains of laden camels and asses, and when we could not we suffered the misery of being mashed up against perpendicular walls of rock and having our legs bruised by the passing freight. Jack was caught two or three times, and Dan and Moult as often. One horse had a heavy fall on the slippery rocks, and the others had narrow escapes. However, this was as good a road as we had found in Palestine, and possibly even the best, and so there was not much grumbling.

Sometimes, in the glens, we came upon luxuriant orchards of figs, apricots, pomegranates, and such things, but oftener the scenery was rugged, mountainous, verdureless, and forbidding. Here and there, towers were perched high up on acclivities which seemed almost inaccessible. This fashion is as old as Palestine itself, and was adopted in ancient times for security against enemies.

We crossed the brook which furnished David the stone that killed Goliah, and, no doubt, we looked upon the very ground whereon that noted battle was fought. We passed by a picturesque old gothic ruin whose stone pavements had rung to the armed heels of many a valorous Crusader, and we rode through a piece of country which we were told once knew Samson as a citizen.

We stayed all night with the good monks at the convent of Ramleh, and in the morning got up and galloped the horses a good part of the distance from there to Jaffa, or Joppa, for the plain was as level as a floor and free from stones, and besides this was our last march in Holy Land. These two or three hours finished, we and the tired horses could have rest and sleep as long as we wanted it. This was the plain of which Joshua spoke when he said," Sun, stand thou still on Gibeon, and thou moon in the valley of Ajalon." As we drew near to Jaffa, the boys spurred up the horses and indulged in the excitement of an actual race — an experience we had hardly had since we raced on donkeys in the Azores islands.

We came finally to the noble grove of orange trees in which the Oriental city of Jaffa lies buried; we passed through the walls, and rode again down narrow streets and among swarms of animated rags, and saw other sights and had other experiences we had long been familiar with. We dismounted, for the last time, and out in the offing, riding at anchor, we saw the ship! I put an exclamation point there because we felt one when we saw the vessel. The long pilgrimage was ended, and somehow we seemed to feel glad of it.

[For description of Jaffa, see Universal Gazetteer.] Simon the Tanner formerly lived here. We went to his house. All the pilgrims visit Simon the Tanner's house. Peter saw the vision of the beasts let down in a sheet when he lay upon the roof of Simon the Tanner's house. It was from Jaffa that Jonah sailed when he was told to go and prophesy against Nineveh, and, no doubt, it was not far from the town that the whale threw him up when he discovered that he had no ticket. Jonah was disobedient, and of a fault-finding, complaining disposition, and deserves to be lightly spoken of, almost. The timbers used in the construction of Solomon's temple were floated to Jaffa in rafts, and the narrow opening in the reef through which they passed to the shore is not an inch wider or a shade less dangerous to navigate than it was then. Such is the sleepy nature of the population Palestine's only good seaport has now and always had. Jaffa has a history and a stirring one. It will not be discovered anywhere in this book. If the reader will call at the circulating library and mention my name, he will be furnished with books which will afford him the fullest information concerning Jaffa.

So ends the pilgrimage. We ought to be glad that we did not make it for the purpose of feasting our eyes upon fascinating aspects of nature, for we should have been disappointed — at least at this season of the year. A writer in " Life in the Holy Land " observes:

" Monotonous and uninviting as much of the Holy Land will appear to persons accustomed to the almost constant verdure of flowers, ample streams, and varied surface of our own country, we must remember that its aspect to the Israelites after the weary march of forty years through the desert must have been very different."

Which all of us will freely grant. But it truly *is* " monotonous and uninviting," and there is no sufficient reason for describing it as being otherwise.

Of all the lands there are for dismal scenery, I think Palestine must be the prince. The hills are barren, they are dull of color, they are unpicturesque in shape. The valleys are unsightly deserts fringed with a feeble vegetation that has an expression about it of being sorrowful and despondent. The Dead Sea and the Sea of Galilee sleep in the midst of a vast stretch of hill and plain wherein the eye rests upon no pleasant tint, no striking object, no soft picture dreaming in a purple haze or mottled with the shadows of the clouds. Every outline is harsh, every feature is distinct, there is no perspective —

distance works no enchantment here.   It is a hope-less, dreary, heart-broken land.

Small shreds and patches of it must be very beau-tiful in the full flush of spring, however, and all the more beautiful by contrast with the far-reaching desolation that surrounds them on every side.   I would like much to see the fringes of the Jordan in spring time, and Shechem, Esdraelon, Ajalon, and the borders of Galilee — but even then these spots would seem mere toy gardens set at wide intervals in the waste of a limitless desolation.

Palestine sits in sackcloth and ashes.   Over it broods the spell of a curse that has withered its fields and fettered its energies.   Where Sodom and Gomor-rah reared their domes and towers, that solemn sea now floods the plain, in whose bitter waters no living thing exists — over whose waveless surface the blistering air hangs motionless and dead — about whose borders nothing grows but weeds, and scat-tering tufts of cane, and that treacherous fruit that promises refreshment to parching lips, but turns to ashes at the touch.   Nazareth is forlorn; about that ford of Jordan where the hosts of Israel entered the Promised Land with songs of rejoicing, one finds only a squalid camp of fantastic Bedouins of the desert; Jericho the accursed lies a moldering ruin to-day, even as Joshua's miracle left it more than three thousand years ago; Bethlehem and Bethany, in their poverty and their humiliation, have nothing about them now to remind one that they once knew the high honor of the Saviour's presence; the hallowed spot where the shepherds watched their flocks by night, and where the angels sang Peace on earth, good will to men, is untenanted by any living creature, and unblessed by any feature that is pleasant to the eye. Renowned Jerusalem itself, the stateliest name in history, has lost all its ancient grandeur, and is become a pauper village; the riches of Solomon are no longer there to compel the admiration of visiting Oriental queens; the wonderful temple which was the pride and the glory of Israel is gone, and the Ottoman crescent is lifted above the spot where, on that most memorable day in the annals of the world, they reared the Holy Cross. The noted Sea of Galilee, where Roman fleets once rode at anchor and the disciples of the Saviour sailed in their ships, was long ago deserted by the devotees of war and commerce, and its borders are a silent wilderness; Capernaum is a shapeless ruin; Magdala is the home of beggared Arabs; Bethsaida and Chorazin have vanished from the earth, and the "desert places" round about them where thousands of men once listened to the Saviour's voice and ate the miraculous bread sleep in the hush of a solitude that is inhabited only by birds of prey and skulking foxes.

Palestine is desolate and unlovely. And why should it be otherwise? Can the *curse* of the Deity beautify a land?

Palestine is no more of this work-day world. It is sacred to poetry and tradition — it is dream-land.

CHAPTER XXX.

IT was worth a kingdom to be at sea again. It was a relief to drop all anxiety whatsoever — all questions as to where we should go; how long we should stay; whether it were worth while to go or not; all anxieties about the condition of the horses; all such question as "Shall we *ever* get to water?" "Shall we *ever* lunch?" "Ferguson, how many *more* million miles have we got to creep under this awful sun before we camp?" It was a relief to cast all these torturing little anxieties far away — ropes of steel they were, and every one with a separate and distinct strain on it — and feel the temporary contentment that is born of the banishment of all care and responsibility. We did not look at the compass; we did not care, now, where the ship went to, so that she went out of sight of land as quickly as possible. When I travel again, I wish to go in a pleasure ship. No amount of money could have purchased for us, in a strange vessel and among unfamiliar faces, the perfect satisfaction and the sense of being *at home* again which we experienced when we stepped on board the *Quaker City,* — *our own ship* — after this wearisome pilgrimage. It is a something we have felt always when we returned to her, and a something we had no desire to sell.

We took off our blue woolen shirts, our spurs and heavy boots, our sanguinary revolvers and our buckskin-seated pantaloons, and got shaved, and came out in Christian costume once more. All but Jack, who changed all other articles of his dress, but clung to his traveling pantaloons. They still preserved their ample buckskin seat intact; and so his short pea-jacket and his long, thin legs assisted to make him a picturesque object whenever he stood on the forecastle looking abroad upon the ocean over the bows. At such times his father's last injunction suggested itself to me. He said:

"Jack, my boy, you are about to go among a brilliant company of gentlemen and ladies, who are refined and cultivated, and thoroughly accomplished in the manners and customs of good society. Listen to their conversation, study their habits of life, and learn. Be polite and obliging to all, and considerate towards every one's opinions, failings, and prejudices. Command the just respect of all your fellow-voyagers, even though you fail to win their friendly regard. And Jack — don't you ever dare, while you live, appear in public on those decks in fair weather, in a costume unbecoming your mother's drawing-room!"

It would have been worth any price if the father of this hopeful youth could have stepped on board

some time, and seen him standing high on the forecastle, pea-jacket, tasseled red fez, buckskin patch
and all,— placidly contemplating the ocean — a rare
spectacle for anybody's drawing-room.

After a pleasant voyage and a good rest, we drew
near to Egypt, and out of the mellowest of sunsets
we saw the domes and minarets of Alexandria rise
into view. As soon as the anchor was down, Jack
and I got a boat and went ashore. It was night by
this time, and the other passengers were content to
remain at home and visit ancient Egypt after breakfast. It was the way they did at Constantinople.
They took a lively interest in new countries, but
their schoolboy impatience had worn off, and they
had learned that it was wisdom to take things easy
and go along comfortably — these old countries do
not go away in the night; they stay till after breakfast.

When we reached the pier we found an army of
Egyptian boys with donkeys no larger than themselves, waiting for passengers — for donkeys are the
omnibuses of Egypt. We preferred to walk, but
we could not have our own way. The boys
crowded about us, clamored around us, and slewed
their donkeys exactly across our path, no matter
which way we turned. They were good-natured
rascals, and so were the donkeys. We mounted,
and the boys ran behind us and kept the donkeys in
a furious gallop, as is the fashion at Damascus. I
believe I would rather ride a donkey than any beast

in the world. He goes briskly, he puts on no airs,
he is docile, though opinionated. Satan himself
could not scare him, and he is convenient — very
convenient. When you are tired riding you can
rest your feet on the ground and let him gallop from
under you.

We found the hotel and secured rooms, and were
happy to know that the Prince of Wales had stopped
there once. They had it everywhere on signs. No
other princes had stopped there since, till Jack and
I came. We went abroad through the town, then,
and found it a city of huge commercial buildings,
and broad, handsome streets brilliant with gaslight.
By night it was a sort of reminiscence of Paris.
But finally Jack found an ice-cream saloon, and that
closed investigations for that evening. The weather
was very hot, it had been many a day since Jack
had seen ice-cream, and so it was useless to talk of
leaving the saloon till it shut up.

In the morning the lost tribes of America came
ashore and infested the hotels and took possession
of all the donkeys and other open barouches that
offered. They went in picturesque procession to
the American Consul's; to the great gardens; to
Cleopatra's Needles; to Pompey's Pillar; to the
palace of the Viceroy of Egypt; to the Nile; to the
superb groves of date-palms. One of our most
inveterate relic-hunters had his hammer with him,
and tried to break a fragment off the upright Needle
and could not do it; he tried the prostrate one

and failed; he borrowed a heavy sledge-hammer from a mason and failed again. He tried Pompey's Pillar, and this baffled him. Scattered all about the mighty monolith were sphinxes of noble countenance, carved out of Egyptian granite as hard as blue steel, and whose shapely features the wear of five thousand years had failed to mark or mar. The relic-hunter battered at these persistently, and sweated profusely over his work. He might as well have attempted to deface the moon. They regarded him serenely with the stately smile they had worn so long, and which seemed to say, "Peck away, poor insect; we were not made to fear such as you; in tenscore dragging ages we have seen more of your kind than there are sands at your feet; have they left a blemish upon us?"

But I am forgetting the Jaffa Colonists. At Jaffa we had taken on board some forty members of a very celebrated community. They were male and female; babies, young boys and young girls; young married people, and some who had passed a shade beyond the prime of life. I refer to the "Adams Jaffa Colony." Others had deserted before. We left in Jaffa Mr. Adams, his wife, and fifteen unfortunates who not only had no money but did not know where to turn or whither to go. Such was the statement made to us. Our forty were miserable enough in the first place, and they lay about the decks seasick all the voyage, which about completed their misery, I take it. However, one or two young

men remained upright, and by constant persecution
we wormed out of them some little information.
They gave it reluctantly and in a very fragmentary
condition, for, having been shamefully humbugged
by their prophet, they felt humiliated and unhappy.
In such circumstances people do not like to talk.

The colony was a complete *fiasco*. I have already
said that such as could get away did so, from time
to time. The prophet Adams — once an actor,
then several other things, afterward a Mormon and
a missionary, always an adventurer — remains at
Jaffa with his handful of sorrowful subjects. The
forty we brought away with us were chiefly destitute,
though not all of them. They wished to get to
Egypt. What might become of them then they did
not know and probably did not care — anything to
get away from hated Jaffa. They had little to hope
for; because after many appeals to the sympathies
of New England, made by strangers of Boston,
through the newspapers, and after the establishment
of an office there for the reception of moneyed con-
tributions for the Jaffa colonists, one dollar was
subscribed. The consul-general for Egypt showed
me the newspaper paragraph which mentioned the
circumstance, and mentioned also the discontinuance
of the effort and the closing of the office. It was
evident that practical New England was not sorry to
be rid of such visionaries and was not in the least
inclined to hire anybody to bring them back to her.
Still, to get to Egypt was something, in the eyes of

26**

the unfortunate colonists, hopeless as the prospect seemed of ever getting further.

Thus circumstanced, they landed at Alexandria from our ship. One of our passengers, Mr. Moses S. Beach, of the New York *Sun*, inquired of the consul-general what it would cost to send these people to their home in Maine by the way of Liverpool, and he said fifteen hundred dollars in gold would do it. Mr. Beach gave his check for the money, and so the troubles of the Jaffa colonists were at an end.*

Alexandria was too much like a European city to be novel, and we soon tired of it. We took the cars and came up here to ancient Cairo, which *is* an Oriental city and of the completest pattern. There is little about it to disabuse one's mind of the error if he should take it into his head that he was in the heart of Arabia. Stately camels and dromedaries, swarthy Egyptians, and likewise Turks and black Ethiopians, turbaned, sashed, and blazing in a rich variety of Oriental costumes of all shades of flashy colors, are what one sees on every hand crowding the narrow streets and the honeycombed bazaars. We are stopping at Shepherd's Hotel, which is the worst on earth except the one I stopped at once in

---

* It was an unselfish act of benevolence; it was done without any ostentation, and has never been mentioned in any newspaper, I think. Therefore it is refreshing to learn now, several months after the above narrative was written, that another man received all the credit of this rescue of the colonists. Such is life.

a small town in the United States.   It is pleasant to
read this sketch in my note-book, now, and know
that I can stand Shepherd's Hotel, sure, because I
have been in one just like it in America and
survived:

I stopped at the Benton House. It used to be a good hotel, but
that proves nothing — I used to be a good boy, for that matter. Both
of us have lost character of late years. The Benton is not a good
hotel.

The Benton lacks a very great deal of being a good hotel.   Perdition
is full of better hotels than the Benton.

It was late at night when I got there, and I told the clerk I would
like plenty of lights, because I wanted to read an hour or two.   When
I reached No. 15 with the porter (we came along a dim hall that was
clad in ancient carpeting, faded, worn out in many places, and patched
with old scraps of oil cloth — a hall that sank under one's feet, and
creaked dismally to every footstep) he struck a light — two inches of
sallow, sorrowful, consumptive tallow candle, that burned blue, and
sputtered, and got discouraged and went out. The porter lit it again,
and I asked if that was all the light the clerk sent.   He said, "Oh no,
I've got another one here," and he produced another couple of inches
of tallow candle.   I said, "Light them both — I'll have to have one to
see the other by."   He did it, but the result was drearier than darkness
itself. He was a cheery, accommodating rascal. He said he would
go "somewheres" and steal a lamp.   I abetted and encouraged him in
his criminal design. I heard the landlord get after him in the hall ten
minutes afterward.

"Where are you going with that lamp?"

"Fifteen wants it, sir."

"Fifteen! why he's got a double lot of candles — does the man
want to illuminate the house? — does he want to get up a torchlight
procession? — what is he up to, any how?"

"He don't like them candles — says he wants a lamp."

"Why, what in the nation does — why I never heard of such a
thing? What on earth can he want with that lamp?"

"Well, he only wants to read — that's what he says."

"Wants to read, does he? — ain't satisfied with a thousand candles, but has to have a lamp! — I do wonder what the devil that fellow wants that lamp for? Take him another candle, and then if — ''

" But he wants the lamp — says he'll burn the d—d old house down if he don't get a lamp! '' [A remark which I never made.]

" I'd like to see him at it once. Well, you take it along — but I swear it beats *my* time, though — and see if you can't find out what in the very nation he *wants* with that lamp.''

And he went off growling to himself and still wondering and wondering over the unaccountable conduct of No. 15. The lamp was a good one, but it revealed some disagreeable things — a bed in the suburbs of a desert of room — a bed that had hills and valleys in it, and you'd have to accommodate your body to the impression left in it by the man that slept there last, before you could lie comfortably; a carpet that had seen better days; a melancholy washstand in a remote corner, and a dejected pitcher on it sorrowing over a broken nose; a looking-glass split across the center, which chopped your head off at the chin and made you look like some dreadful unfinished monster or other; the paper peeling in shreds from the walls.

I sighed and said: " This is charming; and now don't you think you could get me something to read? ''

The porter said, " Oh, certainly; the old man's got dead loads of books; '' and he was gone before I could tell him what sort of literature I would rather have. And yet his countenance expressed the utmost confidence in his ability to execute the commission with credit to himself. The old man made a descent on him.

" What are you going to do with that pile of books? ''

" Fifteen wants 'em, sir.''

" Fifteen, is it? He'll want a warming-pan, next — he'll want a nurse! Take him everything there is in the house — take him the bar-keeper — take him the baggage-wagon — take him a chambermaid! Confound me, I never saw anything like it. What did he say he wants with those books? ''

" Wants to read 'em, like enough; it ain't likely he wants to eat 'em, I don't reckon.''

" Wants to read 'em — wants to read 'em this time of night, the infernal lunatic! Well he can't have them.''

" But he says he's mor'ly bound to have 'em: he says he'll just go a-rairin' and a-chargin' through this house and raise more — well, there's no tellin' what he won't do if he don't get 'em; because he's drunk and crazy and desperate, and nothing'll soothe him down but them cussed books." [I had not made any threats and was not in the condition ascribed to me by the porter.]

"Well, go on; but I will be around when he goes to rairing and charging, and the first rair he makes I'll make him rair out of the window." And then the old gentleman went off growling as before.

The genius of that porter was something wonderful. He put an armful of books on the bed and said "Good night" as confidently as if he knew perfectly well that those books were exactly my style of reading matter. And well he might. His selection covered the whole range of legitimate literature. It comprised "The Great Consummation," by Rev. Dr. Cummings — theology; " Revised Statutes of the State of Missouri " — law; "The Complete Horse-Doctor " — medicine; "The Toilers of the Sea," by Victor Hugo — romance; "The works of William Shakspeare "— poetry. I shall never cease to admire the tact and the intelligence of that gifted porter.

But all the donkeys in Christendom, and most of the Egyptian boys, I think, are at the door, and there is some noise going on, not to put it in stronger language. We are about starting to the illustrious Pyramids of Egypt, and the donkeys for the voyage are under inspection. I will go and select one before the choice animals are all taken.

CHAPTER XXXI.

THE donkeys were all good, all handsome, all strong and in good condition, all fast and all willing to prove it. They were the best we had found anywhere, and the most *recherche*. I do not know what *recherche* is, but that is what these donkeys were, anyhow. Some were of a soft mouse-color, and the others were white, black, and vari-colored. Some were close-shaven, all over, except that a tuft like a paint-brush was left on the end of the tail. Others were so shaven in fanciful land-scape garden patterns, as to mark their bodies with curving lines, which were bounded on one side by hair and on the other by the close plush left by the shears. They had all been newly barbered, and were exceedingly stylish. Several of the white ones were barred like zebras with rainbow stripes of blue and red and yellow paint. These were indescribably gorgeous. Dan and Jack selected from this lot because they brought back Italian reminiscences of the "old masters." The saddles were the high, stuffy, frog-shaped things we had known in Ephesus and Smyrna. The donkey-boys were lively young

Egyptian rascals who could follow a donkey and keep him in a canter half a day without tiring. We had plenty of spectators when we mounted, for the hotel was full of English people bound overland to India and officers getting ready for the African campaign against the Abyssinian King Theodorus. We were not a very large party, but as we charged through the streets of the great metropolis, we made noise for five hundred, and displayed activity and created excitement in proportion. Nobody can steer a donkey, and some collided with camels, dervishes, effendis, asses, beggars, and everything else that offered to the donkeys a reasonable chance for a collision. When we turned into the broad avenue that leads out of the city toward Old Cairo, there was plenty of room. The walls of stately date-palms that fenced the gardens and bordered the way, threw their shadows down and made the air cool and bracing. We rose to the spirit of the time and the race became a wild rout, a stampede, a terrific panic. I wish to live to enjoy it again.

Somewhere along this route we had a few startling exhibitions of Oriental simplicity. A girl apparently thirteen years of age came along the great thoroughfare dressed like Eve before the fall. We would have called her thirteen at home; but here girls who look thirteen are often not more than nine, in reality.

Occasionally we saw stark-naked men of superb build, bathing, and making no attempt at concealment. However, an hour's acquaintance with this

cheerful custom reconciled the pilgrims to it, and
then it ceased to occasion remark. Thus easily do
éven the most startling novelties grow tame and
spiritless to these sight-surfeited wanderers.

Arrived at Old Cairo, the camp-followers took up
the donkeys and tumbled them bodily aboard a small
boat with a lateen sail, and we followed and got
under way. The deck was closely packed with
donkeys and men; the two sailors had to climb over
and under and through the wedged mass to work the
sails, and the steersman had to crowd four or five
donkeys out of the way when he wished to swing his
tiller and put his helm hard down. But what were
their troubles to us? We had nothing to do; nothing to do but enjoy the trip; nothing to do but
shove the donkeys off our corns and look at the
charming scenery of the Nile.

On the island at our right was the machine they
call the Nilometer, a stone column whose business it
is to mark the rise of the river and prophesy whether
it will reach only thirty-two feet and produce a
famine, or whether it will properly flood the land at
forty and produce plenty, or whether it will rise to
forty-three and bring death and destruction to flocks
and crops — but how it does all this they could not
explain to us so that we could understand. On the
same island is still shown the spot where Pharaoh's
daughter found Moses in the bulrushes. Near the
spot we sailed from, the Holy Family dwelt when
they sojourned in Egypt till Herod should complete

his slaughter of the innocents. The same tree they rested under when they first arrived was there a short time ago, but the Viceroy of Egypt sent it to the Empress Eugenie lately. He was just in time, otherwise our pilgrims would have had it.

The Nile at this point is muddy, swift, and turbid, and does not lack a great deal of being as wide as the Mississippi.

We scrambled up the steep bank at the shabby town of Ghizeh, mounted the donkeys again, and scampered away. For four or five miles the route lay along a high embankment which they say is to be the bed of a railway the Sultan means to build for no other reason than that when the Empress of the French comes to visit him she can go to the Pyramids in comfort. This is true Oriental hospitality. I am very glad it is our privilege to have donkeys instead of cars.

At the distance of a few miles the Pyramids, rising above the palms, looked very clean-cut, very grand and imposing, and very soft and filmy, as well. They swam in a rich haze that took from them all suggestions of unfeeling stone, and made them seem only the airy nothings of a dream — structures which might blossom into tiers of vague arches, or ornate colonnades, maybe, and change and change again into all graceful forms of architecture while we looked, and then melt deliciously away and blend with the tremulous atmosphere.

At the end of the levee we left the mules and went

in a sailboat across an arm of the Nile or an over-flow, and landed where the sands of the Great Sahara left their embankment, as straight as a wall, along the verge of the alluvial plain of the river. A laborious walk in the flaming sun brought us to the foot of the great Pyramid of Cheops. It was a fairy vision no longer. It was a corrugated, unsightly mountain of stone. Each of its monstrous sides was a wide stairway which rose upward, step above step, narrowing as it went, till it tapered to a point far aloft in the air. Insect men and women — pilgrims from the *Quaker City* — were creeping about its dizzy perches, and one little black swarm were waving postage stamps from the airy summit — handkerchiefs will be understood.

Of course we were besieged by a rabble of muscular Egyptians and Arabs who wanted the contract of dragging us to the top — all tourists are. Of course you could not hear your own voice for the din that was around you. Of course the Sheiks said *they* were the only responsible parties; that all contracts must be made with them, all moneys paid over to them, and none exacted from us by any but themselves alone. Of course they contracted that the varlets who dragged us up should not mention bucksheesh once. For such is the usual routine. Of course we contracted with them, paid them, were delivered into the hands of the draggers, dragged up the Pyramids, and harried and bedeviled for bucksheesh from the foundation clear to the summit.

We paid it, too, for we were purposely spread very far apart over the vast side of the Pyramid. There was no help near if we called, and the Herculeses who dragged us had a way of asking sweetly and flatteringly for bucksheesh, which was seductive, and of looking fierce and threatening to throw us down the precipice, which was persuasive and convincing.

Each step being full as high as a dinner table; there being very, very many of the steps; an Arab having hold of each of our arms and springing upward from step to step and snatching us with them, forcing us to lift our feet as high as our breasts every time, and do it rapidly and keep it up till we were ready to faint, — who shall say it is not lively, exhilarating, lacerating, muscle-straining, bone-wrenching, and perfectly excruciating and exhausting pastime, climbing the Pyramids? I beseeched the varlets not to twist *all* my joints asunder; I iterated, reiterated, even *swore* to them that I did not wish to beat anybody to the top; did all I could to convince them that if I got there the last of all I would feel blessed above men and grateful to them forever; I begged them, prayed them, pleaded with them to let me stop and rest a moment — only one little moment: and they only answered with some more frightful springs, and an unenlisted volunteer behind opened a bombardment of determined boosts with his head which threatened to batter my whole political economy to wreck and ruin.

Twice, for one minute, they let me rest while they

extorted bucksheesh, and then continued their maniac
flight up the Pyramid. They wished to beat the
other parties. It was nothing to them that I, a
stranger, must be sacrificed upon the altar of their
unholy ambition. But in the midst of sorrow joy
blooms. Even in this dark hour I had a sweet consolation. For I knew that except these Mohammedans repented they would go straight to perdition
some day. And *they* never repent — they never for-
sake their paganism. This thought calmed me, cheered
me, and I sank down, limp and exhausted, upon the
summit, but happy, *so* happy and serene within.

On the one hand, a mighty sea of yellow sand
stretched away towards the ends of the earth, solemn,
silent, shorn of vegetation, its solitude uncheered by
any forms of creature life; on the other, the Eden
of Egypt was spread below us — a broad green floor,
cloven by the sinuous river, dotted with villages, its
vast distances measured and marked by the diminish-
ing stature of receding clusters of palms. It lay
asleep in an enchanted atmosphere. There was no
sound, no motion. Above the date-plumes in the
middle distance, swelled a domed and pinnacled
mass, glimmering through a tinted, exquisite mist;
away toward the horizon a dozen shapely pyramids
watched over ruined Memphis; and at our feet the
bland impassible Sphinx looked out upon the picture
from her throne in the sands as placidly and pensively as she had looked upon its like full fifty lagging centuries ago.

We suffered torture no pen can describe from the hungry appeals for bucksheesh that gleamed from Arab eyes and poured incessantly from Arab lips. Why try to call up the traditions of vanished Egyptian grandeur; why try to fancy Egypt following dead Rameses to his tomb in the Pyramid, or the long multitude of Israel departing over the desert yonder? Why try to think at all? The thing was impossible. One must bring his meditations cut and dried, or else cut and dry them afterward.

The traditional Arab proposed, in the traditional way, to run down Cheops, cross the eighth of a mile of sand intervening between it and the tall pyramid of Cephren, ascend to Cephren's summit and return to us on the top of Cheops — all in nine minutes by the watch, and the whole service to be rendered for a single dollar. In the first flush of irritation, I said let the Arab and his exploits go to the mischief. But stay. The upper third of Cephren was coated with dressed marble, smooth as glass. A blessed thought entered my brain. He must infallibly break his neck. Close the contract with dispatch, I said, and let him go. He started. We watched. He went bounding down the vast broadside, spring after spring, like an ibex. He grew small and smaller till he became a bobbing pigmy, away down toward the bottom — then disappeared. We turned and peered over the other side — forty seconds — eighty seconds — a hundred — happiness, he is dead already? — two minutes — and a quarter — "There he goes!" Too

true — it was too true. He was very small, now.
Gradually, but surely, he overcame the level ground.
He began to spring and climb again. Up, up, up
— at last he reached the smooth coating — now for
it. But he clung to it with toes and fingers, like a
fly. He crawled this way and that — away to the
right, slanting upward — away to the left, still slanting upward — and stood at last, a black peg on the
summit, and waved his pigmy scarf! Then he crept
downward to the raw steps again, then picked up his
agile heels and flew. We lost him presently. But
presently again we saw him under us, mounting with
undiminished energy. Shortly he bounded into our
midst with a gallant war-whoop. Time, eight minutes, forty-one seconds. He had won. His bones
were intact. It was a failure. I reflected. I said
to myself, he is tired, and must grow dizzy. I will
risk another dollar on him.

He started again. Made the trip again. Slipped
on the smooth coating — I almost had him. But an
infamous crevice saved him. He was with us once
more — perfectly sound. Time, eight minutes,
forty-six seconds.

I said to Dan, "Lend me a dollar — I can beat
this game, yet."

Worse and worse. He won again. Time, eight
minutes, forty-eight seconds. I was out of all
patience, now. I was desperate. Money was no
longer of any consequence. I said, "Sirrah, I will
give you a hundred dollars to jump off this pyramid

head first. If you do not like the terms, name your bet. I scorn to stand on expenses now. I will stay right here and risk money on you as long as Dan has got a cent."

I was in a fair way to win, now, for it was a dazzling opportunity for an Arab. He pondered a moment, and would have done it, I think, but his mother arrived, then, and interfered. Her tears moved me — I never can look upon the tears of woman with indifference — and I said I would give her a hundred to jump off, too.

But it was a failure. The Arabs are too high-priced in Egypt. They put on airs unbecoming to such savages.

We descended, hot and out of humor. The dragoman lit candles, and we all entered a hole near the base of the pyramid, attended by a crazy rabble of Arabs who thrust their services upon us uninvited. They dragged us up a long inclined chute, and dripped candle-grease all over us. This chute was not more than twice as wide and high as a Saratoga trunk, and was walled, roofed, and floored with solid blocks of Egyptian granite as wide as a wardrobe, twice as thick, and three times as long. We kept on climbing, through the oppressive gloom, till I thought we ought to be nearing the top of the pyramid again, and then came to the "Queen's Chamber," and shortly to the Chamber of the King. These large apartments were tombs. The walls were built of monstrous masses of smoothed granite, neatly joined together. Some of them were nearly as large square as an ordinary parlor. A great stone sarcophagus like a bathtub stood in the center of the King's Chamber. Around it were gathered a picturesque group of Arab savages and soiled and tattered pilgrims, who held their candles aloft in the gloom while they chattered, and the winking blurs of light shed a dim glory down upon one of the irrepressible memento-seekers who was pecking at the venerable sarcophagus with his sacrilegious hammer. We struggled out to the open air and the bright sunshine, and for the space of thirty minutes received ragged Arabs by couples, dozens, and platoons, and paid them bucksheesh for services they swore and proved by each other that they had rendered, but which we had not been aware of before — and as each party was paid, they dropped into the rear of the procession and in due time arrived again with a newly-invented delinquent list for liquidation.

We lunched in the shade of the pyramid, and in the midst of this encroaching and unwelcome company, and then Dan and Jack and I started away for a walk. A howling swarm of beggars followed us — surrounded us — almost headed us off. A sheik, in flowing white bournous and gaudy headgear, was with them. He wanted more bucksheesh. But we had adopted a new code — it was millions for defense, but not a cent for bucksheesh. I asked him if he could persuade the others to depart if we paid

him.   He said yes — for ten francs.   We accepted
the contract, and said —

"Now persuade your vassals to fall back."

He swung his long staff round his head and three
Arabs bit the dust.   He capered among the mob
like a very maniac.   His blows fell like hail, and
wherever one fell a subject went down.   We had to
hurry to the rescue and tell him it was only necessary
to damage them a little, he need not kill them.   In
two minutes we were alone with the sheik, and remained so.   The persuasive powers of this illiterate
savage were remarkable.

Each side of the Pyramid of Cheops is about as
long as the Capitol at Washington, or the Sultan's
new palace on the Bosporus, and is longer than the
greatest depth of St. Peter's at Rome — which is to
say that each side of Cheops extends seven hundred
and some odd feet.   It is about seventy-five feet
higher than the cross on St. Peter's.   The first time
I ever went down the Mississippi, I thought the
highest bluff on the river between St. Louis and New
Orleans — it was near Selma, Missouri — was probably the highest mountain in the world.   It is four
hundred and thirteen feet high.   It still looms in
my memory with undiminished grandeur.   I can
still see the trees and bushes growing smaller and
smaller as I followed them up its huge slant with my
eye, till they became a feathery fringe on the distant
summit.   This symmetrical Pyramid of Cheops —
this solid mountain of stone reared by the patient
27**

hands of men — this mighty tomb of a forgotten
monarch — dwarfs my cherished mountain. For it
is four hundred and eighty feet high. In still earlier
years than those I have been recalling, Holliday's
Hill, in our town, was to me the noblest work of
God. It appeared to pierce the skies. It was
nearly three hundred feet high. In those days I
pondered the subject much, but I never could understand why it did not swathe its summit with never-
failing clouds, and crown its majestic brow with everlasting snows. I had heard that such was the custom
of great mountains in other parts of the world. I remembered how I worked with another boy, at odd
afternoons stolen from study and paid for with
stripes, to undermine and start from its bed an immense boulder that rested upon the edge of that hilltop; I remembered how, one Saturday afternoon, we
gave three hours of honest effort to the task, and saw
at last that our reward was at hand; I remembered
how we sat down, then, and wiped the perspiration
away, and waited to let a picnic party get out of the
way in the road below — and then we started the
boulder. It was splendid. It went crashing down
the hillside, tearing up saplings, mowing bushes
down like grass, ripping and crushing and smashing
everything in its path — eternally splintered and scattered a woodpile at the foot of the hill, and then
sprang from the high bank clear over a dray in the
road — the negro glanced up once and dodged —
and the next second it made infinitesimal mincemeat

of a frame cooper-shop, and the coopers swarmed out like bees. Then we said it was perfectly magnificent, and left. Because the coopers were starting up the hill to inquire.

Still, that mountain, prodigious as it was, was nothing to the Pyramid of Cheops. I could conjure up no comparison that would convey to my mind a satisfactory comprehension of the magnitude of a pile of monstrous stones that covered thirteen acres of ground and stretched upward four hundred and eighty tiresome feet, and so I gave it up and walked down to the Sphinx.

After years of waiting, it was before me at last. The great face was so sad, so earnest, so longing, so patient. There was a dignity not of earth in its mien, and in its countenance a benignity such as never anything human wore. It was stone, but it seemed sentient. If ever image of stone thought, it was thinking. It was looking toward the verge of the landscape, yet looking *at* nothing — nothing but distance and vacancy. It was looking over and beyond everything of the present, and far into the past. It was gazing out over the ocean of Time — over lines of century-waves which, further and further receding, closed nearer and nearer together, and blended at last into one unbroken tide, away toward the horizon of remote antiquity. It was thinking of the wars of departed ages; of the empires it had seen created and destroyed; of the nations whose birth it had witnessed, whose progress it had

27**

watched, whose annihilation it had noted; of the joy
and sorrow, the life and death, the grandeur and decay, of five thousand slow revolving years. It was
the type of an attribute of man — of a faculty of his
heart and brain. It was MEMORY — RETROSPEC-
TION — wrought into visible, tangible form. All
who know what pathos there is in memories of days
that are accomplished and faces that have vanished
— albeit only a trifling score of years gone by — will
have some appreciation of the pathos that dwells in
these grave eyes that look so steadfastly back upon
the things they knew before History was born — before Tradition had being — things that were, and
forms that moved, in a vague era which even Poetry
and Romance scarce know of — and passed one by
one away and left the stony dreamer solitary in the
midst of a strange new age, and uncomprehended
scenes.

The Sphinx is grand in its loneliness; it is imposing in its magnitude; it is impressive in the mystery
that hangs over its story. And there is that in the
overshadowing majesty of this eternal figure of stone,
with its accusing memory of the deeds of all ages,
which reveals to one something of what he shall feel
when he shall stand at last in the awful presence of
God.

There are some things which, for the credit of
America, should be left unsaid, perhaps; but these
very things happen sometimes to be the very things
which, for the real benefit of Americans, ought to

have prominent notice.   While we stood looking, a
wart, or an excrescence of some kind, appeared on
the jaw of the Sphinx.   We heard the familiar clink
of a hammer, and understood the case at once.   One
of our well-meaning reptiles — I mean relic-hunters
— had crawled up there and was trying to break a
"specimen" from the face of this the most majestic
creation the hand of man has wrought.   But the great
image contemplated the dead ages as calmly as ever,
unconscious of the small insect that was fretting at its
jaw.   Egyptian granite that has defied the storms
and earthquakes of all time has nothing to fear from
the tack hammers of ignorant excursionists — high-
waymen like this specimen.   He failed in his enterprise.   We sent a sheik to arrest him if he had the
authority, or to warn him, if he had not, that by the
laws of Egypt the crime he was attempting to commit
was punishable with imprisonment or the bastinado.
Then he desisted and went away.

The Sphinx: a hundred and twenty-five feet long,
sixty feet high, and a hundred and two feet around
the head, if I remember rightly — carved out of one
solid block of stone harder than any iron.   The
block must have been as large as the Fifth Avenue
Hotel before the usual waste (by the necessities of
sculpture) of a fourth or a half of the original mass
was begun.   I only set down these figures and these
remarks to suggest the prodigious labor the carving
of it so elegantly, so symmetrically, so faultlessly,
must have cost.   This species of stone is so hard

AA**

that figures cut in it remain sharp and unmarred after exposure to the weather for two or three thousand years. Now did it take a hundred years of patient toil to carve the Sphinx?   It seems probable.

Something interfered, and we did not visit the Red Sea and walk upon the sands of Arabia. I shall not describe the great mosque of Mehemet Ali, whose entire inner walls are built of polished and glistening alabaster; I shall not tell how the little birds have built their nests in the globes of the great chandeliers that hang in the mosque, and how they fill the whole place with their music and are not afraid of anybody because their audacity is pardoned, their rights are respected, and nobody is allowed to interfere with them, even though the mosque be thus doomed to go unlighted; I certainly shall not tell the hackneyed story of the massacre of the Mamelukes, because I am glad the lawless rascals were massacred, and I do not wish to get up any sympathy in their behalf; I shall not tell how that one solitary Mameluke jumped his horse a hundred feet down from the battlements of the citadel and escaped, because I do not think much of that — I could have done it myself; I shall not tell of Joseph's well which he dug in the solid rock of the citadel hill and which is still as good as new, nor how the same mules he bought to draw up the water (with an endless chain) are still at it yet and are getting tired of it, too; I shall not tell about Joseph's granaries which he built to store the grain in, what time the Egyptian brokers were "selling short," unwitting that there would be no corn in all the land when it should be time for them to deliver; I shall not tell anything about the strange, strange city of Cairo, because it is only a repetition, a good deal intensified and exaggerated, of the Oriental cities I have already spoken of; I shall not tell of the Great Caravan which leaves for Mecca every year, for I did not see it; nor of the fashion the people have of prostrating themselves and so forming a long human pavement to be ridden over by the chief of the expedition on its return, to the end that their salvation may be thus secured, for I did not see that either; I shall not speak of the railway, for it is like any other railway — I shall only say that the fuel they use for the locomotive is composed of mummies three thousand years old, purchased by the ton or by the graveyard for that purpose, and that sometimes one hears the profane engineer call out pettishly, "D — n these plebeians, they don't burn worth a cent — pass out a King;"* I shall not tell of the groups of mud cones stuck like wasps' nests upon a thousand mounds above high-water mark the length and breadth of Egypt — villages of the lower classes; I shall not speak of the boundless sweep of level plain, green with luxuriant grain, that gladdens the eye as far as it can pierce through the soft, rich atmosphere of Egypt; I shall

---

* Stated to me for a fact. I only tell it as I got it. I am willing to believe it. I can believe anything.

not speak of the vision of the Pyramids seen at a distance of five and twenty miles, for the picture is too ethereal to be limned by an uninspired pen; I shall not tell of the crowds of dusky women who flocked to the cars when they stopped a moment at a station, to sell us a drink of water or a ruddy, juicy pomegranate; I shall not tell of the motley multitudes and wild costumes that graced a fair we found in full blast at another barbarous station; I shall not tell how we feasted on fresh dates and enjoyed the pleasant landscape all through the flying journey; nor how we thundered into Alexandria, at last, swarmed out of the cars, rowed aboard the ship, left a comrade behind (who was to return to Europe, thence home), raised the anchor, and turned our bows homeward finally and forever from the long voyage; nor how, as the mellow sun went down upon the oldest land on earth, Jack and Moult assembled in solemn state in the smoking-room and mourned over the lost comrade the whole night long, and would not be comforted. I shall not speak a word of any of these things, or write a line. They shall be as a sealed book. I do not know what a sealed book is, because I never saw one, but a sealed book is the expression to use in this connection, because it is popular.

We were glad to have seen the land which was the mother of civilization — which taught Greece her letters, and through Greece Rome, and through Rome the world; the land which could have human-ized and civilized the hapless children of Israel, but allowed them to depart out of her borders little better than savages. We were glad to have seen that land which had an enlightened religion with future eternal rewards and punishment in it, while even Israel's religion contained no promise of a hereafter. We were glad to have seen that land which had glass three thousand years before England had it, and could paint upon it as none of us can paint now; that land which knew, three thousand years ago, well nigh all of medicine and surgery which science has *discovered* lately; which had all those curious surgical instruments which science has *invented* recently; which had in high excellence a thousand luxuries and necessities of an advanced civilization which we have gradually contrived and accumulated in modern times and claimed as things that were new under the sun; that had paper untold centuries before we dreamt of it — and waterfalls before our women thought of them; that had a perfect system of common schools so long before we boasted of our achievements in that direction that it seems forever and forever ago; that so embalmed the dead that flesh was made almost immortal — which we cannot do; that built temples which mock at destroying time and smile grimly upon our lauded little prodigies of architecture; that old land that knew all which we know now, perchance, and more; that walked in the broad highway of civilization in the gray dawn of creation, ages and ages before we

were born; that left the impress of exalted, cultivated Mind upon the eternal front of the Sphinx to
confound all scoffers who, when all her other proofs
had passed away, might seek to persuade the world
that imperial Egypt, in the days of her high renown,
had groped in darkness.

CHAPTER XXXII.

WE were at sea now, for a very long voyage — we were to pass through the entire length of the Levant; through the entire length of the Mediterranean proper, also, and then cross the full width of the Atlantic — a voyage of several weeks. We naturally settled down into a very slow, stay-at-home manner of life, and resolved to be quiet, exemplary people, and roam no more for twenty or thirty days. No more, at least, than from stem to stern of the ship. It was a very comfortable prospect, though, for we were tired and needed a long rest.

We were all lazy and satisfied, now, as the meager entries in my note-book (that sure index, to me, of my condition) prove. What a stupid thing a note-book gets to be at sea, any way. Please observe the style:

'' *Sunday* — Services, as usual, at four bells. Services at night, also. No cards.

'' *Monday* — Beautiful day, but rained hard. The cattle purchased at Alexandria for beef ought to be shingled. Or else fattened. The water stands in deep puddles in the depressions forward of their after shoulders. Also here and there all over their backs. It is well they are not cows — it would soak in and ruin the milk. The poor devil eagle* from Syria

---

* Afterwards presented to the Central Park.

looks miserable and droopy in the rain perched on the forward capstan. He appears to have his own opinion of a sea voyage, and if it were put into language and the language solidified, it would probably essentially dam the widest river in the world.

" *Tuesday* — Somewhere in the neighborhood of the island of Malta. Can not stop there. Cholera. Weather very stormy. Many passengers seasick and invisible.

" *Wednesday* — Weather still very savage. Storm blew two land birds to sea, and they came on board. A hawk was blown off, also. He circled round and round the ship, wanting to light, but afraid of the people. He was so tired, though, that he had to light, at last, or perish. He stopped in the foretop, repeatedly, and was as often blown away by the wind. At last Harry caught him. Sea full of flying-fish. They rise in flocks of three hundred and flash along above the tops of the waves a distance of two or three hundred feet, then fall and disappear.

" *Thursday* — Anchored off Algiers, Africa. Beautiful city, beautiful green hilly landscape behind it. Stayed half a day and left. Not permitted to land, though we showed a clean bill of health. They were afraid of Egyptian plague and cholera.

" *Friday* — Morning, dominoes. Afternoon, dominoes. Evening, promenading the deck. Afterwards, charades.

" *Saturday* — Morning, dominoes. Afternoon, dominoes. Evening, promenading the decks. Afterwards, dominoes.

" *Sunday* — Morning service, four bells. Evening service, eight bells. Monotony till midnight. — Whereupon, dominoes.

" *Monday* — Morning, dominoes. Afternoon, dominoes. Evening, promenading the decks. Afterwards, charades and a lecture from Dr. C. Dominoes.

" *No date* — Anchored off the picturesque city of Cagliari, Sardinia. Stayed till midnight, but not permitted to land by these infamous foreigners. They smell inodorously — they do not wash — they dare not risk cholera.

" *Thursday* — Anchored off the beautiful cathedral city of Malaga, Spain. — Went ashore in the captain's boat — not ashore, either, for they would not let us land. Quarantine. Shipped my newspaper correspondence, which they took with tongs, dipped it in sea water, clipped it full of holes, and then fumigated it with villainous vapors till it smelt like a Spaniard. Inquired about chances to run the blockade and visit the

Alhambra at Granada. Too risky — they might hang a body. Set sail — middle of afternoon.

"And so on, and so on, and so forth, for several days. Finally, anchored off Gibraltar, which looks familiar and home-like."

It reminds me of the journal I opened with the New Year, once, when I was a boy and a confiding and a willing prey to those impossible schemes of reform which well-meaning old maids and grandmothers set for the feet of unwary youths at that season of the year — setting oversized tasks for them, which, necessarily failing, as infallibly weaken the boy's strength of will, diminish his confidence in himself, and injure his chances of success in life. Please accept of an extract:

"*Monday* — Got up, washed, went to bed.
"*Tuesday* — Got up, washed, went to bed.
"*Wednesday* — Got up, washed, went to bed.
"*Thursday* — Got up, washed, went to bed.
"*Friday* — Got up, washed, went to bed.
"*Next Friday* — Got up, washed, went to bed.
"*Friday fortnight* — Got up, washed, went to bed.
"*Following month* — Got up, washed, went to bed."

I stopped, then, discouraged. Startling events appeared to be too rare, in my career, to render a diary necessary. I still reflect with pride, however, that even at that early age I washed when I got up. That journal finished me. I never have had the nerve to keep one since. My loss of confidence in myself in that line was permanent.

The ship had to stay a week or more at Gibraltar to take in coal for the home voyage.

It would be very tiresome staying here, and so

four of us ran the quarantine blockade and spent seven delightful days in Seville, Cordova, Cadiz, and wandering through the pleasant rural scenery of Andalusia, the garden of Old Spain. The experiences of that cheery week were too varied and numerous for a short chapter, and I have not room for a long one. Therefore I shall leave them all out.

CHAPTER XXXIII.

TEN or eleven o'clock found us coming down to breakfast one morning in Cadiz. They told us the ship had been lying at anchor in the harbor two or three hours. It was time for us to bestir ourselves. The ship could wait only a little while because of the quarantine. We were soon on board, and within the hour the white city and the pleasant shores of Spain sank down behind the waves and passed out of sight. We had seen no land fade from view so regretfully.

It had long ago been decided in a noisy public meeting in the main cabin that we could not go to Lisbon, because we must surely be quarantined there. We did everything by mass-meeting, in the good old national way, from swapping off one empire for another on the programme of the voyage down to complaining of the cookery and the scarcity of napkins. I am reminded, now, of one of these complaints of the cookery made by a passenger. The coffee had been steadily growing more and more execrable for the space of three weeks, till at last it had ceased to be coffee altogether and had assumed

and the lovely vistas of blue water that went curving in and out, disappearing and anon again appearing through jungle walls of brilliant foliage, restored the energies dulled by long drowsing on the ocean, and fitted us for our final cruise — our little run of a thousand miles to New York — America — HOME.

We bade good-bye to " our friends the Bermudians," as our programme hath it — the majority of those we were most intimate with were negroes — and courted the great deep again. I said the majority. We knew more negroes than white people, because we had a deal of washing to be done, but we made some most excellent friends among the whites, whom it will be a pleasant duty to hold long in grateful remembrance.

We sailed, and from that hour all idling ceased. Such another system of overhauling, general littering of cabins and packing of trunks we had not seen since we let go the anchor in the harbor of Beirout. Everybody was busy. Lists of all purchases had to be made out, and values attached, to facilitate matters at the custom-house. Purchases bought by bulk in partnership had to be equitably divided, outstanding debts canceled, accounts compared, and trunks, boxes, and packages labeled. All day long the bustle and confusion continued.

And now came our first accident. A passenger was running through a gangway, between decks, one stormy night, when he caught his foot in the iron staple of a door that had been heedlessly left off a hatchway, and the bones of his leg broke at the ankle. It was our first serious misfortune. We had traveled much more than twenty thousand miles, by land and sea, in many trying climates, without a single hurt, without a serious case of sickness, and without a death among five and sixty passengers. Our good fortune had been wonderful. A sailor had jumped overboard at Constantinople one night, and was seen no more, but it was suspected that his object was to desert, and there was a slim chance, at least, that he reached the shore. But the passenger list was complete. There was no name missing from the register.

At last, one pleasant morning, we steamed up the harbor of New York, all on deck, all dressed in Christian garb — by special order, for there was a latent disposition in some quarters to come out as Turks — and, amid a waving of handkerchiefs from welcoming friends, the glad pilgrims noted the shiver of the decks that told that ship and pier had joined hands again, and the long, strange cruise was over. Amen.

A NEWSPAPER VALEDICTORY

IN this place I will print an article which I wrote
for the New York *Herald* the night we arrived.
I do it partly because my contract with my publishers makes it compulsory; partly because it is a
proper, tolerably accurate, and exhaustive summing-
up of the cruise of the ship and the performances of
the pilgrims in foreign lands; and partly because
some of the passengers have abused me for writing
it, and I wish the public to see how thankless a task
it is to put one's self to trouble to glorify unappre-
ciative people. I was charged with "rushing into
print" with these compliments. I did not rush. I
had written news letters to the *Herald* sometimes,
but yet when I visited the office that day I did not
say anything about writing a valedictory. I did go
to the *Tribune* office to see if such an article was
wanted, because I belonged on the regular staff of
that paper and it was simply a duty to do it. The
managing editor was absent, and so I thought no
more about it. At night when the *Herald's* request
came for an article, I did not "rush." In fact, I
demurred for a while, because I did not feel like

writing compliments then, and therefore was afraid
to speak of the cruise lest I might be betrayed into
using other than complimentary language. However, I reflected that it would be a just and righteous
thing to go down and write a kind word for the
Hadjis — Hadjis are people who have made the pilgrimage — because parties not interested could not
do it so feelingly as I, a fellow-Hadji, and so I
penned the valedictory. I have read it, and read it
again; and if there is a sentence in it that is not
fulsomely complimentary to captain, ship, and passengers, *I* cannot find it. If it is not a chapter that
any company might be proud to have a body write
about them, my judgment is fit for nothing. With
these remarks I confidently submit it to the un-
prejudiced judgment of the reader:

RETURN OF THE HOLY LAND EXCURSIONISTS — THE STORY OF THE CRUISE.

TO THE EDITOR OF THE HERALD:

The steamer *Quaker City* has accomplished at last her extraordinary
voyage and returned to her old pier at the foot of Wall street. The expedition was a success in some respects, in some it was not. Originally it
was advertised as a " pleasure excursion." Well, perhaps it was a pleasure excursion, but certainly it did not look like one; certainly it did not act
like one. Anybody's and everybody's notion of a pleasure excursion
is that the parties to it will of a necessity be young and giddy and
somewhat boisterous. They will dance a good deal, sing a good deal,
make love, but sermonize very little. Anybody's and everybody's
notion of a well-conducted funeral is that there must be a hearse and a
corpse, and chief mourners and mourners by courtesy, many old people,
much solemnity, no levity, and a prayer and a sermon withal. Three-
fourths of the *Quaker City's* passengers were between forty and seventy
years of age! There was a picnic crowd for you! It may be supposed

BB**

that the other fourth was composed of young girls. But it was not. It was chiefly composed of rusty old bachelors and a child of six years. Let us average the ages of the *Quaker City's* pilgrims and set the figure down as fifty years. Is any man insane enough to imagine that this picnic of patriarchs sang, made love, danced, laughed, told anecdotes, dealt in ungodly levity? In my experience they sinned little in these matters. No doubt it was presumed here at home that these frolicsome veterans laughed and sang and romped all day, and day after day, and kept up a noisy excitement from one end of the ship to the other; and that they played blindman's buff or danced quadrilles and waltzes on moonlight evenings on the quarter-deck; and that at odd moments of unoccupied time they jotted a laconic item or two in the journals they opened on such an elaborate plan when they left home, and then skurried off to their whist and euchre labors under the cabin lamps. If these things were presumed, the presumption was at fault. The venerable excursionists were not gay and frisky. They played no blindman's buff; they dealt not in whist; they shirked not the irksome journal, for alas! most of them were even writing books. They never romped, they talked but little, they never sang, save in the nightly prayer-meeting. The pleasure ship was a synagogue, and the pleasure trip was a funeral excursion without a corpse. (There is nothing exhilarating about a funeral excursion without a corpse.) A free, hearty laugh was a sound that was not heard oftener than once in seven days about those decks or in those cabins, and when it was heard it met with precious little sympathy. The excursionists danced, on three separate evenings, long, long ago (it seems an age) quadrilles, of a single set, made up of three ladies and five gentlemen (the latter with handkerchiefs around their arms to signify their sex), who timed their feet to the solemn wheezing of a melodeon; but even this melancholy orgie was voted to be sinful, and dancing was discontinued.

The pilgrims played dominoes when too much Josephus or Robinson's Holy Land Researches, or book-writing, made recreation necessary —for dominoes is about as mild and sinless a game as any in the world, perhaps, excepting always the ineffably insipid diversion they call croquet, which is a game where you don't pocket any balls and don't carom on any thing of any consequence, and when you are done nobody has to pay, and there are no refreshments to saw off, and, consequently, there isn't any satisfaction whatever about it—they played dominoes till they were rested, and then they blackguarded each other privately till prayer-time. When they were not seasick they were uncommonly prompt when the dinner-gong sounded. Such was our daily life on board the ship — solemnity, decorum, dinner, dominoes, devotions, slander. It was not lively enough for a pleasure trip; but if we had only had a corpse it would have made a noble funeral excursion. It is all over now; but when I look back, the idea of these venerable fossils skipping forth on a six-months picnic, seems exquisitely refreshing. The advertised title of the expedition — "The Grand Holy Land Pleasure Excursion" — was a misnomer. "The Grand Holy Land Funeral Procession" would have been better — much better.

Wherever we went, in Europe, Asia, or Africa, we made a sensation, and, I suppose I may add, created a famine. None of us had ever been any where before; we all hailed from the interior; travel was a wild novelty to us, and we conducted ourselves in accordance with the natural instincts that were in us, and trammeled ourselves with no ceremonies, no conventionalities. We always took care to make it understood that we were Americans — Americans! When we found that a good many foreigners had hardly ever heard of America, and that a good many more knew it only as a barbarous province away off somewhere, that had lately been at war with somebody, we pitied the ignorance of the Old World, but abated no jot of our importance. Many and many a simple community in the Eastern hemisphere will remember for years the incursion of the strange horde in the year of our Lord 1867, that called themselves Americans, and seemed to imagine in some unaccountable way that they had a right to be proud of it. We generally created a famine, partly because the coffee on the *Quaker City* was unendurable, and sometimes the more substantial fare was not strictly first-class; and partly because one naturally tires of sitting long at the same board and eating from the same dishes.

The people of those foreign countries are very, very ignorant. They looked curiously at the costumes we had brought from the wilds of America. They observed that we talked loudly at table sometimes. They noticed that we looked out for expenses, and got what we conveniently could out of a franc, and wondered where in the mischief we came from. In Paris they just simply opened their eyes and stared when we spoke to them in French! We never did succeed in making those idiots understand their own language. One of our passengers said to a shopkeeper, in reference to a proposed return to buy a pair of gloves, "*Allong restay trankeel — may be ve coom Moonday;*" and would you believe it, that shopkeeper, a born Frenchman, had to ask what it was that had been said. Sometimes it seems to me, somehow, that there must be a difference between Parisian French and *Quaker City* French.

The people stared at us everywhere, and we stared at them. We generally made them feel rather small, too, before we got done with them, because we bore down on them with America's greatness until we crushed them. And yet we took kindly to the manners and customs, and especially to the fashions of the various people we visited. When we left the Azores, we wore awful capotes and used fine tooth combs — successfully. When we came back from Tangier, in Africa, we were topped with fezzes of the bloodiest hue, hung with tassels like an Indian's scalp-lock. In France and Spain we attracted some attention in these costumes. In Italy they naturally took us for distempered Garibaldians, and set a gunboat to look for anything significant in our changes of uniform. We made Rome howl. We could have made any place howl when we had all our clothes on. We got no fresh raiment in Greece — they had but little there of any kind. But at Constantinople, how we turned out! Turbans, scimetars, fezzes, horse-pistols, tunics, sashes, baggy trowsers, yellow slippers — Oh, we were gorgeous! The illustrious dogs of Constantinople barked their under jaws off, and even then failed to do us justice. They are all dead by this time. They could not go through such a run of business as we gave them and survive.

And then we went to see the Emperor of Russia. We just called on him as comfortably as if we had known him a century or so, and when we had finished our visit we variegated ourselves with selections from Russian costumes and sailed away again more picturesque than ever. In Smyrna we picked up camel's hair shawls and other dressy things from Persia; but in Palestine — ah, in Palestine — our splendid career ended. They didn't wear any clothes there to speak of. We were satisfied, and stopped. We made no experiments. We did not try their costume. But we astonished the natives of that country. We antonished them with such eccentricities of dress as we could muster. We prowled through the Holy Land, from Cesarea Philippi to Jerusalem and the Dead Sea, a weird procession of pilgrims, gotten up regardless of expense, solemn, gorgeous, green-spectacled, drowsing under blue umbrellas, and astride of a sorrier lot of horses, camels, and asses than those that came out of Noah's ark, after eleven months of seasickness and short rations. If ever those children of Israel in Palestine forget when Gideon's Band went through there from America, they ought to be cursed once more and finished. It was the rarest spectacle that ever astounded mortal eyes, perhaps.

Well, we were at home in Palestine. It was easy to see that that was the grand feature of the expedition. We had cared nothing much about Europe. We galloped through the Louvre, the Pitti, the Uffizzi, the Vatican—all the galleries—and through the pictured and frescoed churches of Venice, Naples, and the cathedrals of Spain; some of us said that certain of the great works of the old masters were glorious creations of genius (we found it out in the guide-book, though we got hold of the wrong picture sometimes), and the others said they were disgraceful old daubs. We examined modern and ancient statuary with a critical eye in Florence, Rome, or anywhere we found it, and praised it if we saw fit, and if we didn't we said we preferred the wooden Indians in front of the cigar stores of America. But the Holy Land brought out all our enthusiasm. We fell into raptures by the barren shores of Galilee; we pondered at Tabor and at Nazareth; we exploded into poetry over the questionable loveliness of Esdraelon; we meditated at Jezreel and Samaria over the missionary zeal of Jehu; we rioted— fairly rioted among the holy places of Jerusalem; we bathed in Jordan and the Dead Sea, reckless whether our accident-insurance policies were extra-hazardous or not, and brought away so many jugs of precious water from both places that all the country from Jericho to the mountains of Moab will suffer from drouth this year, I think. Yet, the pilgrimage part of the excursion was its pet feature—there is no question about that. After dismal, smileless Palestine, beautiful Egypt had few charms for us. We merely glanced at it and were ready for home.

They wouldn't let us land at Malta—quarantine; they would not let us land in Sardinia; nor at Algiers, Africa; nor at Malaga, Spain, nor Cadiz, nor at the Madeira Islands. So we got offended at all foreigners and turned our backs upon them and came home. I suppose we only stopped at the Bermudas because they were in the programme. We did not care anything about any place at all. We wanted to go home. Homesickness was abroad in the ship—it was epidemic. If the authorities of New York had known how badly we had it, they would have quarantined us here.

The grand pilgrimage is over. Good-bye to it, and a pleasant memory to it, I am able to say in all kindness. I bear no malice, no ill-will toward any individual that was connected with it, either as passenger or officer. Things I did not like at all yesterday I like very well to-day, now that I am at home, and always hereafter I shall be able to poke fun at the whole gang if the spirit so moves me to do, without ever saying a malicious word. The expedition accomplished all that its programme promised that it should accomplish, and we ought all to be satisfied with the management of the matter, certainly. Bye-bye!

MARK TWAIN.

I call that complimentary. It *is* complimentary; and yet I never have received a word of thanks for it from the Hadjis; on the contrary, I speak nothing but the serious truth when I say that many of them even took exceptions to the article. In endeavoring to please them I slaved over that sketch for two hours, and had my labor for my pains. I never will do a generous deed again.

CONCLUSION.

NEARLY one year has flown since this notable pilgrimage was ended; and as I sit here at home in San Francisco thinking, I am moved to confess that day by day the mass of my memories of the excursion have grown more and more pleasant as the disagreeable incidents of travel which encumbered them flitted one by one out of my mind — and now, if the *Quaker City* were weighing her anchor to sail away on the very same cruise again, nothing could gratify me more than to be a passenger. With the same captain and even the same pilgrims, the same sinners. I was on excellent terms with eight or nine of the excursionists (they are my staunch friends yet), and was even on speaking terms with the rest of the sixty-five. I have been at sea quite enough to know that that was a very good average. Because a long sea-voyage not only brings out all the mean traits one has, and exaggerates them, but raises up others which he never suspected he possessed, and even creates new ones. A twelve months' voyage at sea would make an ordinary man a very miracle of meanness. On the other hand, if a man has good qualities, the spirit seldom moves him to exhibit them on shipboard, at least with any sort of emphasis. Now I am satisfied that our pilgrims are pleasant old people on shore; I am also satisfied that at sea on a second voyage they would be pleasanter, somewhat, than they were on our grand excursion, and so I say without hesitation that I would be glad enough to sail with them again. I could at least enjoy life with my handful of old friends. They could enjoy life with *their* cliques as well — passengers invariably divide up into cliques, on *all* ships.

And I will say, here, that I would rather travel with an excursion party of Methuselahs than have to be changing ships and comrades constantly, as people do who travel in the ordinary way. Those latter are always grieving over some *other* ship they have known and lost, and over *other* comrades whom diverging routes have separated from them. They learn to love a ship just in time to change it for another, and they become attached to a pleasant traveling companion only to lose him. They have that most dismal experience of being in a strange vessel, among strange people who care nothing about them, and of undergoing the customary bullying by strange officers and the insolence of strange servants, repeated over and over again within the compass of every month. They have also that other misery of packing and unpacking trunks — of running the distressing gauntlet of custom-houses —

of the anxieties attendant upon getting a mass of baggage from point to point on land in safety. I had rather sail with a whole brigade of patriarchs than suffer so. We never packed our trunks but twice — when we sailed from New York, and when we returned to it. Whenever we made a land journey, we estimated how many days we should be gone and what amount of clothing we should need, figured it down to a mathematical nicety, packed a valise or two accordingly, and left the trunks on board. We chose our comrades from among our old, tried friends, and started. We were never dependent upon strangers for companionship. We often had occasion to pity Americans whom we found traveling drearily among strangers with no friends to exchange pains and pleasures with. Whenever we were coming back from a land journey, our eyes sought one thing in the distance first — the ship — and when we saw it riding at anchor with the flag apeak, we felt as a returning wanderer feels when he sees his home. When we stepped on board, our cares vanished, our troubles were at an end — for the ship was home to us. We always had the same familiar old stateroom to go to, and feel safe and at peace and comfortable again.

I have no fault to find with the manner in which our excursion was conducted. Its programme was faithfully carried out — a thing which surprised me, for great enterprises usually promise vastly more than they perform. It would be well if such an excursion could be gotten up every year and the system regularly inaugurated. Travel is fatal to prejudice, bigotry, and narrow-mindedness, and many of our people need it sorely on these accounts. Broad, wholesome, charitable views of men and things cannot be acquired by vegetating in one little corner of the earth all one's lifetime.

The excursion is ended, and has passed to its place among the things that were. But its varied scenes and its manifold incidents will linger pleasantly in our memories for many a year to come. Always on the wing, as we were, and merely pausing a moment to catch fitful glimpses of the wonders of half a world, we could not hope to receive or retain vivid impressions of all it was our fortune to see. Yet our holiday flight has not been in vain — for above the confusion of vague recollections, certain of its best prized pictures lift themselves and will still continue perfect in tint and outline after their surroundings shall have faded away.

We shall remember something of pleasant France; and something also of Paris, though it flashed upon us a splendid meteor, and was gone again, we hardly knew how or where. We shall remember, always, how we saw majestic Gibraltar glorified with the rich coloring of a Spanish sunset and swimming in a sea of rainbows. In fancy we shall see Milan again, and her stately cathedral with its marble wilderness of graceful spires. And Padua — Verona — Como, jeweled with stars; and patrician Venice, afloat on her stagnant flood — silent, desolate, haughty — scornful of her humbled state — wrapping herself in memories of her lost fleets, of battle and triumph, and all the pageantry of a glory that is departed.

We cannot forget Florence — Naples — nor the foretaste of heaven that is in the delicious atmosphere of Greece — and surely not Athens and the broken temples of the Acropolis. Surely not venerable Rome — nor the green plain that compasses her round about, contrasting its brightness with her gray decay — nor the ruined arches that stand apart in the plain and clothe their looped and windowed raggedness with vines. We shall remember St. Peter's; not as one sees it when he walks the streets of Rome and fancies all her domes are just alike, but as he sees it leagues away, when every meaner edifice has faded out of sight and that one dome looms superbly up in the flush of sunset, full of dignity and grace, strongly outlined as a mountain.

We shall remember Constantinople and the Bosporus — the colossal magnificence of Baalbec — the Pyramids of Egypt — the prodigious form, the benignant countenance of the Sphynx — Oriental Smyrna — sacred Jerusalem — Damascus, the "Pearl of the East," the pride of Syria, the fabled Garden of Eden, the home of princes and genii of the Arabian Nights, the oldest metropolis on earth, the one city in all the world that has kept its name and held its place and looked serenely on while the Kingdoms and Empires of four thousand years have risen to life, enjoyed their little season of pride and pomp, and then vanished and been forgotten!

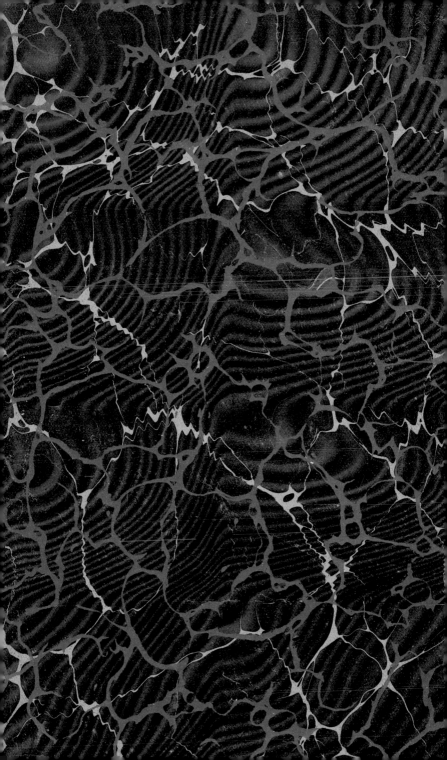